ANTIQUES ROADSHOW

WORLD WAR ONE

IN 100 FAMILY

·TREASURES·

Gottfried Sandrock's trunk
(see page 372)

PAUL ATTERBURY

ANTIQUES ROADSHOW

WORLD WAR ONE

IN 100 FAMILY

·TREASURES·

BBC
BOOKS

CONTENTS

Introduction **10**

FINDING A FORGOTTEN
GREAT-UNCLE
Lewis John Rowley Atterbury **16**

1914

A SCOUT TROOP TRAPPED BY
THE OUTBREAK OF WAR
George Stanley Walmsley **22**

A ROYAL MARINE WHO WENT DOWN
WITH HMS *ABOUKIR*
David Page **25**

A FAMOUS HORSEMAN AND ONE
OF THE FIRST BRITISH CASUALTIES
IN FRANCE
Arthur Hughes-Onslow **28**

A NEW ZEALANDER WHO
TOOK PART IN THE CAPTURE
OF GERMAN SAMOA
Arthur Frederick Webb **32**

A RECORD-BREAKING CRICKETER
WHO DIED AT YPRES
Arthur Edward James Collins **34**

AN OLD CONTEMPTIBLE SAVED
BY HIS WALLET
William Edward Taylor **38**

A SOLDIER FROM A GERMAN FAMILY
FIGHTING FOR BRITAIN
Max Jordan **42**

A FULL LIFE IN THE
REGULAR ARMY – AND THE
1914 CHRISTMAS TRUCE
James John Paice **46**

A PROFESSIONAL FOOTBALLER
INTERNED IN GERMANY
Samuel Wolstenholme **50**

A COLDSTREAM GUARDSMAN
WHO BECAME A POLICEMAN
Gaious John Humber **53**

A QUEEN ALEXANDRA'S ARMY NURSE
WHO SERVED THROUGHOUT THE WAR
Catherine Murray Roy **56**

A SOLDIER WHO FOUGHT WITH THE
BEDFORDSHIRE REGIMENT
Charles Percy Hawkes **60**

1915

A PIONEER WOMAN DOCTOR WHO
SERVED IN FRANCE AND MALTA
Isabella Stenhouse **64**

A BRITISH-BORN CANADIAN SOLDIER
WHO ESCAPED FROM A GERMAN
PRISONER-OF-WAR CAMP
Ernest Samuel Lovell **68**

A YOUNG COUPLE SURVIVE THE
SINKING OF THE *LUSITANIA*
Harold & Alice Smethurst **72**

A SCIENTIST WHO SAVED
THOUSANDS OF SOLDIERS
William Watson **78**

A PIONEER PILOT PROTECTED
BY JOAN OF ARC
Percy Edward Francis **82**

THE EXECUTION OF GERMAN
SPIES AT THE TOWER OF LONDON
John George Douglas **86**

A SUBMARINER'S DARDANELLES
ADVENTURE
Robert Brown **90**

A MASTER MARINER CLAIMED
BY DYSENTERY
John McNicol **94**

A RIFLEMAN WHO KICKED OFF
A BATTLE
Francis Edwards **98**

A SOLDIER'S DEATH CONFIRMED
BY A LETTER FROM A FRIEND
Thomas Henry Mowbray **102**

A NORFOLK MAN WHO FOUGHT
AT GALLIPOLI AND IN PALESTINE
John Edward Lock **106**

A NURSE TRAINED BY
EDITH CAVELL
Muriel Ruth Moore **110**

A SAPPER WHO USED HIS
VIOLIN AS A WAR DIARY
Ernest Alfred Johnson **114**

A SOLDIER WHO FOUGHT
WITH THE AUSTRALIANS
AND THE BRITISH
Walter Hubert Lester **118**

AN EGG THAT TRAVELLED
TO FRANCE AND BACK
Vida Olive Sheppard **122**

A LAD WHO DID HIS BIT
BY BUILDING TANKS
George Henry Atkin **124**

CHAUFFEUR TO THE
PRINCE OF WALES
John Henry Brenton **128**

A SOLDIER WHO RECORDED
HIS WAR IN PHOTOGRAPHS
Hugh Bourn Fortune Godfrey **130**

1916

A SAILOR KILLED IN AN
ACCIDENT AT SEA
Thomas Groves **136**

AN ARCHITECT AND ARTIST
KILLED IN KUT
Gilbert Marshall Mackenzie **140**

A SAILOR LOST WITH LORD
KITCHENER ON HMS *HAMPSHIRE*
John Thomas Buckenham **144**

A TYNESIDER KILLED ON THE
FIRST DAY OF THE SOMME
James Gardiner **148**

A CONSCIENTIOUS OBJECTOR WHO
WON A DISTINGUISHED CONDUCT
MEDAL FOR BRAVERY
John Powis **152**

A SOLDIER WHO SAVED HIS
COMMANDING OFFICER
Major Phillips **156**

TWO BROTHERS KILLED ON THE
SOMME TWO MONTHS APART
Donald Ryan Leatherdale &
Alan Richard Leatherdale **159**

A SOLDIER'S LIFE FOUND
IN A SUITCASE
Richard Walford **164**

A FAMOUS ARTIST PAINTS
HIS LOST SON
William Alexander Stanhope
Forbes **170**

A NARROW ESCAPE FROM
A GERMAN AIRSHIP
Florence Maude Gray **174**

AN ARTIST WITH THE LONDON
IRISH RIFLES
Rudolph Alfred Tanner **178**

A VOLUNTEER FROM BERMUDA
WHO DIED IN FRANCE
Nathaniel Benjamin Harriott **182**

THE RECRUITING SERGEANT AND
THE CONSCIENCE BATON
Archibald Frederick Ashton **186**

A WELSHMAN CAPTURED ON
THE SOMME
Richard Ivor Davies **190**

A CHRISTMAS PRESENT FOR
HIS MOTHER ARRIVED AFTER
HIS DEATH
William Sanders **194**

A MAN WHOSE LIFE WAS DESTROYED
BY WARTIME INJURIES
Amos Finn **196**

AN ARTIST WHO CONTINUED
TO SCULPT WHILE FIGHTING WITH
THE ARTILLERY
Alexander Carrick **200**

THE SOLDIER WHO RESCUED RATTY
Maurice Wells **204**

A SOLDIER WHO MADE HIS
OWN MASCO
Arthur HickmanT **206**

A SOLDIER WHO FOUGHT WITH
THE INTELLIGENCE SECTION
Albert Victor Pullin **208**

1917

A SAILOR CAPTURED BY
A COMMERCE RAIDER
Stanley Orritt **214**

A SOLDIER ALWAYS LOVED
BY HIS WIDOW
Frederick Charles Sewell **218**

A DOCTOR, AND AN ARTIST,
WHO LOVED HORSES
Herbert Arnold Lake **222**

A LADY WHO LOST HER SWEETHEART
Marion Forbes Baird **225**

A SOLDIER KILLED THREE MONTHS
BEFORE HIS SON'S BIRTH
Arthur Turner **228**

WOUNDED FOUR TIMES AND
SAVED BY HIS CAMERA
Ralfe Allen Fuller Whistler **230**

A YOUNG LAD MADE INTO
A 'BLOOD-THIRSTY OLD WARRIOR'
Albert Hall **233**

A CHILD KILLED IN LONDON'S
FIRST BLITZ
Rose Tuffin **236**

A MERCHANT SERVICE SAILOR
TORPEDOED THREE TIMES AND
SAVED BY HIS CANARY
Walter Edward Thorp **240**

A SOLDIER CAPTURED WHILE
SAVING A WOUNDED PAL
Frank Parker **244**

A PADRE WORKING WITH
THE AMERICANS
Arthur E. Boyce **248**

A PHOTOGRAPHER WITH
THE ROYAL FLYING CORPS
William Charles Cambray **252**

A SOLDIER SAVED BY HIS BIBLE
Wilfrid Norman Bush **256**

A SOLDIER SAVED BY A WHISTLE
Joseph Thomas Clucas **258**

A SOLDIER WHO WAS WITH HIS
BROTHER WHEN HE WAS KILLED
George Trevor Hancock **260**

A SOLDIER WHO DID MORE
MARCHING THAN FIGHTING
IN PALESTINE
Geoffrey Carr **264**

DEATH IN ACTION CONFIRMED
BY A RETURNED LETTER
Thomas Preston **268**

POACHER TURNED GAMEKEEPER
– FROM GERMAN INFANTRY TO
BRITISH MEDICAL OFFICER
Stephan Kurt Westmann **271**

1918

A SAILOR LOST IN A SUBMARINE
HE SHOULD NOT HAVE BEEN ON
Ernest John Hunt **276**

A DOCTOR'S PAINTING FROM
MESOPOTAMIA
Richard William Mathewson **280**

A FAMILY DESTROYED
BY THE WAR
William Hugh King &
John Headly King **284**

A SOLDIER WHOSE DEATH LED,
INDIRECTLY, TO A DISCOVERY
OF REGIMENTAL SILVER
Wilfrid Ernest Prew **288**

A WITNESS TO THE
RED BARON'S DEATH
Gladstone Adams **292**

A SAILOR WHO TOOK PART IN
THE ZEEBRUGGE RAID
John Joseph Crowley **295**

A TALE OF TWO BROTHERS
Joel Halliwell &
Thomas Halliwell **298**

A CONCEALED FIRST MARRIAGE
DISCOVERED YEARS LATER
Maria King & Jacob John Franks **302**

A SOLDIER WHO COLLECTED
SOUVENIRS ON THE BATTLEFIELD
Percy Weeks **305**

A SOLDIER WHO SENT HIS WIFE
188 POSTCARDS
Thomas James Draper **308**

A SOLDIER WHO LOOKED AFTER
TURKISH PRISONERS OF WAR
Hyman Levy **311**

A ROYAL FLYING CORPS PILOT
ON DUTY DURING THE FIRST
TRANSATLANTIC FLIGHT
James William White **314**

A MUNITIONS GIRL WHO
COURTED A SOLDIER
Keturah Mary Coombs **316**

A SOLDIER WHO OUTLIVED
HIS DEATH CERTIFICATE
William Henry Bell **320**

A SOLDIER WHO RESCUED
A WOUNDED GERMAN
William Turney **323**

A DRIVER WHO LOVED
HIS HORSES
Harry Wainwright **326**

A CONSCIENTIOUS OBJECTOR
WHO SERVED IN THE
NON-COMBATANT CORPS
William Lowman Stone **328**

A WELSH MINER WHO SERVED
THROUGH THE WAR WITH THE RAMC
David Thomas Jenkins **332**

A SOLDIER WHO HELPED A
WOUNDED GERMAN
Frederick William Gleed **336**

AN ARCHITECT KILLED AT
THE END OF THE WAR
Alfred Tinniswood **339**

A TALE OF TWO GRANDFATHERS
William John Taylor &
Reginald Cuffe **342**

POST WAR

TEN BROTHERS GO TO WAR
The Calpin Brothers **348**

A DORSET MAN WHO DIED
FOR AUSTRALIA
Edwin Henry Dibben **350**

A SAILOR BROUGHT TO LIFE
BY A CHANCE DISCOVERY
Henry Jenkins **354**

A CYCLIST WHO FOUGHT ON
THE NORTH WEST FRONTIER
Charles John Davis **358**

THE SOLDIER GIVEN A WALKING
STICK BY QUEEN ALEXANDRA
Benjamin Frederick Whiteley **362**

A SAILOR WHO FOUGHT IN RUSSIA
William Leslie Tokeley **366**

A STAFF OFFICER AND
CLASSICAL SCHOLAR WHO
WAS A PHOTOGRAPHER
Thomas Perowne Coe **369**

THE STORY OF MY
GRANDFATHER'S TRUNK
Gottfried Sandrock **372**

AN OLD BANJO TELLS THE
STORY OF CANADA'S WAR
Canadian Expeditionary Force **378**

THE CHAPLAIN WHO WITNESSED
THE START AND END OF THE WAR
Reverend George Kendall **382**

Timeline **386**
Index **392**
Acknowledgements **400**

INTRODUCTION

When the First World War started in August 1914 it was an event destined to change Britain fundamentally. In its immediate aftermath, the war was described in Britain as the Great War, the War to End Wars, the Great War for Civilization. A century on, such titles seem inadequate and inappropriate for a war that killed millions and redefined the political, social and economic shape of the modern world. In Britain, every family was affected, in one way or another, and today the war's long shadow has reached the third and fourth generations of those families who took part. Family stories, memories, photographs and mementoes are the war's modern legacy. Passing these down to future generations will ensure that the real history of the First World War will not be forgotten.

In 2011, the *Antiques Roadshow* marked Remembrance Day, the national commemoration of the end of the First World War on 11 November 1918, with a special edition of the show. It was filmed at the National Memorial Arboretum in Staffordshire and a number of families took part, with stories ranging from the First World War to the Falklands, covering many aspects of 20th-century conflict. The result was powerful and moving.

Two years later, with the centenary of the outbreak of the First World War approaching fast, the Roadshow team decided to do something similar, but on a much larger scale. Early in 2013 Fiona Bruce launched an appeal, asking for families who had stories to tell about the war to get in touch. The brief was very simple, and three things were required: a relative who took part in the war, in any capacity, an object that was part of the story, and a modern family member to tell that story. The response was staggering, with over 3000 viewers contacting the programme.

The responses were read in the Roadshow's Bristol office and by the programme's militaria team. It became immediately apparent to everyone involved that a massive family-based archive, hitherto completely unknown and inaccessible, had been tapped. Most of the stories had never been told before outside the family and they were all personal and sometimes deeply moving. They were whittled down to the 50 or so that would form the backbone of the two special *Antiques Roadshow* programmes that were to be made. The basis of this very difficult selection process was

Paul Atterbury filming at Thiepval with Alec Somerville and his banjo,
inscribed with names of soldiers from the Canadian Expeditionary Force.

diversity, in an attempt to represent the long years of the war, the many
places where fighting took place and the different nations involved. There
had to be stories from all the arms of the services, from men and women,
from civilians as well as soldiers and from the survivors as well as the dead.

After careful thought, it was decided that the *Antiques Roadshow* filming
should take place on the Somme. Sir Edwin Lutyens' great Memorial to
the Missing of the Somme at Thiepval, with the 73,000 names of men who
have no known grave, stood as a symbol for the whole war. In July 2013
the Roadshow team went there with the members of 28 families, and their
objects, who were to tell their stories at Thiepval or other Somme sites.
The sun shone during two glorious and unforgettable days of filming,
with many of those taking part, from family members to specialists and
technicians, feeling that they had experienced some of the best days of
their lives. I know I was not alone in finding that these were days of great

emotional intensity, but we all felt it a privilege to be there and to be part of something so memorable.

Given the richness of the material, there was more than we could ever hope to fit into the television specials. This book picks up where the television left off, to tell the story of the war through the eyes, the objects and the memories of 100 families. Immediately, I became involved in the selection of these 100 stories, a process both exciting and frustrating as so many were so good. My task then was to contact all those who had been selected, to make sure their stories were told in as direct and personal a manner as possible. At this stage the multi-generational nature of

Fiona Bruce (left) with three generations of Joel Halliwell's family (from right to left): his daughter Dora Gartside, granddaughter Joanne Bliss, and great-granddaughter Lois Bliss. During the filming the family saw for the first time the grave of Thomas Halliwell, Joel's brother, in Warloy-Baillon Communal Cemetery Extension.

the project became apparent as contact was made with the sons and daughters, grandsons and granddaughters and great-grandsons and great-granddaughters, as well as the great-nieces and great-nephews, of those who had taken part in the war.

The stories selected are all quite different and, most important, all unknown. Some do enter familiar territory, such as the death of Edith Cavell or the sinking of the *Lusitania*, but only when the family story offers a new insight into a well-known event. The aim has been to make the individual stories feel universal. A particular story may be about someone's grandfather, but it is also a story about all of our grandfathers. The experience of the war was common to a generation, and its impact, its aftermath and its memories shaped that generation.

Some families knew their stories in great detail, while others knew very little. Thanks to the internet, family history can be researched with relative ease, as can military history, with surviving service records and details of soldiers who died also available online. In some cases, I was able to fill out some of the gaps in the stories and, in the process, correct some long-held family myths. A century on, there is also a generational aspect, with grandchildren and great-grandchildren often more interested in their relatives' war experiences than their parents had been. Schools, and the National Curriculum, have encouraged this interest in various ways.

Until the 1980s, much of the history of the First World War was based on the memories of veterans, a process prone to all the excitement, generalizations and inaccuracies inherent in oral history. Now there are no veterans and so history has become much more document-based, much more to do with research, with families all over the world able to find out about their own relatives, and their own stories, should they wish to do so. With each year, the range and accessibility of historical records improves, and with it the chance for families to find out about their own stories.

The stories cover many areas of conflict, including the Western Front, the Dardanelles, Italy, Mesopotamia, Palestine, the North West Frontier, Italy, Russia, and even Western Samoa. They also feature many of the participating nations, including Britain, Canada, Australia, New Zealand, the United States and Germany and all the services: army, navy, air force, merchant navy and medical. On the Home Front there are munitions and armaments workers, Conscientious Objectors and civilian victims of bombing and torpedo attacks. Also remarkably diverse are the objects that help to tell the stories: letters, diaries, official documents, drawings and paintings, photographs, mascots, items of uniform or clothing, watches, jewellery, books, medals, battlefield souvenirs, handkerchiefs, embroidery, even a stuffed rat. They have been grouped by year, based on the key event or moment in each story. Each one is followed to its conclusion, whether this was a return to civilian life in Britain, or death in a foreign field.

While each story is individual and distinct, and the family responses to the impact of the war are infinitely varied, there are some common themes. Love and emotion are constant, although they take many forms, along with the events that inspired them. One theme, however, is universal, namely that those who took part in the war rarely if ever talked about it – to their wives, their children or their grandchildren. In the days before post-traumatic stress and counselling, people who had experienced dreadful and life-changing events had no choice but to deal with it themselves. Most did this by trying to put their memories away forever, and by never talking about the war and its effect on them and their friends.

In each case the personal story is the core. Attached to that core is the relevant military and historical background that gives each story a context. This information is, inevitably, general and broadly drawn and, like most history, open to interpretation. This book is, indirectly, the history of the war, but it is that history seen through the prism of memory and family stories. As a result, some inaccuracies are probably inevitable, although great care has been taken to avoid them.

There are many reasons that made me want to write this book, but high on the list is my own family story. Both my grandfathers fought in the war, and both survived, although their experiences were very different, with one fighting on the Western Front and the other based in the Sudan. However, theirs are not the story I want to tell. My great-uncle, Lewis John Rowley Atterbury, was killed on the Somme on 7 October 1916. His is the story I want to tell.

Right: Sir Edwin Lutyens' Memorial to the Missing of the Somme at Thiepval.

Lewis Atterbury's silver watch, marked with the
name of a Canadian department store.

FINDING A FORGOTTEN GREAT-UNCLE

LEWIS JOHN ROWLEY ATTERBURY
1885–1916

When I was about ten my grandmother took me to Westminster Abbey and showed me the Tomb of the Unknown Warrior. While we were standing there, she said, casually, 'That could be your great-uncle.' Nothing further was said and I soon forgot all about it. He was never mentioned in the family and another 40 years had to pass before Lewis John Rowley Atterbury came into my life.

From the late 1980s I was a regular visitor to the Western Front, and to the Somme in particular, looking primarily at cemeteries and monuments. My main interest was architecture, especially the work of Sir Edwin Lutyens, and so I had been several times to the Memorial to the Missing of the Somme at Thiepval. One cold and wet December in about 1996 I was showing a friend some of the First World War sights of the Somme, and we finished the day at Thiepval. I gave her a quick tour and then we set off back to the car, keen to get out of the rain. As we crossed the grass in front of the Memorial, I was compelled to turn round, walk back through the rain across the grass and look up my name in the printed index of all the names listed on the Memorial. I am not a particularly spiritual person, but the force driving me back to the Memorial was hard to resist. I quickly found the relevant entry: Atterbury,

Lewis has become very important to me. His eternal presence
at Thiepval may explain the strong emotional attachment
I feel to the Somme, and all it represents.

PAUL ATTERBURY, GREAT-NEPHEW

Lewis John Rowley, 2nd Lieut, London Regiment, 7th October 1916. Within a minute I was looking at his name on panel 9D, neatly carved in the white Portland stone, among the many thousands listed on the Memorial.

Back in England, I rang my father, Rowley Atterbury, told him what had happened and asked him who this unknown Atterbury was. 'Oh yes,' he said, 'he was my uncle Rowley, I was named after him.' When I replied that this was the first time I had ever heard of him, my father gave some kind of non-committal answer, paused, and then said, 'I've got his watch somewhere, do you want it?'

This was the beginning of a long story, and a deep passion for the Somme. Research around the family and in various archives gradually produced the details of Lewis's life and death. I found photographs of him, took possession of his silver pocket watch, and visited the field where he had died during the Battle of the Transloy Ridges, towards the end of the Somme campaign in 1916. I have since been back to the Somme often, usually two or three times a year, and have walked most of the battlefield, from 1 July 1916, that dreadful opening day, to its end in the freezing cold of mid-November nearly five months later. Whenever I can, I include a visit to Lewis at Thiepval who, I like to think, is pleased to see me.

Born in north London in March 1885, Lewis was one of six children. His father John was an East India merchant with an office in the City of London. The family were well off and enjoyed a comfortable life in a large house in Liphook, Hampshire, until 1901, when John Atterbury was declared bankrupt. Immediately, the family's situation became precarious and they moved to a small terraced house in Portsmouth. In 1903 Lewis was sent to Canada, to escape the wreckage and start a new life in Winnipeg. He became established as an accountant with a mortgage company and was a well-known athlete and cricketer. Sadly, those are the only details of his Canadian life known today.

In September 1914 Lewis enlisted in Valcartier, Quebec and was attached to the 2nd Field Company of the Canadian Engineers. He sailed for Europe with the first contingent of the Canadian Expeditionary Force, two-thirds of which were British-born Canadians. He was in France in February 1915, where he took part in the Second Battle of Ypres, and was one of a group of 27 volunteers who held a bridge over the Yser for a whole day against an overwhelming number of German attackers. In January 1916 he was awarded a commission in the London Regiment (Royal Fusiliers).

Initially 2nd Lieutenant Atterbury was attached to a Reserve battalion but, faced with the prospect of spending the rest of the war in England, he managed to arrange a transfer to the 1/4th Battalion of the London Regiment, part of the 56th Division, and joined them on the Somme in a draft of new officers on about 20 September 1916. At this stage, the British front line was being pushed slowly eastwards. Combles had been captured and the next targets were the villages of Lesboeufs and Morval, on the Transloy Ridge. The attack was launched early in October, and struggled from the start against well-placed German machine guns. After a break for consolidation, the attack was resumed on 7 October, with four companies of the 1/4th Battalion involved. It was not successful and at the end of the day the battalion had suffered 300 casualties and the survivors could not even fill one company. Five officers were killed, including Lewis Atterbury, who was seen to fall under machine gun fire. He was listed as missing, and his next of kin, surprisingly his eldest sister Susan rather than his parents, was informed. Lewis's body was never found and his death was not formally acknowledged until May 1917.

Much of my great-uncle's life remains a mystery. Nothing has come to light about his time in Canada. Family stories talked about land owned by him in Winnipeg, all of which reverted ultimately to the Canadian government, but there is no evidence. An obituary in a Canadian paper described him as 'prominent'. His will listed only his British possessions, a trivial sum of money representing largely his back pay. No one knows why, at the age of 29, and as a Canadian citizen, he left a secure and successful life in Winnipeg to fight for Britain.

As a child, I remember regular visits to my great-aunts Susie and Ivy, two of Lewis's unmarried sisters, and naturally I knew my grandfather, Lewis's older brother, very well. However, as far as I can remember, Lewis was never mentioned, and there was no trace of his life to be seen. I have no idea how his watch came into my father's possession and, when he gave it to me in 1997, he did not explain anything about it. Since then, I have tried to give my great-uncle a kind of life, though it is one still full of gaps.

1914

EVENTS IN THE BALKANS, KNOWN THEN AS 'THE POWDER keg of Europe', triggered the First World War, although the actual causes were wide-ranging and complex. The rising power of Russia challenged the declining Austro-Hungarian Empire, but it was balanced by the threat posed by the modern Turkish army. Driven by militarism and imperial ambitions, a newly unified Germany threatened this balance of power in Europe. Having rapidly defeated France during the Franco-Prussian War in 1870–1, Germany believed it could do it again. Likewise Italy, another recently unified country, was seeking its place in the modern world. The new friendship between Britain and France, confirmed by the Entente Cordiale, was perceived as a threat by other countries. Britain, already with the most powerful navy in the world, had increased that power to defend her trade routes and her extensive Empire and, in the process, launched an international arms race.

Although discussed for years, when it came the war took Britain and France by surprise. In 1914, the British were more concerned about a possible civil war in Ireland than events in the Balkans. The general view was that a war in Europe would be short-lived. Nevertheless, Britain sent a rapidly assembled Expeditionary Force to France and Belgium and by the middle of August 1914 the small but well-trained British professional army was in action. The German invasion of France, following their well-publicized Schlieffen plan, was initially successful but the German armies were stopped on the outskirts of Paris by the combined efforts of British and French forces, and then driven steadily backwards. By the autumn, both sides had dug in, consolidated their positions and trench warfare was established, on a line from the Swiss border to the Channel. The pattern for the next four years was set, as the Allied armies squared up against those of the Central Powers in many different areas of conflict.

The stories in this chapter reflect many aspects of the first few months of the war, from people trapped in Europe by the rapid and generally unexpected outbreak of hostilities to a witness of the unofficial Christmas truces. There are professional soldiers from the regular army fighting through the war's first battles, from Mons to First Ypres, alongside hastily prepared Territorial Forces drawn from volunteers. Others show the effect of submarine warfare on the Royal Navy, the battles in distant parts of the world over colonial possessions, the rise of anti-German feeling in Britain and the important role that was to be played in the conflict by horses. Above all, the stories underline the rapid, and generally unexpected, shift from a conventional war of mobility to the establishment of a trench warfare stalemate, held in place by machine guns and artillery, mechanized and remote killing machines that caused death and injury in numbers that shocked all those involved in the conflict.

A SCOUT TROOP TRAPPED BY THE OUTBREAK OF WAR

GEORGE STANLEY WALMSLEY
1901–1985

The outbreak of the First World War was the culmination of a sequence of predictable but largely unforeseen events across Europe. While the

possibility of war had been extensively discussed during the preceding years, many were taken by surprise when it actually started in August 1914. In many ways, the least prepared were the British, and so through the summer of 1914 life in Britain was carrying on much as normal, and many were planning summer visits to France.

In 1914 George Stanley Walmsley, who had been born in Manchester in March 1901 to a father in the textile industry, was a pupil at Manchester Grammar School and a member of the school's Boy Scout troop. This was in the habit of holding an annual summer camp in Europe, and no one saw any reason why 1914 should be any different. On 28 July 1914, 44 Boy Scouts and their Scoutmaster, Mr Hope, set off from Manchester for the

'My father was an engineer, and a very knowledgeable and intensely practical man. He mended everything in the house and would never buy anything new if he were able to make or repair a damaged or worn out item. Perhaps his early Boy Scout training helped.'

PETER WALMSLEY, SON

The Boy Scout troop's ceremonial return to Manchester
in September 1914, after they were forced to march across
France to return home after the outbreak of war.
George Walmsley is at the head of the right-hand column.

Auvergne, in southwest France. By 1 August they had reached Paris. They were still there on 3 August 1914 when Germany declared war on France. All public transport was immediately requisitioned by the French government as troops were rushed to the front, and so the Scouts were trapped in Paris, with no hope of finding transport to the Channel ports.

Back in Manchester the boys' parents were getting concerned as none of the postcards, which their sons were supposed to send every two days, had arrived. There was much relief when, on 10 August, Mr Paton, the school's High Master, received a card from Mr Hope, the Scoutmaster, saying, 'All well and happy.' He went on to say that, as there were no trains, 'we are now setting out marching back to Havre.'

It took the troop two weeks to cover the 150 miles, marching about 13 miles a day in temperatures up to 90°F. Every night they pitched their camp, except on one occasion when they were looked after and fed by soldiers in a barracks. All along the route, the French people looked after them and gave them fruit, milk, chocolate and flowers. When they reached Le Havre, it took Mr Hope some time to find a boat to take them back to England and they finally arrived at the end of the month, along with many of their postcards. Determined not to miss their annual summer camp, the troop set off for the New Forest and camped for a week near Lyndhurst, and for a second week at Lulworth Cove in Dorset. When they finally made it back to Manchester in mid-September, they marked their return by parading to the school with bugles and drums playing and flags flying from all the countries the troop had visited over the years, with Germany excepted.

George continued his education and was too young to serve in the First World War. In 1918 he joined Mather & Platt and trained as a hydraulic engineer, and then worked in that field for the rest of his career. In the Second World War he had a Reserved Occupation and towards the end of the war was responsible for the pumping machinery for the Pluto (Pipe Line Under The Ocean) network, which supplied the Allied invasion armies with fuel.

George married Elizabeth Morris in 1928 and they had one son, Peter, who remembers his father as a very resourceful man. In the garage he kept a Spitfire wing, which he had found in a field, and he used the aluminium from it for general household repairs, including the replacement of worn-out saucepans.

George Walmsley's adventure was not exceptional. Throughout August and September 1914 Britons trapped in Europe by the outbreak of war struggled to make their way home. Some travelled via Spain and the Mediterranean, some via Holland, some via Scandinavia, journeys made easier by the neutrality of many of the countries that shared borders with the belligerent nations. Many were, of course, trapped in Germany, and for most of these there was only the prospect of spending the duration of the war in an internment camp.

A ROYAL MARINE WHO WENT DOWN WITH HMS ABOUKIR

DAVID PAGE
1883–1914

Born in December 1883 to a farm labourer in Hertfordshire, David Page was one of a family of six children. In 1903 David enlisted in the Royal Marines and at some point joined the Royal Marine Artillery (RMA). This branch of the Royal Marines, originally set up in the early 19th century, was later reorganized and had a variety of duties, including manning the two aftermost gun turrets on a battleship or cruiser. The RMA also supplied two brigades to fight on the Western Front, one an anti-aircraft unit, and the other equipped with 12 massive 15-inch howitzers, each of which required a crew of 60.

It is not known how David spent the years leading up to the First World War, where he was based or on which ships he served but at the outbreak of war he was on HMS *Aboukir*.

Aboukir was a *Cressy*-class cruiser launched in Scotland in 1900 and in service by 1902. However, by 1914 advances in warship design had made her and her sisters obsolete. At the outbreak of war HMS *Aboukir* and her sister ships, HMS *Bacchante*, HMS *Euryalus*, HMS *Hogue* and HMS *Cressy*,

> '*We don't know much about David in the family today, but I am sure he was kind, hardworking and very law-abiding, just like his brothers and sisters.*'

DIANE YOUNG, GREAT-NIECE

were given the task of patrolling the Broad Fourteens of the North Sea, an area to the east of the English Channel, to provide a screen for destroyers and submarines operating out of Harwich. Many senior naval officers felt the patrol was risky because of the vulnerable nature of the old cruisers involved and some even called the patrol the 'live bait squadron'.

On 20 September 1914 four of the ships, *Euryalus*, *Aboukir*, *Hogue* and *Cressy*, went out on patrol, without their usual destroyer escort because of the bad weather. *Euryalus* later returned to port because of a coal shortage, leaving the other three to carry out the patrol. At 06.00 hours on 22 September *Aboukir*, *Hogue* and *Cressy* were sailing at 10 knots in line astern formation, despite standing instructions that they should be zigzagging and travelling faster. The ships were spotted by the German submarine *U-9*, under the command of Otto Weddigen. He made a careful attack at about 06.25 and fired a single torpedo at *Aboukir*, which hit her on the port side. This crippled the cruiser and she began to sink, rolling over about 20 minutes later. *Hogue* and *Cressy*, thinking she had hit a mine, had gone to her aid and stopped to pick up survivors. Manoeuvring carefully, *U-9* fired two torpedoes at *Hogue* from a range of about 300 yards. Both hit, and *Hogue* sank within ten minutes. *U-9* then turned towards *Cressy*, which had started to get underway, and fired two torpedoes, one of which damaged

Opposite: The HMS Aboukir sweetheart brooch, given by
David Page to his sister before his last voyage in 1914.
Above: The cruiser HMS Aboukir.

her. The submarine then hit *Cressy* again with her last torpedo and the cruiser sank within 15 minutes. Other ships were quickly on the scene and 837 men were rescued but 1459 died, many of whom were reservists or cadets. Among the dead was David Page.

The destruction of these three old cruisers so early in the war brought home to the Royal Navy both the vulnerability of large ships to submarines and the danger posed by adhering to tactics and attitudes rendered obsolete by modern warfare.

David's mother died in 1913 and so, in her absence, David gave his sister Beatrice a silver brooch of an anchor with the name Aboukir mounted across it, before sailing on his last voyage in 1914. Such 'sweetheart' brooches became popular during the First World War as gifts for girlfriends or mothers. The object passed from Beatrice to her daughter Ethel, and in turn to her daughter Diane, who treasures it today as the only surviving link to her great-uncle.

Top: Cartoon by Snaffles, depicting Arthur Hughes-Onslow
as a famous amateur jockey. Bottom: Arthur Hughes-
Onslow's Death Plaque, with the original packaging.

A FAMOUS HORSEMAN AND ONE OF THE FIRST BRITISH CASUALTIES IN FRANCE

ARTHUR HUGHES-ONSLOW
1862–1914

Arthur Hughes-Onslow was born in August 1862. His father died when he and his four brothers were young, and they were brought up by his mother on the family estate in Ayrshire. He was sent to the Royal Military College (now the Royal Military Academy) at Sandhurst and afterwards gazetted to

the 5th Lancers, although immediately transferred to the 10th Hussars, one of Britain's most famous cavalry regiments. It has a history stretching back to the 17th century and has fought in the Peninsular War, at the Battle of Waterloo and in the Crimea. In 1861 the regiment was renamed the 10th (Prince of Wales's Own) Royal Hussars, and when Arthur joined it in 1882, it was serving in Lucknow in India. Officers in famous regiments required considerable private means to fund their membership, and Arthur probably paid his way by renting out the Ayrshire estate. His first action with the regiment was in the Sudan, in the Battle of El Teb in 1884, and he also fought in South Africa, before retiring from the army in 1903, with the rank of Major.

'I'm very proud of my great-grandfather. I know suicide was as bad as desertion in those days but he'd proved his courage in two earlier wars. It was his love of horses that led him to do it, he couldn't face what was going to happen to them.'

JOHN FERGUSSON, GREAT-GRANDSON

Arthur was a famous horseman, both with the Hussars and as a jockey. He won the Military Gold Cup at Sandown, Surrey, three times, the Conyngham Cup at Punchestown, County Kildare, three times and countless other steeplechases over a career lasting more than 30 years. He was a well-known writer on country matters and was drawn by Snaffles, the English artist and cartoonist who specialized in sporting and military subjects, in 1913. In 1891 he married Kathleen Whitehead and they had two children, Geoffrey and Dorothy.

When war was declared on 4 August 1914, Arthur, at 52, was old enough to be exempt from military service. However, he immediately returned to the army and was employed at once in the Remount Service, because of his cavalry background and experience with horses, and attached to a depot near Southampton. Set up in 1887, the Remount Service was responsible for the purchase, training and supply of horses and mules for army use. Initially, there were 121 officers and 230 men, with most of the officers, like Arthur, drawn from the landed gentry and other areas where they had active experience with horses. The famous horse and sporting artists Alfred Munnings and Lionel Edwards were Remount officers.

On the outbreak of war in 1914, the British army owned 25,000 horses and mules. Within 12 days this number had been increased to 165,000, in effect by a process of compulsory purchase. A year later the figure was 535,000. During the course of the war, the Remount Service purchased around 470,000 horses in Britain, 429,000 horses and 275,000 mules in the United States, 6000 horses in South America and 4000 mules from Spain and Portugal. The British Remount Service also supplied horses and mules to many of the Allied armies, including the Australian, Canadian, New Zealand, Portuguese and Belgian forces, while the Remount Service in India supplied horses and mules to the Mesopotamian campaign.

As is now well known, hundreds of thousands of these horses and mules were to die during the conflict. It seems that Arthur was acutely aware of the likely fate awaiting so many of his beloved horses, mainly because he had seen horses in his care suffer and die in previous conflicts. On 17 August 1914, the SS *City of Edinburgh*, a transport ship, docked in Le Havre with a cargo of horses for the British Expeditionary Force. Arthur was on board, as the Remount officer in charge of the shipment but, unable to face the prospect of taking horses into battle again, he shot himself while the ship lay by the quayside.

At first, the manner of Arthur's death was concealed from his family. His son Geoffrey, then serving as a Midshipman on the battleship HMS *St Vincent*, was called off watch to be told that his father had died. Two weeks later he was told that his death was from a broken blood vessel. It was only after the war, when Geoffrey received a demand for death duties and inheritance tax, that the truth came out. Death duties were waived for those who died on active service but the tax authorities decided that, as a suicide, Arthur was not exempt. While shocked by the true nature of Arthur's death, the family fought this decision and in the end the government conceded that Arthur's death had been in the service of his country and waived the tax demands. The family then received his medals, including the 1914 Star, popularly known as the Mons Star, and his Death Plaque or 'Death Penny'. In 1917, the British government had decided to issue a named bronze plaque to be given as a token of gratitude to the next of kin of everyone who died on active service in the First World War, accompanied by a printed letter of thanks from the King. A competition for the design attracted over 800 entries and the winner was the Liverpool sculptor Edward Carter Preston. When they began to be distributed after the war, the plaques had a very mixed response and were immediately nicknamed the Widow's Penny or the Death Penny.

Arthur Hughes-Onslow was one of the first casualties of the First World War. His brother Denzil also returned to the army after many years away from the colours and served as a Major with the Dorsetshire Regiment. He too died, killed by a German sniper on the Somme on 10 July 1916, also at the age of 52. But it is Arthur's death, in extraordinary circumstances, that was to make him one of the first, if not the first, soldier in the British Expeditionary Force to die on active service.

A NEW ZEALANDER
WHO TOOK PART IN THE CAPTURE
OF GERMAN SAMOA

ARTHUR FREDERICK WEBB
1890–1942

The building of Germany's Empire in Africa and the Pacific is a little-known story, and even less well known is the role played by these colonies in the First World War. Most were captured or taken over by the Allies, in campaigns radically different from anything experienced on the Western

Front. Arthur Frederick Webb, who was born in Wellington, New Zealand, in April 1890, took part in one of the most remote of these campaigns.

Arthur was educated in New Zealand and then went to work in the government printing office. In common with many of his friends and countrymen, he signed up in August 1914, soon after the outbreak of war, and joined the New Zealand Expeditionary Force (NZEF).

Action came quickly when a force of 1370 volunteers was sent, at the behest of the British government, to capture the radio station at Apia, on German Samoa. They set off across the Pacific in two troopships, escorted by three ancient destroyers. At Fiji the fleet was greatly strengthened by the addition of the battlecruiser HMAS *Australia* and two cruisers, HMAS

> '*My grandfather was a quiet man, very intelligent
> but his confidence was badly damaged by his illness.
> Music was always at the heart of his life.*'

JASON PAYNE, GRANDSON

Melbourne and the French ship *Montcalm*. This added protection was to counter the threat posed by the presence of two German armoured cruisers, *Scharnhorst* and *Gneisenau*, in the area. In the event, there was no German attack on the fleet and the force landed at Apia on 29 August 1914. Faced by a large and well-equipped invading force, the small German garrison did not resist and the colony was successfully occupied. The German warships arrived off Apia on 14 September but Admiral von Spee quickly decided that there was no point in trying to recapture the colony in a region by then dominated by British forces, and the two cruisers sailed for Tahiti and thence to South America. The occupation of German Samoa continued until 1920, after which New Zealand governed what became known as the Western Samoa Trust Territory until 1962.

When the New Zealand force returned home, a number of the volunteers, including Arthur Webb, left the army. The main elements of the NZEF then sailed for Egypt, and thence to Gallipoli, where they merged with the 4th Australian Brigade to form the Australian and New Zealand Division, which in turn became part of ANZAC (the famous Australian and New Zealand Army Corps). Webb returned to his printing job but, in October 1915, he re-enlisted and served as a trombonist and bandmaster in the NZEF in New Zealand until April 1917. The band then sailed for Europe and was used for entertaining the troops, mostly in Britain, until demobilization in 1919.

Webb returned to New Zealand with a serious case of trench fever, and never fully recovered. Breathing problems meant that he could only work irregularly. However, with music his one great love, he continued to work as a musician and ended up as a band leader in the Big Band era. Webb married twice, first to Violet Lepper in May 1920 and second to Winifred Burberry in May 1940, and there was one child from each marriage. He died in August 1942.

Right: Arthur Webb's pocket watch, typical of the kind used in the pre-wristwatch era, is kept today by his grandson.

Above: Arthur Collins, on the day he scored his record innings at the age of 13. Left: A silver cup won by Arthur Collins in a tennis tournament in India in 1910.

A RECORD-BREAKING CRICKETER WHO DIED AT YPRES

ARTHUR EDWARD JAMES COLLINS
1885–1914

Arthur Edward James Collins was born in India in August 1885. His father was a judge in the Indian Civil Service but by the time he started his education at Clifton College, Bristol, both his parents had died and he was

living with guardians in Devon. Clifton College was a school famous for both its sporting and its military achievements, and former pupils included the poet Sir Henry Newbolt and Field Marshal Haig.

In 1899, when he was 13, Arthur Collins, playing in a school house cricket match, achieved the highest individual score ever recorded in cricket, 628 not out. The match was played over four days and Arthur batted for a total of six hours and fifty minutes. As his runs steadily mounted, more and more people came to watch, and when it was finally over, the innings was widely reported, notably in *The Times*, and it has been a famous feature in Wisden, the cricketers' almanac, ever since. The scorecard from this game survives and today, over a century later, Arthur's record still stands, and has never been seriously challenged. In 1999, the centenary of his great feat was

'The river of death has brimmed his banks,
And England's far, and Honour a name,
But the voice of a schoolboy rallies the ranks:
Play up! Play up! and play the game!'

SIR HENRY NEWBOLT, 'VITAI LAMPADA'

35

marked by an article in the *Daily Telegraph*, written by Sir Tim Rice. This gives a sense of Arthur Collins, the schoolboy cricketer:

> A reserved boy, short and stockily built, fair-haired and pale ... remembered by his contemporaries as one who led by example, rather than by inspiration ... He was academically bright, and popular. He was modest – throughout his life more annoyed than grateful for the attention his childhood feat brought him.

Though he continued to play cricket, Arthur never played in a first-class game. His one appearance at Lords was for the Royal Engineers against the Royal Artillery in 1913. He also played rugby and won a medal as a boxer.

After leaving school, Arthur entered the Royal Military Academy at Woolwich and, when his studies there were finished, he was commissioned as a 2nd Lieutenant in the Royal Engineers in December 1904. He was posted to India in 1907, where he served for six years as an engineering officer, returning to Britain in 1913 on a year's leave. With a promising military career ahead of him as an experienced engineer officer, he married Ethel Slater, the daughter of a brother officer, in Castletown on the Isle of Man in April 1914.

Twelve days after the start of the First World War on 4 August 1914, the 5th Field Company of the Royal Engineers landed in France as part of the British Expeditionary Force. The company was attached to the 2nd Division and included four Sapper Sections with Lieutenant Arthur Collins as Section Officer for No. 1. Sapper, or engineer, sections were usually regarded as support staff rather than fighting troops. The company was quickly in action, at Mons and Le Cateau, in the first battles of the Marne and the Aisne, and in the advances into Belgium on 17 October 1914. Next came the First Battle of Ypres, with the 5th Field Company being deployed on 25 October at Polygon Wood. Heavy German artillery fire and bitter fighting caused many casualties, and Arthur found himself in command of the company. His leadership and courage greatly helped the Sappers, who suddenly had to turn themselves from engineers into front-line infantry.

Early on 11 November 1914 the Germans launched a massive artillery barrage on Polygon Wood, the preparation for a ground attack by the Prussian Guards. Sweeping aside British resistance at Nonne Bosschen the Germans advanced rapidly towards Polygon Wood, where they were faced by the 5th Field Company and a hastily assembled infantry force made up of cooks, grooms, clerks and other behind-the-lines soldiers, none of whom would have expected to find themselves fighting in the front line. In fierce and often hand-to-hand fighting this force somehow managed to check the German advance, helped by the fine marksmanship of the well-trained Sappers. At some point, while signalling for reinforcements, Arthur was shot and mortally wounded. Two of his Sappers managed to get him back to the trench but he died an hour later. That afternoon, the 5th Field Company, supported by other infantry units from the Oxfordshire and Buckinghamshire Light Infantry, the Black Watch, the Irish Guards and the Northamptons, counter-attacked and with fixed bayonets put the Prussian Guards to flight. This success brought to an end the First Battle of Ypres, saving the town and ending the German advance towards the Channel ports.

Lieutenant Arthur Collins, and two fellow officers who had also been killed, were formally buried near where they had fallen, but all the graves were destroyed and lost during later fighting in the area. His name is listed among the Missing on the Menin Gate Memorial in Ypres. The 5th Field Company, Royal Engineers, fought on the Western Front for the rest of the war, while Arthur's two younger brothers, Herbert Charles Collins and Norman Cecil Collins, also died on active service in the First World War. Arthur's wife Ethel, heartbroken by the loss of her husband so soon after their marriage, remained a widow until her death in 1966.

In his combination of sporting prowess, military achievement, modest demeanour and devotion to duty, Arthur Collins was in every way the classic Englishman at the heart of fellow Cliftonian Sir Henry Newbold's famous poem, 'Vitai Lampada' (the Torch of Life). Though inspired by battles and campaigns from the late Victorian era, the poem's relevance to the First World War, and to 1914 in particular, was missed by few. Throughout his life Arthur played up and played the game, and it was the loss of his generation during the first months of the war that not only destroyed Britain's highly professional regular army but also blighted Britain's future social and economic development in the changed world of the 1920s and 1930s.

Today, Arthur Collins is remembered widely by the nation as a sporting hero, but his memory as a man is treasured by his family.

AN OLD CONTEMPTIBLE
SAVED BY HIS WALLET

WILLIAM EDWARD TAYLOR
1891–1979

William Edward Taylor was born in Hertford in 1891, into a family whose Hertford connections went back centuries. At some point before the war, he joined the Hertfordshire Regiment as a Territorial Force volunteer.

The origins of the Hertfordshire Regiment lay in local Rifle Volunteer Corps founded in the 1850s. Always closely associated with the Bedfordshire Regiment, the Hertfordshire Regiment was established as an independent body in 1908, with a single regular army battalion.

When the regiment was mobilized at the outbreak of war in 1914 as part of Britain's regular army, William sailed with the regiment's 1/1st Battalion to France to join the British Expeditionary Force, serving initially as a medical orderly or stretcher-bearer. He was at the First Battle of Ypres, which ended on 22 November, thereby receiving the 1914 Star, and qualifying as an Old Contemptible.

'On Sunday morning it was the family tradition to go and see granddad Taylor, he was a proper granddad, a true gentleman. We'd play dominoes or go up to the Working Men's Club to play cribbage. We never tackled him about his war experiences, though we knew bits and pieces.
They just got on with it.'

DAVID TAYLOR, GRANDSON

Above: Family photographs, clearly showing the progress of the bullet.
Below: The wallet that saved William Taylor's life.

The term 'Old Contemptible' is often associated with soldiers mobilized in the first few months of the war. The British Expeditionary Force (BEF) was composed of regular army and territorial regiments. Though small numerically, the BEF fought bravely and successfully during the early months of the war, helping to halt the German advance and thus derail their Schlieffen plan for the conquest of France. Frustrated by these delays, the Kaiser apparently instructed von Kluck, his army commander, to destroy 'Sir John French's contemptible little army'. The regular army troops in the BEF immediately seized upon this and quickly called themselves the Old Contemptibles, a term that became enduringly associated with those who had fought in Belgium and France in 1914 between August and 22 November, the end of the First Battle of Ypres.

In January 1915 William was with the battalion at the Cuinchy Brickstacks battle, supporting the Irish and Coldstream Guards as part of the 4th Guards Brigade. From this point the regiment was popularly known as the Herts Guards. Later that year he took part in the battles of Festubert and Loos. In August 1916 the battalion moved south to the Somme, initially near Thiepval. In October and November 1916 William took part in the Battle of the Ancre Heights, and on 13 November he was involved in the action that captured the Hansa Line, earning a Military Medal for rescuing wounded colleagues under fire. The battalion moved back to Ypres at the end of 1916, remaining there for some months. William was promoted to Lance Corporal and then took part in the Third Battle of Ypres, which started on 31 July 1917, earning a Bar to his Military Medal. A few days earlier he had had a narrow escape when he was shot in the chest but the bullet was stopped by the wallet in his breast pocket.

In the course of the First World War, a surprising number of soldiers owed their lives to objects in their pockets, usually books or wallets, but sometimes whistles, cigarette cases and even cameras. These were often carried in uniform breast pockets and so served by chance as protectors for the heart and other vital organs. Many other soldiers must have been saved by bullets striking metal buckles or buttons, ammunition pouches, water bottles, binoculars, entrenching tools and other pieces of equipment.

In January 1918 the battalion moved south again and on 23 March it was drawn into the heavy fighting as the Allies struggled to halt the German

Spring Offensive. The battalion fought for ten days in the Somme region, suffering heavy losses. The survivors, including William, returned north, to be reformed and rested. In May the battalion was back on the Somme, but was almost obliterated by a gas attack near Fonquevillers. Reformed again, the battalion was in reserve until 23 August 1918 when they joined the Allied Offensive at the Battle of Achiet-le-Petit. William, by then a Corporal, fought with the battalion at Cambrai in October and was with them throughout the final battles that culminated in the Allied victory. He remained in Belgium until April 1919, when he was demobilized.

After the war William Taylor returned to Hertford where he spent the rest of his life. He married in 1928, but two years later his wife died, leaving him with newborn twins. An elderly nanny helped to bring them up but there was no normal family life for him or the children until he remarried in 1944. William worked until his retirement as a gardener for the McMullens, the owners of the local brewery, for whom he also played cricket and bowls. He was always proud of being an Old Contemptible and regularly took part in Old Contemptible events and celebrations, including the 50th anniversary in 1974. William died in 1979.

William Taylor had a remarkable career, fighting throughout the war from the early battles of 1914 to the Armistice in 1918 with the 1/1st Battalion. His Military Medal and Bar show that he was often in the centre of the action, yet he was never wounded. The one time he received what should have been a fatal injury, the bullet hit his wallet which, with his family photographs and other papers, absorbed the impact, and thus saved his life.

A SOLDIER FROM A GERMAN FAMILY FIGHTING FOR BRITAIN

MAX JORDAN
1881–1914

Max Jordan was born in 1881 to a German family who had emigrated to Britain. Originally from farming stock near Stuttgart, the Jordans had

settled in Camberwell, south London, which had a long-established German community and where Max's father worked as a French polisher. After the outbreak of war the Jordans, like many of their German compatriots, were subjected to abuse, hostility and vandalism by their neighbours. This was to continue through the war, even though their son was fighting for Britain.

In May 1897 Max had enlisted at Aldershot into the 1st Battalion of the Manchester Regiment. This was the start of a varied and interesting life as a professional soldier in the Manchesters, a well-respected regiment in Britain's small but highly trained regular army. As part of army reforms,

'I lived with my grandmother until I was three. She was indomitable, very strict, and kept to the rules she had learned in domestic service. I remember sitting upright on a stiff horsehair sofa and not being allowed to move while she wrote her shopping list. She wasn't unkind, but like Queen Victoria she never got over her husband's death. I always felt an outsider as the approach of Christmas made granny more gloomy.'

PATRICIA CREAMER, GRANDDAUGHTER

Right: Max Jordan's Queen's South Africa Medal.
Below: The postcard (front and back) sent by Leah
Jordan to her sister, after her husband Max had
sailed for Europe from India.

SOUTH AFRICA 1901

DEFENCE OF LADYSMITH

ELANDSLAAGTE

The Delhi Gate, Fort Agra.
Built during the Akber's Reign, in 1599 A.D.

the Manchesters had been formed in July 1881 by the merging of two older foot regiments, the 63rd and the 96th.

Max served first in Gibraltar, then was sent to South Africa towards the end of 1899. Apart from a few months in St Helena in 1902 he was in South Africa until October 1906, and fought at the Siege of Ladysmith during the Boer War. The next posting was to India and the Manchesters remained there until the outbreak of the First World War, although Jordan seems to have returned to Britain between the end of 1908 and early 1911. During this period he met Leah Ellis, probably in Manchester, and they were married in 1909. Leah was one of eight children from a Derbyshire mining family and worked as a domestic servant. She had a reputation as a tough, no-nonsense girl, willing to speak her mind and it was said that her employers didn't know what they had taken on. The couple returned to India, in time for Max to take part in the Delhi Durbar of 1911. Leah retained her forceful character, on one famous occasion fetching her husband, who was rather the worse for wear, from the Sergeants' Mess – an area that was completely out of bounds to women.

On the outbreak of war in August 1914 the battalion left their base in the hill station at Dalhousie, marched across the plain to Jullunder, travelled by train to Karachi and then embarked on a ship bound for Egypt on 27 August. From there they set sail for France, reaching the front line by 26 October. The battalion was immediately in action near Festubert, and continued to be involved through November and December. On 18 December British troops attempted to drive the Germans back from the village of Givenchy. Initially successful, the attack was soon broken by aggressive and continuous German counter-attacks, and when the battle ended on 22 December, the British were back at their start lines. There were 4000 British casualties, including Sergeant Max Jordan who was killed in hand-to-hand fighting near Givenchy on 21 December 1914.

Max has no known grave but his name is listed among the Manchester Regiment casualties at the Le Touret Memorial, which serves as a record of over 13,000 soldiers who died in this area before the Battle of Loos but have no known grave. Later the Manchesters, much expanded, served in Mesopotamia and fought at Neuve Chapelle, Loos, the Somme, Arras and Passchendaele.

When the 1st Battalion left the hill station, Leah and her two small children were left to pack up their belongings, ready to move down to the plain and be shipped back to Britain. The day after Max's departure, Leah wrote a postcard to her sister Mary in Rotherham.

> Dear M. Sorry I cannot write a letter, we are full of trouble. Our men went to the plains yesterday, Max included. They are supposed to set sail for Egypt on the 28th of this month. There seems to be nothing but war. I have been upset. I have been moving today … so everything is upside down. I am packing all up ready for us to move on the plain. I hope everything is all right at home. No more now. With fondest love from your loving sister, L.J. xxxx

When soldiers were killed, their wives and children were no longer allowed to live in army accommodation and their income ended, although there was often a small pension. More importantly, it is not known when Leah heard about Max's death – it could have been en route to Britain or after she and her family had settled in South Yorkshire with her sister. Leah never recovered from her husband's death, never remarried, and refused for the rest of her life to celebrate Christmas as Max had died so close to that date. She grieved all her life, living in a sparsely furnished house with no bathroom, and running her life along the strict rules she had learned in domestic service. Her children, Max and Mary, aged three and one when they left India, barely knew their father, and had to come to terms with their grieving mother. Leah died in 1973.

Leah's experience was not uncommon among army wives, particularly in the early months of the war. The professional soldiers, who were the backbone of Britain's regular army, formed a dedicated, well-trained and very efficient force that fought well above expectations in the early battles of the war in Belgium and France but were decimated by the sheer scale of the conflict. They wore their 'Old Contemptible' nickname with pride, along with the 1914 Star which they earned when they helped to stop the German invasion, and derail the Schlieffen plan. The volunteers that replaced them were not from the same mould and, however keen and well trained they were, they would always lack the experience of the professional soldier.

Wt. W1154/2240 7/11. 7,500,000. Sch. 4a.   "S" Form.   Army Form C. 2121.

MESSAGES AND SIGNALS.

Prefix	Code 742 P.m.	Words	Charge	This message is on a/c of:	Recd. at 7.56 P m
Office of Origin and Service Instructions.		42			4 P M

Sent

At _____ m.   _____ Service.   Date 27/12/14

To _____   From H B

By _____   (Signature of "Franking Officer.")   By Sgt Paice

TO   ADT

Sender's Number.	Day of Month	In reply to Number	
			A A A

*

Following message has been

received unsigned from the enemy.

Gentlemen our automatic rifle

has order from the Colonel to

begin the fire again at midnight

We take in honour to award

you of this fact message ends

From   CAPT ONWIN

Place

Time   1.55 Pm

The above may be forwarded as now corrected.   (Z)

Censor. _____   Signature of Addressor or person authorised to telegraph in his name.

* This line should be erased if not required.

A signal form preserved by James Paice, announcing
that the Germans were going to resume hostilities
after a 1914 Christmas truce.

A FULL LIFE IN THE REGULAR ARMY – AND THE 1914 CHRISTMAS TRUCE

JAMES JOHN PAICE
1891–1933

James John Paice was born near Southampton in May 1891 into a farming family. His father was a farm carter and general labourer, and James started his working life as a dairyman. In July 1908, however, he decided to join the army and enlisted into the 1st Battalion of the Hampshire Regiment, signing on for 21 years. The Hampshire Regiment was formed in 1881 by the merger of two long-established local foot regiments, the 37th and the 67th.

Though he was small in stature, James worked hard and was soon well established as a professional regular army soldier. Much later, his commanding officer reported that James was 'a hard-working reliable man of sober habits who has carried out his duties in an exemplary and exceedingly conscientious manner. He has a good way with other men and is a good disciplinarian.'

'I never knew my grandfather but, by all accounts, he was a typical professional soldier, not a man to be trifled with but meticulous in looking after his men. His brother, my uncle Charlie, who I knew well as a child, never talked about James, and I didn't ask, which of course I now regret very much.'

TRISH SWINDELLS, GRANDDAUGHTER

Trained as a Signaller, he was a Sergeant at the start of the First World War. His Battalion went to France in August 1914 as part of the British Expeditionary Force and was quickly in action at Le Cateau and Mons, on the Marne and the Aisne and in other battles of the first months of the war. This was the start of the remarkable military career of the Hampshires, a regiment that won battle honours in most of the major engagements of the war. As a regular member of the 1st Battalion, James Paice was to take part in many of these battles on the Western Front between 1914 and 1918. Unfortunately, the full details of James's wartime service record are not known, although he was wounded twice on the Somme, where he won his Military Medal, and at some point he was gassed. We also know that he witnessed one of the Christmas truces of 1914 and, when on duty as a Signaller, he received and transcribed at 19.56 on 27 December 1914 a signal from the German regiment in the opposite trenches informing the British that, following orders received from their colonel, they were to open fire at midnight. For some reason of his own, James kept this signal, and it survived the rest of the war, eventually finding its way into a scrapbook assembled by his son.

The Christmas truce of 1914 was an unofficial ceasefire that affected large areas of the Western Front. In fact, it was a series of local ceasefires, arranged informally between the opposing troops, usually started by displays of candles and Christmas trees, and the singing of carols. Probably encouraged by their officers and non-commissioned officers (NCOs), soldiers from both sides left their trenches and assembled in No Man's Land, where they exchanged cigarettes, food and alcohol, and souvenirs such as buttons, badges and hats. Joint services were held and football matches were played. The truces also allowed for the collection and burial of dead soldiers.

It is calculated that about 100,000 Allied and German soldiers were involved, and the truces lasted two or three days, though some started on Christmas Eve and continued to New Year. The High Command on both sides quickly issued orders forbidding any kind of fraternization or communication with the enemy, and the war was soon resumed, as James's signal indicates. In Britain there was a news blackout about the truces but, after details and photographs were published in the American press, British newspapers soon followed, and by early January many had carried photographs and descriptions of the truces. A few Christmas truces were held in 1915 but in most sectors fighting continued as usual, as it did for the rest of the war.

In 1919 James, by then a Sergeant-Major, returned to Gosport with the 1st Battalion. Having signed on for 21 years, he remained a professional soldier, enjoying a further decade of active service which included Turkey in 1920 with the army of occupation, Egypt and Cyprus in 1922, where he became a Company Sergeant-Major, Egypt in 1923 and 1924, and India in 1925 where, according to his son, he and his family ate curry and rice, and prunes and custard every day for six weeks. In 1927 he returned to Britain, as Company Sergeant-Major (CSM) for the HQ Company of the 2nd Battalion, and in 1928 he received his last posting, as CSM at the Hampshire Regiment's depot in Winchester. James left the army in July 1932, probably for reasons of ill health as he died in December 1933, from septic broncho-pneumonia. His doctor described his lungs as 'thin as paper', the lasting effect of having been gassed during the war.

James Paice married his wife Elizabeth at Portsea on 2 February 1915, while on leave, and their only son was born the following November. According to James's granddaughter, her father was just like James: meticulous, a keen sportsman and an avid collector of documents and information. He was also awarded a Military Medal, while serving during the Second World War.

A PROFESSIONAL FOOTBALLER INTERNED IN GERMANY

SAMUEL WOLSTENHOLME
1878–1933

Samuel Wolstenholme was a gifted sportsman born in Bolton, Lancashire in 1878. As a young man he was soon playing regularly in local football leagues, and in 1897 he was signed by Everton. Sam made 160 appearances for the team, who described him as 'a brainy and thoughtful right-half, as nimble as a squirrel'. In 1904 he signed for Blackburn Rovers and the same year made the first of his two appearances for England, playing in the team that won the Home Championship in 1904 and 1905. He appeared 97 times for Blackburn and then in 1909 he moved to Norwich City, staying there until the end of his playing career in 1913. Sam then accepted a coaching position in Germany, working for the Norddeutscher Fussball-Verband. He moved to Germany in the spring of 1914, and was there when war broke out in August. As an enemy alien he was interned, along with thousands of other men and women from Britain, France, Belgium and other countries who found themselves trapped in Germany. Sam was sent to the Ruhleben internment camp near Berlin.

Built on the site of a former racing track, Ruhleben was a large camp, capable of holding up to 5500 internees. Most of the inmates were British and included men who were working, studying or on holiday in Germany at the outbreak of war, along with the crews of merchant ships and trawlers

'Everyone says my great-grandfather was a real gentleman who got on with everybody. He was also a great footballer, who had played for England. By bringing those skills together he must have made life much more bearable for many people in the internment camp.'

STEVE PHILLIPS, GREAT-GRANDSON

either stranded in German ports or captured during the early months of the war. According to the rules of the Geneva Convention, which Germany adhered to, civilian camps were to be allowed to administer their own affairs, and Ruhleben became well known for having its own police force, postal service, library and internally printed magazine. There were also a number of private businesses operating within the camp, including a casino. Among those detained were several musicians, who started a music society in 1915, which ran a programme of lectures and concerts. There were also performances of Gilbert and Sullivan operettas, and a winter pantomime. A drama society organized productions of plays by Shakespeare and Oscar Wilde.

The Whitemetal cup, made from a decorated shell case, which was won by Sam Wolstenholme's football team in the 1915–16 season, and has remained in the family ever since.

Sport was also important. Sam was not alone, for several other professional footballers were interned, including fellow internationals Fred Spiksley, Fred Pentland, Steve Bloomer and John Cameron, along with other club players. Together, they formed the Ruhleben Football Association. Leagues were set up and cup competitions organized, with some of the games attracting up to 1000 spectators. The teams in the Ruhleben league adopted the names of famous British clubs and so, in November 1914, Wolstenholme was the referee for a cup final between Tottenham Hotspur and Oldham Athletic. In May 1915 Sam played for an England XI against a World XI. Towards the end of the war there was a triangular international tournament, featuring British, French and Belgian teams. Other sports played in the camp included tennis, golf and cricket. Sam was an accomplished cricketer and helped set up a camp cricket league, again with teams taking the names of famous county clubs.

In the 1915–16 season, Sam's football team won both the league and the cup, with an enviable record of played 23, won 21, lost 1 and drawn 1. The Whitemetal cup, made locally from a decorated shell case, was sent back to Sam's wife in Britain, and has been in the family ever since.

Several books have been written about Ruhleben and its unusual way of life and there are museum displays describing the Ruhleben story. There were four other internment camps in Germany, one of which could hold 10,000. One, Rastatt, was especially for French citizens, while another, Havelberg in Saxony, included 400 Indians among its internees. The camps were predominantly male, but there were some female internees. Most of those interned in Germany, including Samuel Wolstenholme, stayed in their camps until the war ended.

A COLDSTREAM GUARDSMAN WHO BECAME A POLICEMAN

GAIOUS JOHN HUMBER
1891–1968

Gaious (or Gaius) John Humber, who was usually known as Jack, was born in November 1891, one of a family of seven children living in Ampney Crucis in Gloucestershire. Later, they moved to Kilmington, near

Axminster in Devon. His father was a gamekeeper and the family grew up in a completely rural environment. After leaving school Jack worked briefly as a gamekeeper with his father and then, on 18 April 1910, he enlisted for three years in the 1st Battalion of the Coldstream Guards, and was based at Pirbright and other depots in the south of England. His attestation papers reveal that he was 5ft 10in tall, and had grey eyes and brown hair. At the end of his three years, he was transferred to the Reserve. His character references stated that he was 'a smart and thoroughly reliable man' and 'a trustworthy hard-working man'. Probably on the strength of these he was taken on by the Glamorganshire Constabulary, on 6 May 1913.

'I was very close to my grandparents, they brought me up.
I was 19 when Grandpa died. He was a lovely, lovely man, happy
to pass the time of day with anyone. When I was small, he took me
shopping, holding my hand or on his bike. He never mentioned the
war but always wore his Coldstream Guards belt.'

LORRAINE BEALE, GRANDDAUGHTER

Fifteen months later, on 5 August 1914, Jack was recalled to the colours, rejoining the 1st Battalion, the Coldstream Guards. The oldest serving guards regiment in the British army, the Coldstream Guards can trace their origins back to the Civil War but it was in 1670 that it became known as the Coldstream Regiment of Foot Guards. From this point on, the regiment has been associated with most of the important military events in British history, including the Battle of Malplaquet, the Battle of Fontenoy, the American War of Independence, the Peninsular Wars and the Battle of Waterloo, the Crimea and South Africa. On the outbreak of the First World War, the Coldstream Guards, as part of the 1st Guards Brigade, were among the first to be sent to France with the British Expeditionary Force. As a soldier serving in the 1st Battalion, Jack took part in all of the early battles of the war, including the retreat from Mons, the battles of the Aisne and the Marne, and the First Battle of Ypres. The regiment faced some desperate days. On 29 October 1914, after heavy fighting at Gheluvelt, the 1st Battalion had no officers left and only 80 men of an original force of several hundred. Four days later, having been reinforced, it was again reduced to no officers and just 120 men. Somehow, Jack survived all these early battles.

In 1915 the Guards Brigades were reorganized as the Guards Division, and the 1st Battalion, the Coldstream Guards, became part of the 2nd Guards Brigade and remained so for the rest of the war. The battalion fought throughout 1915, 1916, 1917 and 1918, taking part in many of the major battles of those years. Surviving records do not show exactly where Jack served, or what he did, but his discharge papers reveal that he was with Battalion transport for two years and three months. At some point he must have been wounded, for on 15 May 1918 he was discharged from the battalion for being 'no longer physically fit for military service'. In later life he never mentioned this, nor did he have any lasting or visible disability.

On 16 February 1916, during a brief period of leave, Jack married Edith Cawley, a girl he had known for some time. They had one son, also called Jack, and were a devoted couple. Throughout his service, Jack carried a studio portrait photograph of Ede, as she was known, in his knapsack, and she was never far from his thoughts, as the souvenirs he brought back for her indicate. In 1914 Jack rescued from a ruined cottage a French glass bottle, decorated with flowers in enamels, which he then carried with him until he could give it to Ede. This has been passed to his granddaughter, along with a book of Burns's poems whose inscription reads, 'Picked up near some dead soldiers in the Ypres Salient in December 1914.'

After the war, Jack returned to the Glamorganshire Constabulary, and remained a policeman until he retired in May 1939. His service in the early months of 1914 qualified Jack as an Old Contemptible but he never seems to have had any interest in that, and took no part in later reunions and commemorations. He was, however, a member of the Old Coldstreamers Association, and continued to use his Coldstream Guards belt all his life. Lorraine, his granddaughter, who lived with him and Ede throughout much of her childhood, remembers once as a child being threatened by Jack after some naughtiness that 'he would give her his belt' – though her grandmother was so horrified that it never happened again. After retiring, Jack did a variety of odd jobs. He was a great gardener, and was particularly proud of his vegetables. Jack was a staunch Conservative, and Ede a Labour supporter, and Lorraine remembers them often discussing politics, but never arguing. When Ede, who had long suffered from multiple sclerosis, died in 1968, Jack followed her three weeks later.

Opposite: A gold locket containing photographs of Gaious and his wife Edith, which he carried at all times throughout the war.
Above: A popular edition of Burns's poems, found by Gaious Humber.

Portrait of Catherine Murray Roy, CBE, RRC, MM, painted by
Elizabeth Mary Watt, a friend and noted artist who attended
Glasgow School of Art in 1906 and was part of the
circle known as the Glasgow Girls.

A QUEEN ALEXANDRA'S ARMY NURSE WHO SERVED THROUGHOUT THE WAR

CATHERINE MURRAY ROY CBE, RRC, MM
1883–1976

The story of nursing in the army starts with Florence Nightingale and the 38 nurses who served with her during the Crimean War. On her return, Nightingale continued to battle for proper training and official status for army nurses and she remained a consultant to the War Office until 1872. The Royal Victoria Hospital at Netley in Hampshire was opened in 1863 specifically to train surgeons and nurses for the army, and from 1866 nurses were formally attached to military hospitals. In 1881 nurses came under the control of the Army Nursing Service, with nurses serving with the army in Egypt, the Sudan and South Africa. In 1902 the Army Nursing Service was replaced by Queen Alexandra's Imperial Military Nursing Service, which had been set up by Royal Warrant, and it was this organization that Catherine Murray Roy joined in 1909, becoming what was popularly called a QA.

Born in January 1883, Catherine Murray Roy was one of eight children whose father was a Church of Scotland minister in Drymen, a small country parish near Helensburgh. Having decided to go into nursing, at that time still an adventurous and unusual career for a woman, she trained at the Western Infirmary in Glasgow. The conventional route for Catherine would then have been the hospital service but instead she chose the army, because it was better paid and gave more opportunities for travel. At her interview she declared: 'I want foreign service and I want active service.'

'My great-aunt was a lovely woman, always pleased to see you and interested in what you were doing. She was very kindly and a wee petite woman, but she must have been strong to do what she did. She never talked about her life or the war, except to say how awful the food was.'

MARGARET ROY, GREAT-NIECE

When war broke out in 1914, a small group of nurses was sent to France with the British Expeditionary Force, just over a week after the declaration of war on 4 August. This group included Catherine Roy and her friend Annie Baird, the sister of television pioneer John Logie Baird. In action almost at once, Catherine began to experience the demanding and dangerous life faced by an army nurse working near the front line. This service early in the war qualified her for the 1914 Star and the right to the nickname 'Old Contemptible', although the term is not usually applied to women. These nurses faced battlefield conditions for which no training or experience could have prepared them, dealing on a daily basis not only with devastating shell splinter and shrapnel wounds, amputations, gangrene and the effects of gas, but also shell shock, frostbite, diseases such as tetanus and dysentery, and the constant presence of violent death.

Catherine Roy receives her CBE from King George VI in 1940.

Soldiers injured on the battlefield followed a well-determined route. Assuming they made it back to their own lines, on stretchers, carried by soldiers or on their own, they were then quickly patched up in a very rudimentary way at the regimental aid post at the edge of the battlefield. Next was the field dressing station behind the lines where they might receive injections and emergency operations from medical officers and orderlies. From here they went to the casualty clearing station, well behind the lines. This was, in effect, a well-equipped field hospital, often tented and staffed with nurses and doctors. The final stage of this journey in France was the base hospital, to which they were usually transported by train. After a period of recovery they were either sent back to Britain for further treatment, or returned to the battlefield. At every stage of this journey, death was commonplace. In general, nurses were attached to base hospitals and casualty clearing stations, but it was not unknown for them to work closer to the front line.

Catherine served in many of the major campaigns of the war, working mostly in casualty clearing stations or base hospitals. She was at the Somme in 1916, meeting on a few occasions her brother Jim – 2nd Lieutenant James Ferrie Roy – who was fighting there with his regiment, the Black Watch, until his death at High Wood on 30 July. On 29 May 1917, while a Staff Nurse, she was mentioned in despatches. In October the same year she was awarded the Military Medal, for 'Conspicuous gallantry displayed in the performance of her duties on the occasion of hostile raids on Casualty Clearing Stations in the Field'. When the war ended in 1918, Catherine, by now a Sister, stayed on in France to nurse victims of the Spanish influenza epidemic, and was awarded the Medal for Epidemics in Silver Gilt in March 1919. In January 1920 Catherine received the Royal Red Cross 1st Class, an award specifically for nurses introduced at the behest of Queen Victoria in 1883.

During the 1920s and early 1930s, Catherine continued to serve as an army nurse, and travelled frequently to postings overseas, including Syria, China and Hong Kong. A good manager and excellent with people, she rose steadily through the ranks of the nursing service. In 1934 she was appointed Principal Matron at the War Office, an equivalent rank to Lieutenant Colonel, and then in April 1938 she became Matron-in-Chief of the Queen Alexandra's Imperial Military Nursing Service, the most senior post in the service.

In 1940 Catherine retired from the army and returned to Scotland, to look after her mother and her sister. She settled into a way of living that enabled her to pursue her interests in art, music and all the pleasures of an intellectual life offered by Glasgow. At this point she met the artist Elizabeth Mary Watt (1885–1954), one of the famous 'Glasgow Girls', a famous group of avant garde women artists and designers. Watt painted a portrait of Catherine in uniform, wearing her medals. She was also a crossword addict and competed regularly with her brother to see who could complete the *Glasgow Herald*'s daily crossword in the fastest time. Towards the end of her life she moved back to Helensburgh, near her childhood home, and died there in 1976, after a fall. Margaret, her great-niece, who knew her well until she was ten, said that without that fall Catherine could have gone on forever.

A SOLDIER WHO FOUGHT WITH THE BEDFORDSHIRE REGIMENT

CHARLES PERCY HAWKES
1894–1969

 A Bedfordshire man at heart all his life, Charles Percy Hawkes was born in Luton in March 1894. Generally known as Bob, he had a brother and a sister. His father was a hardware and straw hat dealer, and as such was involved in Luton's core industry. After leaving school, Bob joined his father in the straw hat trade. When war broke out, he enlisted in the 1st Battalion of the Bedfordshire Regiment.

With a history dating back to the 17th century, the regiment became known as the Peacemakers through their habit of arriving at the scene of major conflicts too late to take part. In 1881 they were reformed as the Bedfordshire Regiment and served in India and Ireland. On the outbreak of the First World War the 1st Battalion was sent to France as part of the British Expeditionary Force (BEF), landing on 16 August 1914 with the 15th Infantry Brigade. They were then involved in all the major conflicts of the Western Front, from Mons and the early battles of 1914 to the final advance in October 1918, gaining in the process a reputation as one of the most reliable regiments in the BEF.

It is not known exactly when Bob enlisted, but he was certainly in France with the battalion in August 1914, and took part in the battles of Mons, Le Cateau, the Marne and the Aisne. In September 1914 he was wounded

'My step-grandfather had a strong personality, a crushing handshake, was full of colourful language and a great story teller, though he never said much about his war experiences. All his life he supported the Labour Party and Luton Town.'

CHRIS BENNELL, STEP-GRANDSON

at Missy and sent back to Britain to recover, returning to active service in 1915 in time for the Second Battle of Ypres. In 1916 the 1st Battalion fought during the later phases of the Somme, notably at High Wood, Longueval, Guillemont and Flers–Courcelette. In 1917 they took part in the Battle of Arras and the Third Battle of Ypres. At some point Bob was wounded again, probably during the Battle of Arras and, when he had recovered, he was given an Honourable Discharge, in June 1917.

Later, Bob rarely referred to the war but had a number of stories about his time in the trenches. One was that, having been put in jail for helping himself to the unit's rum ration, he suddenly became a hero for saving his gaoler when the prison was shelled. He also claimed that Woodbine cigarettes had kept him alive during gas attacks. Many soldiers took this light-hearted approach as a way of managing their dreadful experiences. One of Bob's treasured possessions was a copy of *The Doings of the Fifteenth Infantry Brigade* by its commander Brigadier General Count Gleichen, in which he wrote numerous comments about the events described.

After the war Bob worked as a chauffeur, and moved down to Somerset, where he married Alma Ash, a local girl, in 1925. In the 1930s Bob studied to be an engineer through various correspondence courses. In the Second World War he was a civilian instructor in engineering at RAF Hereford, and then in the 1950s he became an engineering clerk for the Ministry of Works in London, retiring in 1959. Always proud of being what he called a 'self-made man', Bob was a lifelong Socialist, a commitment based on his First World War experiences. He died in June 1969.

Right: Charles Hawkes's annotated copy of *The Doings of the Fifteenth Infantry Brigade.*

1915

DURING THE WAR'S FIRST FULL YEAR, BOTH SIDES TRIED
to overcome the stalemate imposed by trench warfare. The
Germans, fighting with a conscripted and well-trained army,
were committed to defence, making their trenches into fortresses.
The Allies – France, Belgium and Britain, increasingly supported
by Imperial Forces from India, Canada, Australia, New Zealand
and South Africa – were committed to attack, and believed that
the way to end the war was to break through the enemy trench
lines, allowing cavalry to sweep through into the open country
and destroy the enemy from behind. The battles of 1915, Loos
and Second Ypres, proved this could not be done, but this lesson
was not easily learned. Italy joined the conflict on the Allied side
and took on the Austro-Hungarians. Meanwhile, German troops
were also drawn steadily into the Russian campaign.

 The British government decided to try to end the
war by defeating Turkey and so launched a joint naval and
army invasion of the Dardanelles, designed to capture
Constantinople. Despite help from French and Imperial forces,
notably Australia, the campaign was a failure, with the invading
troops soon trapped in a hostile environment and decimated by
gunfire and disease. Withdrawal from Gallipoli started at the end
of 1915 and was all over by early 1916. Among the few successes
were the withdrawal itself, achieved with little loss of life, and
the daring work done by British submarines.

 The Royal Navy had imposed a blockade on Germany at
the start of the war, and Germany replied by increased use of

her submarines, eventually declaring a policy of unrestricted submarine warfare. Merchant ships became, in German eyes, legitimate targets, and Britain began to suffer as her vital supplies were attacked. In May, the sinking of the liner *Lusitania* caused international outrage, and brought the United States closer to joining the war.

In Britain, and throughout the Empire, powerful advertising campaigns led by Lord Kitchener ensured hundreds of thousands of volunteers continued to sign on. Moral pressure at home helped these campaigns, with civilians increasingly suspicious of anyone not in uniform.

In 1915 gas was first used as an offensive weapon by Germany, provoking a rapid Allied response, and from then on gas, and the measures to protect soldiers from its effects, became a major feature of the war. Aeroplanes were also improving, with the Royal Flying Corps, and its German equivalent, becoming a significant element in military strategy.

This chapter covers most of the major campaigns of 1915, and also highlights themes as diverse as German espionage in Britain, the royal family and the Western Front, British soldiers' fascination with football and amateur photography, the experiences of prisoners of war, support for the war among British schoolchildren, the efficiency of the military postal services, the ways families at home heard about the deaths of their loved ones, and the impact of women on the army medical services.

———————

A PIONEER WOMAN DOCTOR WHO SERVED IN FRANCE AND MALTA

ISABELLA STENHOUSE
1887–1983

Born in Leith, near Edinburgh, in 1887 as one of four sisters, Isabella Stenhouse was clearly an ambitious and determined woman. From 1908 she trained to be a doctor in Edinburgh, at a time when such a course of

action was still very unusual. When she graduated in 1913, she was one of just five women among 90 men, and they had been taught separately as the university would not allow mixed classes. She managed to secure a post as a house surgeon and house physician at Liverpool Royal Infirmary, even though

such posts were rarely accessible to women at the time. The conventional route for women doctors was to work in hospitals run by women, or to take on the areas that did not appeal to men, such as working with women, children, the poor or in public health.

When war broke out, the military authorities were reluctant to employ women in any front-line medical capacity, even though the Queen Alexandra's Imperial Military Nursing Service had been in existence since 1902. Women could work as nurses for various other organizations, such as the First Aid Nursing Yeomanry Corps (the FANYs), the Voluntary Aid

'My grandmother never talked about what she had seen and done and she refused to record her memories. She gave me her medical instruments without telling anyone else but I was too young to realize their importance, and all the questions I should have asked.'

KATRINA KIRKWOOD, GRANDDAUGHTER

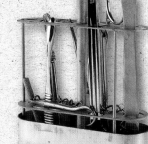

Right: A set of army issue medical instruments used by Isabella Stenhouse in France and Malta, engraved with her name.
Below: Isabella Stenhouse in a group of RAMC doctors and nurses.

D.ʳ Isabel Stenhouse
LEITH N.B.

Detachment (the VADs) or others, usually under the umbrella of the Red Cross. However, there was certainly no army employment for women doctors. As a result, various individuals and organizations set up privately funded hospitals for service in France and other front-line areas, which were sometimes run and often staffed by women. Examples include the field hospitals set up by the Duchess of Westminster, the Duchess of Sutherland, Lady Hatfield, Lady Murray, Dr Elsie Inglis and Mrs Stobart, while others were established by Sick Sisters and the Friends' Ambulance Unit. Some worked with foreign organizations, such as the one run for the French Red Cross by Mrs Lillian Doughty-Wylie, the wife of Lieutenant Colonel Charles Doughty-Wylie VC, a career soldier and diplomat. Isabella joined Mrs Doughty-Wylie, and went to France in March 1915, working as a doctor in the field until the autumn of 1915 when Mrs Doughty-Wylie, devastated by the death of her husband at Gallipoli, moved the hospital away from France. Isabella returned to Edinburgh, to continue her surgical studies and to teach at the university. She was the first woman to teach a mixed anatomy class.

By early 1916 the army authorities, struggling with a great shortage of trained doctors and medical staff, asked for women doctors to volunteer for service in Malta. Isabella was one of the 40 who were appointed, on 24 July 1916, and three weeks later she was in Malta. These women doctors were given neither uniform nor rank and so had no power to ensure that orders were carried out, or discipline maintained. Some more enlightened RAMC officers allowed some women, including Isabella, to wear RAMC badges but this was an informal arrangement. Later, the issue of the status and pay of military women doctors was raised in parliament. Convinced of her right to a rank, Isabella called herself Captain, and used the title, but it was never a formal rank.

Popularly known as 'the Nurse of the Mediterranean' Malta had 25,000 beds but most of the patients were soldiers suffering from dysentery, malaria and other diseases rather than battlefield injuries. Drawing on her experience in Edinburgh and in France, Isabella was employed as a surgeon, and appointed to a surgical hospital. Her medical instruments, now cherished by her granddaughter, were standard army issue and so must have been one of the first sets issued to a woman doctor. The Maltese hospitals were busy through 1916, but much less so in 1917. Many women doctors went home or transferred to Salonika but Isabella stayed on and in May 1918 she was posted to Alexandria. She was attached to General Allenby's Mess and her presence caused some consternation among the more traditional officers who were not only faced by a woman at dinner, but a woman doctor to boot. However, she did meet a charming officer who challenged her to ride his horse. She did, but fell off and broke her arm. Lying on the desert sand and seeing a pair of concerned blue eyes looking down at her, she fell in love and in October 1919 she and Captain Hubert Samuel Lane were married in Edinburgh. Captain Lane was a widower with one son, and together he and Isabella had two children, David and Alison.

The broken arm was the end of Isabella's military career but she continued to work as a doctor back in Britain. First, she took a job at the all-female Elizabeth Garrett Anderson Hospital in London, then worked in mother-and-baby clinics in Newcastle, before doing similar work in Poplar, east London. She continued practising until 1934, but maintained her medical registration until her death in 1983.

Women doctors, nurses and auxiliaries who served during the First World War shared extraordinary experiences, many based on the art of improvisation and facing emergencies with equanimity. They suffered all kinds of hardships, and were exposed to pain and misery on a daily basis. In the field, they lived and worked in tented camps, in ruined buildings, in trains and on ships, in deserts and snow-bound landscapes. They faced frightened and sick children, desperate refugees and wards like bloody battlefields, filled with soldiers with appalling injuries. There were the practical hardships caused by shortages of equipment, food and rest. They served in every sector of the war, in Europe, the Balkans, Russia and the Middle East. For many it was a challenge, almost a rite of passage, an escape from the often predictable and unchallenging lives they had left behind. There was excitement and there was relaxation, in the form of concert parties, dances, excursions, picnics and romance. Many met and married men they had worked alongside, or looked after in the wards. Isabella Stenhouse will have had some of those experiences but she never talked about her life as a doctor in the war. The most she ever told her daughter was that she had once helped someone to remove a patient's appendix.

Pte E. S. Lovell. 9691.

3rd Batt. Can. Inf:

BUCKINGHAM PALACE

1918

The Queen joins me in welcoming you on your release from the miseries & hardships, which you have endured with so much patience & courage.

During these many months of trial, the early rescue of our gallant Officers & Men from the cruelties of their captivity has been uppermost in our thoughts.

We are thankful that this longed for day has arrived, & that back in the old Country you will be able once more to enjoy the happiness of a home & to see good days among those who anxiously look for your return.

George R. I.

Ernest Lovell's copy of the letter sent by King George V to all prisoners of war when they returned to Britain. These letters were facsimiles and could not be personalized aside from the name, added by an office worker to each letter, so there is no mention of Ernest's daring escape.

A BRITISH-BORN CANADIAN SOLDIER WHO ESCAPED FROM A GERMAN PRISONER-OF-WAR CAMP

ERNEST SAMUEL LOVELL
1895–1981

One of ten children, Ernest Samuel Lovell was born in March 1895 in Hemel Hempstead. After the death of his father, a bricklayer, his mother took the family to the country and Ernest grew up working on farms. When he was 17 he was sent to Canada to start a new life, and quickly settled as a farm hand.

When war broke out, Ernest decided to enlist, joining the 3rd Battalion of the Toronto Regiment on 14 August 1914. They sailed from Quebec in September to join the Canadian Expeditionary Force in Europe. The battalion, part of the 1st Canadian Division, arrived in France in February 1915 and first went into the trenches near Armentières. They fought in the Second Battle of Ypres, where Ernest saw the terrible after-effects of the Germans' first use of poison gas. Here, in the chaos and confusion of battle, he was cut off with a group of soldiers by a German advance, and captured. Taken back behind the lines, Ernest was put with a large group of British, Canadian and French colonial troops and eventually transported by train to Giessen prisoner-of-war camp.

'My great-uncle Ernie was a lovely guy, a tall thin streak of a man who always gave me half a crown. The family talked about him as a hero, but he made light of it. Like many other survivors, he had a deep sadness, almost a guilt, about comrades who had been killed.'

JO HUGHES, GREAT-NIECE

In the First World War Germany was divided into 25 army districts, each under an Army Corps whose responsibility included prisoner-of-war camps. There were four kinds: those for officers, for other ranks, for civilians and other enemy nationals, and military hospitals. There were large numbers of camps, the biggest of which could hold 20,000 men, and they were designed to handle soldiers from all nations. When he was 80, Ernest wrote a memoire of his experiences as a prisoner in one of these camps, describing his capture and the conditions in which he was kept. Giessen, where Ernest spent much of his time, was one of nine camps in the Frankfurt region under the control of the XVIII Army Corps. Prisoners' accommodation was basic and sometimes primitive and food was always in short supply, particularly towards the end of the war. Many were kept alive by Red Cross parcels. Most were expected to work, on the land, in mines or in industry. Escapes were rare, partly because unsuccessful attempts were severely punished and partly because the planning and support systems that are well known from the tales of daring escapes during the Second World War simply did not exist in the First World War. German civilians were also often notably unfriendly towards enemy prisoners.

While at Giessen, Ernest was sent to work on the land, and later underground in mines near Larenburg. In January 1916 Ernest was moved to a much larger camp near Oldenburg, designed to hold 18,000 prisoners. He worked in the fields again, digging peat and planting potatoes, but he seemed to spend quite a bit of time in the punishment area. It was here that he and some fellow prisoners began to make escape plans, because the Dutch border was only 80 miles away. Their first attempt was on 26 April 1916. This failed but the second attempt, made with a friend called Joe, was successful and they got away from the camp. After several days' freedom, and many adventures, they were recaptured, returned to the camp and given 14 days of solitary in a dark cell on bread and water.

Early in the morning of 13 July, Ernest and Joe escaped again, this time with two other prisoners, one of whom had a compass. Travelling by night and hiding during the day, they made steady progress towards the border, although their journey was a hazardous one, fraught with danger. Having lost the other two men, Ernest and Joe found themselves faced by a river crossing. Joe couldn't swim but, rather than abandon his friend, Ernest searched the banks and finally managed to steal a small boat and get them both across. Eventually, they reached the border, found an unguarded canal bridge and crossed into Holland. They handed themselves in to the local police, who took them to the British Consul and on 23 July 1916 they stepped off a boat at Gravesend. Next stop was the depot where the 23rd Battalion was based, and a thorough interrogation. Ernest was then given some pay and some leave and went to see his mother in Hemel Hempstead. He had been told she was ill and he arrived just in time to see her before she died on 15 September. All of her four sons were at her funeral.

After seeing the doctor, Ernest was sent to the Royal Mineral Hospital in Bath, suffering from rheumatism, and stayed for two months. Here he discovered that he was deaf in one ear, probably the result of the shelling, and that he had flat feet, and together these could have kept him out of active service. When he returned to the depot, he was told he had been recommended for the Military Medal, mainly because of the way he had helped his friend Joe cross the river. He finally received this in 1920.

On 3 March 1917, Ernest married Margaret Wilson, and they went first to London for a few days on honeymoon and later to Folkestone, where they had a narrow escape from a German air raid. This, on 25 May 1917, was the first daylight attack by a number of large Gotha G.IV bombers, from the German Kagohl 3 unit. London was the planned target but bad weather forced the Gothas to bomb secondary targets at Folkestone and the army camp at Shorncliffe. The attack left 95 dead and 195 injured, and was the first of a series of similar day and night bombing raids by the Gothas.

In December Ernest left Britain on a boat bound for Canada. Later, Margaret came to join him. He was discharged from the army on 25 January 1918. For a while Ernest toured Canada and the United States, talking about his experiences and raising money for prisoners of war. He was on tour when the war ended, on 11 November 1918. Ernest and Margaret bought a farm in Henderson, built it up for some years, sold it and then bought a grocery store and filling station. Ernest died in 1981.

Jo Hughes, Ernest's great-niece, met him several times during his visits to Britain, and he was a firm favourite of her mother's. This inspired a lifelong interest in the war in general, and in Ernest in particular, and she has always been keen to share his story, and keep his memory alive.

A YOUNG COUPLE SURVIVE THE SINKING OF THE LUSITANIA

HAROLD & ALICE SMETHURST
1888–c.1948 & 1890–1970

Alice and Harold Smethurst were a young couple returning to their roots in Britain when they boarded the *Lusitania* in New York on 1 May 1915. Alice, one of seven children, had been born in the United States where her

parents, John and Mary Ann Schofield, had emigrated from Lancashire in the 1880s. However, they returned to Lancashire when Alice was about six, to work in the textile trade there. Harold was also involved in the textile industry, working at the Ellen Road cotton mill in Newhey, Lancashire, where he met Alice.

After their marriage in April 1912, Alice and Harold emigrated to the United States in December 1913 in search of a better life, and lived in Pennsylvania. After 18 months they decided to return to Britain, partly because of Alice's homesickness. At

that time, Alice was six or seven months pregnant with their first child. Initially, Harold booked a passage on a small ship but, thinking they would

'I never knew Harold, but everyone says he was a kind and loving man, always generous in helping his children. I did know Alice though when I was small, she was warm and reassuring to be with. She had a coal fire in her sitting room with a thick green rug in front of it which was lovely to sit on eating hot buttered toast.'

DEB LANCASTER, GREAT-GRANDDAUGHTER

be safer on something larger, he transferred to the RMS *Lusitania*, one of the grandest, fastest and best-equipped ships in Cunard's transatlantic fleet. What happened next is best described in Harold's own words, in an account he wrote soon after the event:

It was a glorious day and New York harbour was crowded with people – relations, friends and sightseers – to watch passengers embark aboard the SS *Lusitania*. The band commenced to play and amidst a great amount of cheering and flag-waving we had started on our voyage. The passengers commenced to settle down, and got acquainted with each other. The topic of conversation was war, and submarines.

Friday morning arrived (7th May) – it was very happy and we were looking forward to seeing the coast of Ireland – about 10.30am that morning we first saw the Irish coast. The gong rang for dinner and everyone began to feel more contented. After dinner I took my wife up on deck – the Old Head of Kinsale was now quite clear. I left my wife with some friends, telling her I was going to our cabin for a shave. I had almost finished shaving (time about 2.50pm) when suddenly I heard a deadening thud and felt the ship give a lurch. I grabbed my coat and rushed up on deck to see what was wrong. Everybody was in a state of panic, women and children screaming and crying, men were rushing about to find their loved ones. After a great struggle I found my wife. She was crying bitterly. I called out 'Alice!' And the next moment she was in my arms. I told her we had been torpedoed, and we must hurry to get to the boat decks.

The ship had now got a terrible list, we had several staircases to mount and in that great rush men, women and children were left behind. Because of the rush very few passengers had got their lifebelts.

We eventually reached the boat station, but you can imagine what it felt like. Everybody was fighting to reach the boats, and some of the crew were calling out for assistance to lower the boats. Leaving my wife in a safe place, I went forward with several other men to give the crew a helping hand. The first boat we attempted to lower was staved in owing to the list of the ship and our inexperience – and these poor souls were all thrown into the water. I say here without fear of contradiction that lots of lives were lost by our crude methods.

After launching several boats, I decided to get my wife into one. Taking her in my arms I told her to keep her spirits up, and that she would have to leave me now. After a lot of persuasion she decided to leave me. I got her into a boat and was pleased to see that boat arrive safely into the water.

I then decided to look after myself. I had become friendly with a ship's steward, he asked me if I could swim. I told him yes and he told me to go along with him. He took me to a rope at the stern of the ship that was hanging over the side. We took off our boots and went down the rope like a couple of monkeys. That was the last I saw of my friend.

I struck out and tried to get as far away from the ship as possible. I had not gone very far when I felt some unseen power taking me under the water. I looked round and just caught sight of that ill-fated ship disappear out of sight. The sea then became very calm.

There was plenty of wreckage floating around and this proved of valuable assistance to anyone that could swim. I saw in the distance a boat that had keeled over, I swam to it, there were only two men clinging to it when I arrived. In a very short time it was crowded with swimmers, and several of them were dead beat, then it was a case of the fittest survive. I saw several men pulled away from that boat and disappear. I decided to leave, I had sighted some more wreckage and started off immediately. I had it all to myself and was able to get a good rest. Shortly afterwards I saw a boat about half full of people – and she appeared to be just drifting. So I struck out towards her. I got to within what I thought was hailing distance – I cried out 'help! help!' But my cry was in vain. They must have been only taking a rest, and the boat moved quickly away from me.

I was by then feeling very cold and my limbs were becoming numb. I turned over on my back and just drifted. I had then given up all hope of being saved. I thought about my wife and wondered if she had been rescued, and I also thought about those poor souls who had gone down. Whilst I was meditating I saw some wreckage a short distance away. I drifted along with the wreckage – a short time afterwards I saw a boat in the distance, and it appeared to be coming in my direction. I waited some considerable time to make sure, yes, I was right.

Opposite: Alice Smethurst's wedding ring, saved with her from the sinking of the *Lusitania*. Above: Popular postcard of RMS *Lusitania*.

I then decided to make what I knew would be my very final effort. I struck out towards it. This appeared to me to be the longest swim I had ever experienced. I got quite close to it and cried out again for help. This time my cry was not in vain. She turned towards me and in a very short time they saved me from my watery grave. I was utterly exhausted, then I heard my name called out. I looked up and found to my surprise it was my wife who had called me. She was at the opposite end of the boat.

The next thing I remembered, I was on a small fishing boat, and one of the sailors was holding a pint pot full of hot tea for me to drink.

In a later conversation with her niece, Alice said that watching the *Lusitania* sink was like seeing a huge cotton mill disappear into the sea.

Harold and Alice were transferred to a warship, landed in Queenstown, and were taken to the Rob Roy Hotel to recover. In due course, they made their way to Lancashire, where they settled for the rest of their lives. They had four children and the eldest, Albert, always said that he was the youngest survivor of the *Lusitania*. Harold worked in a mill and then took over a plumbing business in Royton with his son. In about 1940 he developed angina and died a few years later. Alice never recovered from his death but lived on until 1970. Her daughter Marion is still alive and she inherited her mother's wedding ring. In due course Marion gave it to her daughter and on her death it passed to her daughter. So today, Deb Lancaster, Alice's great-granddaughter, wears the wedding ring that survived the sinking of the *Lusitania*.

When the *Lusitania* sailed from Liverpool on her maiden voyage on 7 September 1907, she was the largest, fastest and most lavishly fitted passenger liner in the world, though soon to be eclipsed by her sister, the *Mauretania*. She quickly captured the Blue Riband, an award for the fastest Atlantic crossing by a passenger liner, thus ending a period of German domination of the North Atlantic. The two ships were commissioned by the Cunard Line, with government funding and naval support, the latter giving the ships Armed Merchant Cruiser status. The *Lusitania* was built on the Clyde, the *Mauretania* on the Tyne. Later, a third sister, the *Aquitania*, was added to the fleet. The Cunard ships took their names from former Roman provinces in Spain and North Africa. The White Star Line followed Cunard's lead by commissioning the larger *Titanic* and *Olympic*, and later the *Britannic*.

When the *Lusitania* left New York on 1 May 1915, carrying 1959 passengers and crew, she was starting her 202nd crossing of the North Atlantic. By then, the threat posed by submarines to merchant vessels had considerably increased, thanks in part to Britain declaring the North Sea a war zone in November 1914, which had provoked Germany to respond in February 1915 by declaring all the seas around Britain a war zone, thus allowing them to attack Allied shipping without warning. Prior to the *Lusitania*'s final departure from New York, the Imperial German Embassy placed notices in 50 American newspapers warning passengers of the dangers they faced by travelling on the ship. By then, the Germans had discovered that the *Lusitania* was aiding Britain's war effort by carrying large quantities of small arms ammunition, artillery shells and raw materials used in the manufacture of explosives, along with more conventional cargo. For the German government this, combined with the *Lusitania*'s listed Armed Merchant Cruiser status, justified any attack on what they saw as a legitimate military target. The Admiralty issued instructions to the

Lusitania's captain, warned him about submarines known to be operating in the Irish Sea, and promised a naval escort through the war zone which, for various reasons, did not materialize. It seems that the *Lusitania*, sailing close to the Irish coast, crossed by chance the course taken by the German submarine *U-20*, giving Kapitan Schwieger the opportunity to fire one torpedo, which hit the ship's starboard bow. This was followed by a second, much larger explosion, the cause of which has never fully been explained, although it seems to have originated in the steam-generating plant of the turbine-driven ship. The *Lusitania* immediately began to list, and sank 18 minutes later. Thanks to panic, inadequate lifeboats, ineffective watertight partitions and an inexperienced crew, 1195 passengers and crew lost their lives, mostly by drowning or from hypothermia.

The impact of the loss of the *Lusitania* was considerable. The British propaganda machine went into overdrive, presenting the attack on the ship as a German war crime. A German commemorative medal depicting the sinking of the *Lusitania*, and attacking Cunard for putting business before passenger safety, was copied in Britain and sold in huge quantities to encourage the British public to see the German government as cruel and uncivilized. Large passenger vessels were subsequently equipped with sufficient lifeboats. Most important, the death of 128 American citizens in the disaster greatly advanced the slow process that would bring the United States into the war on the Allied side two years later. In response to American pressure, the German government announced in September 1915 that all attacks on passenger liners would cease. In January 1917, however, the German government re-introduced unrestricted submarine warfare, by which time the American public was increasingly in favour of the war.

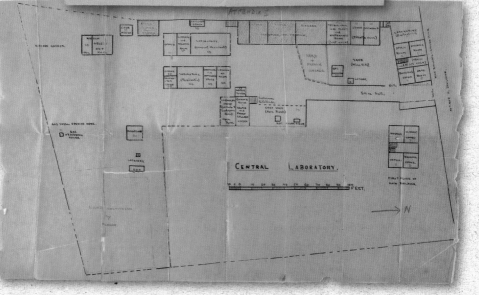

Miss Watson
7 Upper Cheyne Row
Chelsea · S.W.3

1.

5. 3. 79

Dear Miss Watson,

I was present at the post-mortem examination today. The operation itself was quite satisfactory, but the very dilated stomach had not lessened in size at all as a result of it. There was a small growth at the Pylorus (the opening of the Stomach into the bowel)

CENTRAL LABORATORY.

→ N

Above: The layout of the Central Laboratory, St Omer,
where Professor Watson led a team working on combating
scientific warfare, including gas attacks. Top: Letter to
William Watson's sister informing her of his death.

A SCIENTIST WHO SAVED THOUSANDS OF SOLDIERS

WILLIAM WATSON
1868–1919

Unlike any conflict in earlier history, the outcome of the First World War was greatly influenced by science and technology. There were many firsts, including the widespread application of technologies that facilitated

remote and long-distance killing, the aerial bombardment of civilian populations, the use of telephone and wireless communication, the development and exploitation of new war machines, such as aircraft, tanks and submarines, and the emergence of chemical weapons. Tear gas was first used as an offensive weapon in 1914 but with little effect. The first significant use of poison gas was in April 1915, when the Germans unleashed a massive chlorine gas attack against French troops near Langemarck. Further gas attacks followed in the Ypres sector, with nearly 150 British soldiers dying near Hill 60 on 5 May 1915. From this point onwards, poisonous gases, either released from canisters or fired in shells, became a regular feature of First World War battles. As a result, protecting soldiers from the effects of gas became an immediate concern for all countries involved in the conflict.

'For me he comes through as an intense kind of man and his singular devotion to duty demonstrates that. He was clearly something of a workaholic with diverse interests, and achievements, in the scientific field. My aunt knew him but, of course, I never asked the right questions while she was alive.'

JEREMY WATSON, GREAT-NEPHEW

A PIONEER PILOT PROTECTED BY JOAN OF ARC

PERCY EDWARD FRANCIS
1895–1940

As a child, Percy Edward Francis had always been fascinated by engineering and machinery, and this set the pattern for his life. The second son of a family with a large retail business in the Tottenham Court Road area of

London, he had qualified as a pilot by the age of 17, in 1912, and the same year was a Steward at the first Aerial Derby and Show held at Hendon in north London. In September 1914 he tried to enlist in the Royal Flying Corps but was turned down, apparently on medical grounds, so instead he joined the 4th Battalion of the Seaforth Highlanders, choosing that regiment partly because a friend had bet him £5 that he would never wear a kilt. Later, he talked about the discomfort and impracticality of wearing a kilt in muddy and water-filled trenches, and the great variety of undergarments – all completely unofficial – developed by soldiers to overcome these difficulties.

The Seaforths were formed in 1881 from a merger of two long-established Highland foot regiments, the 72nd and the 78th. The 4th Battalion was one

'According to the family, my grandfather was a remarkable character, always good fun to be with, loved children, enjoyed jokes and was always tinkering with machinery. He was passionate about flying, always talking about his flying memories. I wish I had met him.'

GORDON LE PARD, GRANDSON

The French 19th-century biscuit-porcelain figure of Joan of Arc, rescued by Percy Francis. This was a popular small-scale copy of a well-known statue.

of three front-line Territorial battalions, part of the rapid expansion of the regiment during the First World War. Sent to France in November 1914, the 4th Battalion joined the Dehra Dun Brigade in the 7th Meerut (Indian) Division in December. This Division, part of the Indian Expeditionary Force sent to Europe to join the war, had landed in Marseilles in October 1914. It fought through much of 1915, including in the Battle of Neuve Chapelle and the Second Battle of Ypres, and then in November 1915 it was transferred briefly to the 46th North Midland Division and then a Scottish Division. In January 1916, it joined the famous 51st Highland Division.

While fighting in the Ypres area in 1915, Percy found in a ruined church a small biscuit-porcelain figure of Joan of Arc. Her head had been knocked off but he repaired her, and from that moment she became his mascot and good luck charm. He carried her through the rest of his service career. The figure was a popular small-scale reproduction of a well-known lifesize 19th-century statue of St Joan, originally made in marble, bronze and other materials and widely replicated across France.

In early 1916 Percy was, according to the family, offered either a medal or a commission. He chose the latter, transferred to the Royal Flying Corps and was trained in aerial photography, the technical aspects of which had always interested him. By the late summer of 1916 he was flying in action and continued to do so until the spring of 1918, working primarily in the field of aerial reconnaissance. His job was vital, dangerous and repetitive and involved the constant taking of photographs of the enemy trench lines so that British trench maps could be regularly updated.

Percy flew in slow, two-seater aircraft such as the BE2c. Designed for reconnaissance, this came into service in France with the Royal Flying Corps early in 1915 and by the end of that year 16 squadrons were in operation. In the early days the BE2c was often unarmed and so could be easily attacked and destroyed by enemy fighters, particularly the Fokker E.I, the first German aircraft with a machine gun synchronized to fire through the propeller. The cameras in use were large, bulky and with a slow exposure, requiring the aircraft to be flown in a straight line and at slow speeds over long periods. While the aircraft was very stable, to aid the pilot in the reconnaissance and the photography, it was also relatively un-manoeuvrable, making it difficult to evade anti-aircraft fire and attacking fighters. The losses were correspondingly high, and by 1916 crews had a life expectancy of a few weeks. By the end of 1917 the BE2c had largely been replaced by the much improved RE8 and Armstrong Whitworth FK8. Somehow, Percy survived, perhaps protected by Joan of Arc, who always flew with him wrapped in a bag.

In the spring of 1918 he was granted a period of leave, and was asked to fly to Britain to deliver an aircraft back to its base. He set off and over the Channel flew into fog. He lost height and direction and crashed into the White Cliffs of Dover. Seriously injured, he lay in the wreckage of the aircraft on the undercliff for three days, before being discovered by a local gamekeeper. By then, it had been assumed that he had crashed into the sea and been lost. He recovered in hospital, and begged to be allowed to fly again, but to no avail. Promoted to Acting Major, he was sent back to France by the Royal Air Force, which had taken over from the Royal Flying Corps on 1 April 1918, but to a desk job, organizing aircraft movements to support the great Allied advance that had started on 8 August 1918. At the end of 1918 he was demobilized, largely for medical reasons.

Back in Britain, Percy continued to fly for pleasure, and retained all his old enthusiasms. He became a friend of Geoffrey de Havilland, the aviation pioneer, and helped in the development of some of his aircraft. He married in 1921 and had three children, ran small engineering businesses, a wireless shop and a motorcycle garage but never really settled, moving house three times and owning a constantly changing series of motorcars. His wife, a forthright woman who had been a pioneer Girl Guide, coped well with her husband's erratic existence.

In a way, Percy was typical of the generation that survived the First World War, either permanently marked by the experience or, like him, never able to find in peacetime the stimulation and excitement of wartime action. Percy died in 1940, partly because of the lasting effects of his 1918 crash.

In later life, he talked endlessly about flying, but rarely about the war itself or any actions he had been in. His view was that he had been very lucky to have been paid to fly, doing what he loved best.

The flask given to Alice Douglas by the condemned German spy, Haike Janssen, shortly before his death in July 1915. His name is scratched into the base of the detachable cup.

THE EXECUTION OF GERMAN SPIES AT THE TOWER OF LONDON

JOHN GEORGE DOUGLAS
1861–1940

John George Douglas was born in Aldershot, Surrey, in 1861. His father and his grandfather had been career soldiers in the British army, with his father, John George senior, serving in Burma and India and taking part in the Relief of Lucknow during the Indian Mutiny. John George senior's regiment had returned to Britain in 1859, by which time he was a Colour-Sergeant. Soon after John George's birth the regiment was sent to Ireland, and his father died there from consumption in 1865.

Nothing is known about John George's childhood until 1877, when he enlisted for 12 years in his father's old regiment, the 84th Regiment of Foot. He then served in Britain for five years and in 1882 the regiment went to Egypt and John George fought at the Battle of Tel-el-Kebir. The next seven years were spent in Britain and then his period of service ended in 1889. Within a few months he had re-enlisted, however, signing on for another nine years and serving in the Royal Hampshire Regiment. The years were spent in Britain and Ireland and he reached the rank of Colour-Sergeant. In 1897, John George married Alice Pratt, the daughter of a policeman, and they had five children. In 1898 John George re-enlisted again, in the Royal Southern Reserve Regiment,

'My grandfather was Barrack Warden at the Tower of London and my grandmother cooked meals for German spies awaiting execution. Then came the volley of rifle shots disturbing the quiet morning air.'

BOB DOUGLAS, GRANDSON

set up to provide home defence while large numbers of regular troops were in South Africa. This was disbanded in 1901 and John George was out of the army.

For a couple of years he was the verger at the Garrison Church, Portsmouth, and then he was employed as a civilian at the Royal Arsenal, Woolwich. In about 1907 he was appointed Barrack Warden at the Tower of London. Barrack Wardens, usually retired army Warrant Officers, were civilians employed by the army to look after the maintenance and day-to-day running of military barracks. At the time of his appointment, Waterloo Barracks at the Tower of London housed about 1000 soldiers. John George and his family lived in The Casemates, a row of married quarters built against the Tower's curtain wall, facing the covered shooting range used by the soldiers.

With the outbreak of war in 1914, John George and his family became drawn into the conflict in an unexpected way. Between the autumn of 1914 and 1916, a number of people were arrested in Britain on suspicion of spying for Germany. This was a very real concern among the British authorities, both before and during the war and there is no doubt that Germany made extensive use of agents. This theme was highlighted by writers such as John Buchan in *The Thirty-Nine Steps* and Erskine Childers in *The Riddle of the Sands*, novels that reflected contemporary concerns about German militarism and the spy networks upon which it depended. In the event, the number of German spies sent to operate in Britain was quite limited and around 24 were caught, including several women. Those caught were interrogated and, if the evidence was strong enough, tried before a court martial. If the verdict was guilty, they were sentenced to be shot by firing squad, under the wide-ranging regulations brought into force by the Defence of the Realm Act in August 1914. In 11 cases, the executions were held at the Tower of London. Convicted spies were brought to the Tower the evening before their execution and housed overnight in The Casemates, next door to John George and his family. On several occasions his wife Alice supplied meals to the condemned spies, at the request of the Tower authorities. On the day of execution, the family were woken early by the sound of the prisoner being taken under escort past their windows to the rifle range opposite. Soon would come the volley of rifle shots.

On 12 May 1915 a Dutchman, Haike Janssen, landed at Hull on a ship from Amsterdam and travelled south to Southampton. The next day another Dutchman, Willem Roos, arrived by ship in London and travelled north to Newcastle. Both claimed to be cigar salesmen, and carried samples. The British Security Services were quickly suspicious and telegrams, letters and postcards sent by the two men back to the Netherlands, which was neutral in the First World War, were intercepted, and found to contain coded messages concealed in information about cigars. Janssen was arrested on 30 May and Roos on 2 June. Both were taken to London and interrogated together and separately. Immediately apparent was their lack of knowledge about cigars and equally damaging was their claim to have visited naval ports to sell cigars to sailors, as British sailors only smoked pipes and cigarettes. In addition, notebooks containing coded information and map references were found among their papers. Janssen was tried by court martial in Westminster on 16 July, offered no defence and was found guilty. Roos was tried the next day, with the same outcome. On 29 July 1915, the two men were brought to the Tower of London and housed in The Casemates. As before, Alice Douglas was asked to supply them with meals. In gratitude, Haike Janssen asked Alice to accept a small leather-covered hip flask, set in a detachable cup, on the base of which he had scratched his name. She thanked him and accepted his gift.

At 06.00 the next morning Janssen was taken under escort by a detachment of Scots Guards to the old Tower moat and shot. Roos followed ten minutes later. A contemporary report described how both men died bravely, and met their fate 'with a courage which could evoke nothing but admiration'.

John George Douglas retired to Norfolk with his wife and he died there in 1940. One of his sons, Frederick, maintained the Tower connection by marrying a Yeoman Warder's daughter in 1925. Frederick's son Bob, John George's grandson, is today the proud owner of Haike Janssen's hip flask.

A SUBMARINER'S DARDANELLES ADVENTURE

ROBERT BROWN
1887–1947

While the dismal story of the Dardanelles campaign is well known, less familiar today are the achievements of the Allied submarines in support of that campaign. As the troops were struggling to make progress at

Robert Brown (left) and Guy D'Oyley-Hughes (right) on the submarine *E11*.

Gallipoli, a small flotilla of British E-class submarines continuously harassed Turkish shipping in the Sea of Marmora. One of the most successful was the *E11*, captained by Lieutenant Commander Martin Nasmith. The submarine's navigating officer was Lieutenant Robert Brown. Born at sea off Cape Horn in January 1887, Robert, the eldest of three children, was delivered by his father, the Master of the barque *John Gambles* who, luckily, had undertaken a midwifery course in San Francisco. Robert Brown senior had a long career at sea, and was Master of a number of steam and sailing ships, often operating out of Maryport in Cumbria. Robert junior followed his father to sea and served on several ships, including the iron barque *Lady Elizabeth* from May 1904 to January 1906. This ship

'According to a family story Robert was indirectly the cause of his father's death. After a long period with no news about Robert and E11, the postman brought news that he was alive and well. His father, overcome with relief, had a heart attack and died.'

LYNNE COOPER, GREAT-NIECE

survives as a beached hulk near Port Stanley, in the Falkland Islands.

In 1914 Robert was a second officer with the Holt Line, based in Liverpool. He had earlier volunteered for the Royal Naval Reserve and so was called into the Royal Navy at the outbreak of war. After training, he joined the submarine service. This new arm of the navy had developed rapidly since the early 1900s. Still unproven in war, the submarine was looked on by many as a dangerous and unprincipled weapon, and those who served on them were often described rather dismissively as 'the Trade', because the informal way of dressing associated with life underwater was considered to be not up to the Royal Navy's usual immaculate standard. The E-class, introduced from 1912, formed the backbone of the British submarine service throughout the First World War. By 1915 German U-boats were becoming a serious menace, mainly because they enjoyed the freedom of the seas to find and attack targets at will. British submarines, by contrast, had to work harder to find their targets as there were fewer German ships on the high seas, and much of the German navy stayed in the harbours and bases.

The Dardanelles campaign gave the submarines their first real challenge, and they seized the opportunity, with the Allies mounting regular submarine patrols around the Turkish coast and into the Sea of Marmora. There were many successes, despite the Turkish counter-measures which included mines, nets, shore batteries and patrolling gun boats which could easily spot the periscope of a submarine in the shallow coastal waters. During a patrol in May 1915 Lieutenant Commander Nasmith sank or disabled 11 Turkish vessels and took E11 through the Dardanelles Straits and into Constantinople harbour, causing chaos and consternation. For this, he was awarded the Victoria Cross. On 5 August 1915, E11 set out on another patrol along the Dardanelles Straits and towards the Sea of Marmora. This turned out to be even more dramatic as the submarine narrowly escaped being caught in nets and blown up by a mine. Turkish transports were attacked and sunk or damaged, columns of troops were shelled and on 8 August the last remaining Turkish battleship, the *Barbaros Hayreddin*, was torpedoed and sunk. This adventurous patrol continued for several more days, with E11 sometimes operating together with her sister submarine E2, and more ships were sunk, including transports and supply vessels.

No.3 Australian General
Hospital
Lemnos
27-9-15

My Dear Wife As you are doubtless aware by now I
have been very ill in hospital for eleven days or so. I
came to a head last night, it came to a crisis and I
believe I will get better slowly now. I am in
good heart myself and apparently getting a little
stronger all the time. I have had the best medical
and nursing attention or I would not be here now
I will write to you again as soon as

possible Love to the girls, yourself, and grandma

your loving husband
John

Written by Major Upjohn 3rd Aust Gen Hosp at the dictation of Capt McNicol

Letters to Lieut McNicol can be addressed to
him at this hospital

Right: The letter from John McNicol to his wife, Mary, taken down by a doctor at No.3 Australian General Hospital on Lemnos. It was received after the telegram, below, sent by the Admiralty to Mary, informing her of his death.

POST OFFICE TELEGRAPHS.

OHms admiralty London

TO Reply Paid McNicol Burnbank Gourock

Deeply regret inform you Lieut
John McNicol R N R
Died on 29th September from
dysentery please report name address
and relationship of his nearest
relatives admiralty

A MASTER MARINER CLAIMED BY DYSENTERY

JOHN MCNICOL
1859–1915

The Royal Naval Reserve (RNR) was set up in 1859 to create a voluntary reserve of trained and professional seamen from the Merchant Service who could be called upon in times of war to assist the Royal Navy. Additional training was offered, usually for one month each year. RNR seamen served with distinction in a number of conflicts, including South Africa. At the start of the First World War, there were 30,000 officers and men attached to the RNR, a figure that had more than doubled by the

end of the war, and they were soon involved, serving on and commanding a wide range of ships including destroyers, auxiliary cruisers, submarines, Q-ships and minesweeping trawlers. Some RNR officers qualified as pilots with the Royal Naval Air Service, and many RNR ratings served as infantry in the Royal Naval Division, fighting in Gallipoli and the Somme. In addition, merchant officers and men who served on Armed Merchant Cruisers, hospital ships, transports and fleet auxiliaries were drafted into the RNR for the duration of the war.

'By all accounts John was affectionate, caring and kindly, a great family man who loved his wife and children and always took an interest in their lives and friends. My great-aunt and my mother often talked about him.'

CATHY JEWELL, GREAT-GRANDDAUGHTER

This is probably how John McNicol joined the RNR. He was born in July 1859 in Gourock, near Glasgow, one of seven children, five of whom died in childhood. His father was a master mariner and John followed in his father's footsteps, joining his first ship, the *Eastward*, in 1877. He spent some years on his second ship, the *Return*. In 1888 he qualified as a master mariner, and then worked for two years as a pilot on the Clyde. Later, he sailed on a number of ships owned by Gem Line, one of Britain's largest coastal trading fleets, a Dundee-based shipping business founded by William Robertson in 1852. In September 1891 John married Mary Virginia Jones and they had two daughters. John and Mary had met when she was, literally, the girl next door in Gourock. Their two daughters, Mary and Elizabeth, sometimes sailed with their father on local voyages, although Elizabeth, Cathy's grandmother, suffered from seasickness.

In 1915 John, with the rank of Lieutenant, was in command of SS *Turquoise*, a small Gem Line ship built in 1893. On 31 July, while on passage carrying supplies for Gallipoli, she was sunk by gunfire from the submarine U-28, 60 miles from the Isles of Scilly. One crew member was killed, but the remainder escaped in the lifeboats and spent 14 hours adrift before being rescued. John's next command was the SS *Silverfield*, a brand-new ship serving as a supply vessel in the Dardanelles. *Silverfield* was one of over 135 troopships, hospital ships and transports that took part in the Dardanelles campaign, and most would have been commanded and crewed by RNR officers and men.

Letters sent home in August 1915 indicate that all was well, but in September John became ill with dysentery. A number of diseases and infections greatly increased the death toll during the First World War, notably typhoid, cholera, dysentery, influenza and gangrene. These were mostly universal but some were much more significant in warmer regions. The total for Allied deaths in the eight months of the Dardanelles campaign was over 55,000, and a number of these deaths were the result of diseases. The combination of poor sanitation, unburied corpses and summer heat caused a dysentery epidemic, which affected over 100,000 Allied soldiers. Many recovered but the worst cases were taken to hospital. John was among these and so he found himself at No. 3 Australian General Hospital (AGH) at Mudros on the island of Lemnos. This had been set up in July and August 1915, primarily to treat the casualties from the Allied August offensives. Later, most of the patients brought there were suffering from dysentery or para typhoid, and many of the staff also became infected. By the winter, many of the patients were suffering from frostbite. No. 3 AGH was disbanded at the end of the Dardanelles campaign, and then re-established in Egypt before moving to Abbeville in France in 1917.

John never recovered and died on 29 September 1915, at the age of 56. His last days are well documented. A doctor, who had become a good friend, wrote to his wife Mary on 26 September, telling her about his illness and that it was serious. The next day John dictated a letter to Mary, which was taken down by another doctor, a Major Upjohn:

> My dear wife
>
> As you are doubtless aware by now I have been very ill in hospital for 11 days or so. It came to a head last night, it came to a crisis and I believe I will get better slowly now. I am in good heart myself and apparently getting a little stronger all the time. I have had the best medical and nursing attention or I would not be here now. I will write to you again as soon as possible.
>
> Love to the girls, yourself and grandma
>
> Your loving husband, John

On 12 October 1915 Mary McNicol received a telegram from the Admiralty, informing her of her husband's death. Some days later, she received the sadly mistaken letter quoted above, assuring her that he was getting better.

John is buried in Portianos Military Cemetery at Mudros, on Lemnos. His widow Mary went to London to live with her daughter, also Mary, who was a senior official at the Post Office, rising in due course to the highest level attainable by women. John's widow Mary McNicol lived to a great age, dying in 1953. Their daughter Mary, Cathy's great-aunt, had a long-held ambition to visit her father's grave, which was unfulfilled. Her sister Elizabeth's daughter, Cathy's mother, held the same ambition, also unfulfilled. So now it is up to Cathy, John McNicol's great-granddaughter, to complete that emotional journey.

A RIFLEMAN WHO KICKED OFF
A BATTLE

FRANCIS EDWARDS

1893–1964

Francis Edwards, better known as Frank (on right of photograph), was the sixth in a family of seven children. His father Alfred was a coachman and his mother Emily a domestic servant. In 1907 he left school to become a

stationer's assistant. By then the family were living near Chelsea's football ground at Stamford Bridge, with Fulham's Craven Cottage not far away, and Frank became a football enthusiast, both as a player and a spectator. When war broke out, Frank volunteered for service with the local Territorial regiment, the London Irish Rifles. He was soon able to show off his sporting talents, becoming captain of the London Irish football team.

Formed in 1859, the London Irish Rifles became a part of the Territorial Force in 1908 when it was renamed the 18th (County of London) Battalion, the London Regiment (London Irish Rifles). At the start of the First World War, the London Irish Rifles raised three battalions, with the 1st in France in time to join the 47th Division in the Battle of Festubert in May 1915.

'I knew my grandfather until I was ten, he lived with us.
He was a kind man, tall and upright, but he never talked to me
about the war, or to my mother but we knew the story. I was very
possessive of my grandfather, he was my footballer of Loos.'

SUE HARRIS, GRANDDAUGHTER

Right: A later bronze of Francis Edwards, the footballer of Loos, cast to commemorate his historic act. Below: The football used by Francis Edwards to kick off the Battle of Loos.

The letter from Ed Crow, one of Thomas Mowbray's friends, that told
Emma Mowbray about her husband's death.

A SOLDIER'S DEATH CONFIRMED BY A LETTER FROM A FRIEND

THOMAS HENRY MOWBRAY
1881–1915

The eldest of the four children of Thomas Mowbray and Violetta Parton, Thomas Henry Mowbray was born in Croydon, south London, in December 1881. His mother remarried in 1894, becoming Mrs White, and had three more children. In June 1899, when he was 18, Thomas enlisted in the Chatham Division of the Royal Marines and was trained as a Military Boatman. During his period of service the records reveal that, while his ability was rated highly, his character rating dropped steadily, from very good to fair, and then from indifferent to objectionable, when he was discharged. The family story, according to his eldest daughter, was that he struck an officer while defending another soldier but there is no record of this. The records do reveal that he was of  average height with brown eyes and grey-brown hair and had a tattoo on his left arm. It is not known what he did after leaving the army, except that the 1911 census lists him as a 'wash horseman laundry', probably in a laundry in Surrey run by his stepfather's family. In 1905 he married Emma Collins, by whom he had four children between 1907 and 1914.

'I never knew my grandfather, and my grandmother was a frail little grey-haired old lady when I was a child. My mother told me about him and research both confirmed and contradicted stories I had been told. I'm sure he was brave, impetuous, tough and big-hearted. I'm very proud of my grandfather.'

CHRIS EASTON, GRANDSON

A NORFOLK MAN WHO FOUGHT AT GALLIPOLI AND IN PALESTINE

JOHN EDWARD LOCK
1896–1991

In an age when the choice of employment available to many was either unskilled labour or service, John Edward Lock's father was a jack-of-all-trades who took on a range of jobs to keep the family alive. John, always known as Jack, was born in Thetford, Norfolk, in November 1896 and was

the second of eight children, two of whom died in childhood. His father was a strict disciplinarian and Jack had to leave school at 12 to take on a variety of jobs, including working for a butcher, being a groom, a gardener and a stoker for Thetford gas works. Early in 1914 he joined the Territorial Force and at the outbreak of war he enlisted in the 4th Battalion of the Norfolk Regiment, as a bugler and stretcher-bearer.

This famous county regiment had been formed in 1881 from the long-established 9th (East Norfolk) Regiment of Foot. The 4th Battalion had been raised in Norwich in August 1914. After training in Colchester, the battalion embarked at Liverpool on the SS *Aquitania* and sailed to the Dardanelles, arriving in Mudros on 5 August 1915. During the voyage Jack earned extra pay working

'I learned so much at the feet of my grandfather. Granfa Lock was my role model, my working-class hero and best man at my wedding. He was an NUR [National Union of Railwaymen] shop steward, a chorister and church warden, a brilliant poacher and his parsnip wine was really potent.'

ROGER LOCK, GRANDSON

as a stoker in the ship's boiler room. From this point on, Jack kept a diary, a graphic record of his daily life and the chaos of the Dardanelles. He describes the battalion landing at Gallipoli on 10 August, amid shell fire and search lights, and his first sight of dead and wounded soldiers. He writes about the shortage of food and water in the front-line trenches, and the better rations in the so-called rest trenches. On 25 August 1915 Jack was wounded while working as a stretcher-bearer and taken first to a hospital ship and then to the hospital at Lemnos to recover. After convalescence he was back in the trenches on 9 October and wrote about what he found there:

> I returned to duty with the boys who were at Anzack [sic] I was rather surpise [sic] to find such a small battalion but the rest of them still stuck it. Some of the boys had altered some I did not know some of them had got so thin and wore out. Well the next day I was sent out with a party trench digging I saw some sights as I was going along the sap I saw a dead mans fingers sticking out of the ground ... next day I was sent out to our own trenches ... 5 yards in front of the trench a grope [sic] of dead men laying some turks and some of our own men ...

The Dandanelles campaign, and its main element, the attack on the Gallipoli peninsula, was one of the most notorious Allied offensives of the First World War, mainly because of the lack of success and high cost in casualties. The plan, developed and promoted by Winston Churchill, the First Lord of the Admiralty, was for the Allies to attack and capture Constantinople, and thus take Turkey and the Ottoman Empire out of the war. In principle, it was sound but relied on surprise and speed of movement. The first phase was an attack by naval forces, which might have succeeded had it been pursued with greater determination. Its failure made inevitable a much more difficult attack using both ground and naval forces, the main aspect of which was an armed landing on the Gallipoli peninsula to open up an attack on Constantinople by land. On 25 April 1915 a large Allied force was landed at various places along the peninsula, and from the start chaos reigned. Troops were landed at the wrong places or could not advance beyond the beaches and Turkish opposition was much greater than expected, the element of surprise having been lost.

The Allies responded by pouring more troops on to the peninsula, including many Australian and New Zealand forces, and battles continued for months. Advances were made but at great expense, with the terrain, the conditions, the weather and the closeness of the opposing trenches making fighting very difficult. There was also a major outbreak of dysentery.

When Jack's battalion first landed at Suvla Bay on Gallipoli in August 1915 in the full heat of summer, it joined a campaign that was still being fought fiercely towards its original, and ever less attainable, conclusion, the capture of the peninsula. When Jack returned to the front line in October, things had changed, including the weather, and the Allies were beginning to accept that the campaign had failed. A withdrawal started in December 1915, and the last troops had left Gallipoli by 9 January 1916. The evacuation, done in secret, and with minimal losses, was the campaign's only real success. The death toll in the Dardanelles campaign was horrendous: 43,000 British, 15,000 French, nearly 9000 Australians, 2700 New Zealanders, 1400 Indians and around 60,000 Turks. The losses of the ANZAC (Australian and New Zealand Army Corps) forces, in their first significant involvement in the First World War, had a lasting impact upon the national and cultural identity of those nations.

The 4th Battalion arrived back in Alexandria on 18 December 1915, becoming part of the 54th East Anglian Division. There was then a period of rest and the arrival and training of new drafts to make good the Gallipoli losses. Throughout 1916 Jack served in Egypt and on the Suez Canal defences, as part of the Egypt Expeditionary Force, which spent the year gradually driving the Turks out of Egypt. In early 1917 they prepared for the next phase, the capture of Gaza to open up the way into Palestine. The first Battle of Gaza in March 1917 was initially successful, but then failed through lack of support and poor communications, the constant problem in so many First World War battles. The Second Battle of Gaza, in April 1917, was also a failure. On 19 April Jack was reported dead, but a letter received by his parents a month later confirmed that he was still alive, though wounded. As so often, poor communications left families with an agonizing wait for news. He recovered again, in time to take part in the third, and finally successful, Battle of Gaza in November 1917. From this point on, the Allies enjoyed a sequence of battle successes, driving the Turks out of Palestine and Syria and capturing Jerusalem and ultimately Damascus. Following the Armistice Jack returned to Egypt with the battalion, and then to Britain in January 1919 to be demobilized.

Jack came back to Britain expecting a hero's welcome but, like so many other former soldiers, he found little gratitude and no work. So he re-enlisted in the army in 1919, signing on for three years in the Norfolk Regiment's 2nd (Regular) Battalion, and served in India and in the tribal conflicts in Waziristan and the Khyber Pass. In 1919 he also married Annie Jackson, and they went on to have three children. His period of engagement ended in March 1922 and so Jack left the army again, and joined the Great Eastern Railway as a linesman near Fakenham. This was the start of a railway career that was to last 39 years, with Jack working for the Great Eastern, the London and North Eastern Railway and British Railways. A strong union man with clear political views, Jack became chairman of his branch and a shop steward.

Unlike so many of his contemporaries, Jack Lock survived his wartime experiences relatively unscathed. He was a man of firm principles and many interests, which included gardening, goat-, pig- and chicken-rearing, wine-making, choral singing and playing various musical instruments, playing bowls, helping the St John Ambulance, watch-mending, riding his motorcycle and sidecar, and smoking. At an earlier period in his life he was also an excellent poacher. When he died in 1991, aged 94, he was one of the few surviving Gallipoli veterans.

Daisies picked by John Lock near Jerusalem on 1 January 1918, pressed for preservation and later framed.

A NURSE TRAINED BY EDITH CAVELL

MURIEL RUTH MOORE
1892–1977

The story of Edith Cavell is universally familiar, mainly because at the time of her death she was seen as a national heroine, and the victim of a German atrocity. For Britain, and for America, the execution of a nurse ranked up there with the sinking of the *Lusitania* as examples of despicable behaviour by a ruthless enemy. For a century the case has been debated endlessly. It seems clear now that, while Edith Cavell was probably not a spy for the British government, she had helped Allied soldiers escape from occupied Belgium, and for the Germans that was enough to justify their action. What has been lost in the debate is any sense of who Edith Cavell was as a person, and so a rare insight is offered by the story of a nurse who worked alongside her.

Born in Liverpool in June 1892, Muriel Ruth Moore moved with her family to Antwerp in 1897 as her father worked for a shipping company. Along with her brothers and sisters she was educated there, becoming multilingual. In January 1912 she enrolled in a nursing college in Brussels run by Edith Cavell. The following year her family moved to Morocco but Ruth stayed on at the Hospital St Gilles in Brussels to finish her training.

When war broke out Brussels was soon occupied by the Germans. Ruth stayed on and, when the Royal Palace became a military hospital, the Ambulance du Palais, she was sent to work there. Thanks to her fluency in German, she was put in charge of a German ward. Encouraged by Edith Cavell, her matron, who told her that her patients had no more right to ask her nationality than to ask her age or her Christian name, Ruth hid as far as she could the fact that she was British. By now, after several years in her

'My grandmother collected documents, letters, photographs and newspaper cuttings about the war and her involvement in it. This seemed to be the most important part of her life, which she re-lived regularly by writing and talking about it.'

MIRIAM TAYLOR, GRANDDAUGHTER

Top: A group of nurses in Brussels, including Ruth Moore (middle row, 6th from left). Bottom left: Pass issued to Ruth Moore by the German forces occupying Brussels. Bottom right: Ruth Moore's identity card and the enamel badge she wore when attending Edith Cavell's nursing college in Brussels.

care, Ruth knew and respected Edith as a reserved, independent, serious-minded and highly principled woman.

Edith had originally come to Brussels to work as a governess. After five years, resolved to do something useful with her life, she returned to England to train as a nurse. By the time she qualified, Edith was a determined woman with a clear sense of duty. After some years of hard and dedicated work in hospitals in impoverished parts of London, she returned to Brussels to open one of the first independent nursing colleges.

By the end of 1914, Ruth's position in Brussels was becoming precarious. Apart from Edith, she was the only English nurse working at the hospital, and this knowledge was becoming quite widely known. Her brother Jack was also in Belgium, working in a business in Antwerp, and he managed to remain there throughout the war. He and Ruth were in contact but were able to keep their relationship a secret.

Early in 1915 the Germans issued an order that all nationals from enemy countries who were in occupied Belgium had to present themselves to the authorities, or run the risk of being arrested, imprisoned or even executed. Ruth felt she had to obey this and so, in March 1915, armed with the necessary papers, she was allowed to leave Belgium for Holland. A group of her Belgian colleagues planned to leave at the same time. However, because they were not allowed to exit their country openly, Edith arranged for them to be smuggled out, using the routes and connections she had developed for helping soldiers leave occupied Belgium. She saved the nurses, and a large number of Allied soldiers, but at the cost of her own life. In August 1915 she was arrested, tried for treason and, despite appeals from the American consul, executed on 12 October. The night before her execution, Edith Cavell made her famous statement, 'Patriotism is not enough, I must have no hatred or bitterness towards anyone.'

After some dramatic adventures, the Belgian nurses met Ruth in Maastricht and then the whole group travelled on to England. There they separated, the Belgian nurses going to a Belgian hospital in England, and Ruth to a military hospital in Worcestershire.

Determined to return to the Western Front, Ruth did not stay there long. Family reasons took her to Tangiers, where she worked as a nurse, while looking all the time for posts with the Red Cross in France. Nothing came up, partly because the British authorities did not want her to return to the Western Front, fearful of the risks she might be exposed to if captured. So, in 1916 she took a post as a nursing sister in the Colonial Hospital in Gibraltar, where she spent the rest of the war. The hospital looked after sick and injured passengers and crew from merchant vessels, and was always busy, notably after the Spanish influenza outbreak which started late in 1917. She also nursed malaria and typhoid cases, and survivors from torpedoed and wrecked ships. After the war Ruth wrote about her Gibraltar experiences, noting that not all her patients' problems were caused by diseases or injuries.

> As the war dragged on we had to open yet another ward for officers who were brought in mostly suffering from nervous strain – it was pathetic to see men of such splendid physique reduced to nervous wrecks, but was it to be wondered at, when one considered the dangers and fears they had to face?

Ruth witnessed in Gibraltar the celebrations that marked the signing of the Armistice on 11 November 1918, an event overshadowed for her and all her colleagues by the sinking the day before near Cape Trafalgar of the battleship HMS *Britannia* by the submarine U-50. The afternoon of Armistice Day they all attended the funeral of 23 sailors who had died on the *Britannia*.

After the war Ruth worked in Spain for a while and then returned to England, became a State Registered Nurse and qualified as a midwife. In the late 1920s she married an engineer, James Hellyer, whose grandfather had worked with Florence Nightingale in the Crimea.

Throughout the rest of her life, Ruth often talked and wrote about her wartime experiences, and her connection with Edith Cavell. She contributed to articles and books about Edith, and had a long correspondence with the actress Anna Neagle, who played Edith in the 1939 film, *Nurse Edith Cavell*. In this way Ruth was able to keep alive the character and personality of a woman who, through the nature of her death, has become for the British an iconic heroine, almost a Joan of Arc figure.

A SAPPER WHO USED HIS VIOLIN AS A WAR DIARY

ERNEST ALFRED JOHNSON
1883–1948

In December 1883 Ernest Alfred Johnson was born in North Shields. His father, who had come from an Irish farming background, was an engineer and his mother was a mariner's daughter. After attending the Jubilee

School, Ernest was taught wood-carving by a Miss Spence. He became a skilled and creative carver, making interesting and attractive items at various times in his life. The family today have some candlesticks, and a bowl ornamented with a carved model of a squirrel. The use of this squirrel may support the family story that he had some connection with Robert Thompson, the famous Mouseman carver of Kilburn, Yorkshire. In 1908, Ernest signed on as a carpenter on the SS *London City* and sailed from North Shields to New York and back. His discharge papers described him as: 'everything to be desired & strictly sober', not perhaps surprising for a Methodist with Irish Protestant roots. Meanwhile, his father had remarried and had another son, also called Ernest. This Ernest Johnson

'I never knew my grandfather, and my grandmother never mentioned him. But now I have his fiddle, it is fantastic, I feel I have a connection to him. It's been very moving for me, thinking of him playing it in those dreadful places and remembering his family at home. And here I am, playing it again, that's why I learned, to bring him back to life.'

JAN EVANS, GRANDDAUGHTER

was the navigator on the *R101* airship, and died when it crashed in Northern France on 5 October 1930.

In March 1911 the first Ernest married a local girl, Jane Hepple, whose father was a pattern maker. They took on a grocer's shop and Ernest had a workshop where he made furniture and decorative objects from wood. They had two children and then, in late 1914 or early 1915, Ernest enlisted as a Sapper in the Royal Engineers and was attached to a Field Company. After training, they sailed to France in August 1915 and Ernest took with him a violin from the Irish side of the family. This instrument, on which he could only play popular tunes such as 'Roses of Picardy', apparently his favourite, was to accompany him throughout his war service.

The violin became his war diary for he scratched on the back the names of all the places where he served, along with important details of his life in the army. The list starts with: 'Left Buxton for France 8/8/1915' and ends with 'FINISHED WITH ARMY 18.2.19'. In between are 20 place names with dates, along with details of leave periods and the interesting comment: 'Spoke to King George at Messines'. The King and Queen spent a fortnight touring the Western Front in July 1917, visiting Messines on the 4th, a month after the famous battle. The place names, with occasional erratic spellings, list some famous battle locations apart from Messines, including La Couture, Neuve Chapelle, Richebourg and Laventie.

However, the dates on the violin do not always coincide with the

Ernest Johnson's violin (above), with a detail (right) of his war diary carved on the back of the instrument.

known dates of the battles and some have no obvious connection with the place they are attached to. This raises the possibility that he added the dates to the violin when he got home, working from memory, and sometimes made mistakes, both in spelling and chronology. They are also scratched in a very consistent manner, as though they had all been done together at one time, rather than spread over a couple of years. It is, therefore, difficult to establish for certain exactly what Ernest's movements were. The details of his service record are not known, though it seems likely that he was a Field Company carpenter.

Field companies were attached to every division and supplied general and technical expertise to support the front lines. Their work included trench building and repair, road construction and maintenance, communications and signals and general building work. There were over 200 field companies in the British army in the First World War. Each company comprised about 200 men, and included bricklayers, carpenters, plumbers, blacksmiths, painters, surveyors, drivers, farriers and other specialist tradesmen. Other specialist companies within the Royal Engineers looked after tunnelling, chemical warfare, field surveying, the operation of railways, docks and coastal fortresses.

After a spell of duty in Belgium, the violin indicates that Ernest was next posted to Italy with his company. Ten Italian locations are listed, some of which are difficult to identify because of the spelling. Among the clearest are Mantova, Vicenza, Verona, Castelfranco, Lake Garda and Piave.

Although a member of the Triple Alliance with Germany and Austro-Hungary, Italy did not immediately join the war. For its own political reasons and after lengthy discussions with Britain, Italy finally agreed to join the Allies, declaring war on Germany and Austria in April 1915. Italy's campaign started with the first of a series of offensives along the Isonzo river. As so often happened in the First World War, there were gains but no breakthroughs, and 11 further Isonzo offensives were launched in 1915 and 1917. Meanwhile, in March 1916 the Austrians launched their own equally inconclusive offensive on the Asagio. Unlike the Western Front, these battles were fought over mountainous country, and sometimes in the snow, and the casualty rates for both sides were extremely high. In the summer of 1917 large numbers of German reinforcements were sent to support the Austrians, significantly shifting the balance away from the Italians. In October 1917 the joint German and Austrian armies launched the Battle of Caporetto, and swept through the Italian lines, forcing the Italian army into a 12-mile retreat on the first day. This is the background to Ernest Hemingway's novel, *A Farewell to Arms*. The advance continued, driving the Italians to the Piave, where it stopped, mainly because the Austrians had outrun their supply lines. In November, the British and French, fearing an Italian collapse, sent large numbers of troops to bolster their army, along with significant amounts of strategic material, much of which came from United States sources. In early 1918, Germany took its troops out of Italy, to prepare for its forthcoming Spring Offensive on the Western Front. The Austrians, keen to end the war, launched an offensive on the Piave in June but this was repulsed by the now much strengthened Italians, supported by the British and French. In October the Italians retaliated and launched the Battle of Vittorio Veneto which was a decisive success. Over 300,000 Austrian soldiers surrendered, heralding the collapse of the Austro-Hungarian army. The war ended with the signing of an armistice on 3 November 1918, after which Italy took control of Dalmatia. British forces were fully involved until the end of the Italian campaign.

After the war Ernest returned to North Shields, a changed man, quiet and withdrawn. His wife later told their daughter that, had he been like that when she had first met him, she probably wouldn't have married him. He spent his time in his shed on the allotment, or in his room playing wartime tunes on his violin. Nevertheless, they had three more children. They gave up the shop and Ernest took odd jobs while his wife worked as a dressmaker. Luckily his wife was a very strong woman, and she looked after everything. In the 1930s Ernest began to work in the shipyards, and this kept him occupied through the Second World War, fitting out ships. In 1940 the death of his daughter Jenny at the age of 16 deeply affected him, and he was never the same again, until his death in 1948.

In 2011 Ernest's granddaughter Jan found the violin in an attic. It was in a sorry state but she had it repaired and decided to learn to play it, to preserve the memory of the grandfather she had never met. Jan can now play a selection of First World War tunes, including 'Roses of Picardy', and feels that she has brought Ernest back to life for the family.

ANZAC Memorial Medallion, instituted in 1967 for those from Australia and New Zealand who took part in the campaign in Gallipoli. This one was given to Walter Lester's family.

A SOLDIER WHO FOUGHT WITH THE AUSTRALIANS AND THE BRITISH

WALTER HUBERT LESTER
1896–1981

Among the hundreds of thousands of soldiers who took part in the First World War, there are not many who fought for two nations. Walter Hubert Lester was born in Leeds in June 1896, the eldest of four children.

His father, and his grandfather, were Church of England clergymen. Walter's childhood and upbringing were comfortable but at school his family's expectations were not fulfilled and so, at the age of 17, he was packed off to Australia, to work as a farm hand on a large sheep station near Perth, under the care of a maternal uncle, Frank Laverack. On 21 November 1913 Walter sailed from London on board the Orient Line's SS *Orvieto*, bound for Fremantle. Walter settled quickly into his new life in the isolation of the outback, developing both skills and confidence and becoming an excellent rider.

When war broke out, Britain was quick to seek support from the countries that were part of the British Empire. Among the first to respond were Canada, Australia and New Zealand, each setting up their own

'Walter Lester was a warmly welcoming and generous man, with an ever-present twinkle in his eye. His life was filled with adventures and anecdotes yet, like all those who fought and survived the war, things would never be the same again.'

ANTHONY POOLE, SON-IN-LAW

AN EGG THAT TRAVELLED TO FRANCE AND BACK

VIDA OLIVE SHEPPARD
1902–1977

Vida Olive Sheppard was born in August 1902 in Frome, Somerset, and lived all her early life in that town. As a child, she attended Christ Church School. In 1915 she and the other children in her class were encouraged to help the soldiers fighting in the trenches by collecting and sending them gifts, such as small items of food or warm clothing.

At the time, there was little understanding in Britain of the real nature of trench life on the front line, as information came mostly from letters home which were usually censored before being sent, or from newspaper reports, which never highlighted either the heavy losses or the actualities of day-to-day life on the front line. By 1915 the government propaganda machine was getting into its stride and working hard at maintaining public support for the war, in all sorts of ways. Posters encouraged recruitment, crucial in the years before the introduction of conscription in 1916, and articles in magazines promoted ways in which families at home could improve the life of the soldier at the front. The postal service was well organized and efficient and so parcels containing food and other gifts sent to the soldiers were generally quickly delivered, and genuinely appreciated by the recipients.

'I don't recall my mother – or my father for that matter – talking of their experiences of the First World War. For all her married life my mother was a housewife, and devoted herself to me and my father and maintained a happy family life.'

BRIAN FRENCH, SON

This kind of propaganda, which with hindsight can seem simplistic and patronizing, was actually quite effective. It was also directed at schools, where many children had fathers, uncles or brothers away on active service.

In this case, the pupils in Vida's class were encouraged to bring to school something that could be sent to the soldiers in France, packed together as a class gift. Vida took an egg as her gift, and the parcel was duly sent off, via one of the well-publicized distribution depots. Vida wrote a message on her egg : 'Vida Olive Sheppard Christ Church School Frome – Health and Luck to dear Tommy Atkins God Bless Him.' Normally, that would have been the end of the matter. However, in this case the egg was returned, stuffed with cotton wool and carefully packed in a cigarette tin, with a new message 'Returned with thanks, Pt. E Devall, 23.5.15' in blue ink. The sender, a Private E Devall from the Royal Army Medical Corps No. 12 General Depot, also wrote Vida a letter, explaining that he had received the egg, extracted and enjoyed the contents while carefully preserving the shell and returned it to her as 'a souvenir of this terrible war'. He ended by saying, 'I must conclude thanking you for your kind wishes and please accept the same from me in return.' So far, it has not proved possible to identify Private Devall with certainty, or establish what happened to him.

Vida clearly treasured the egg and all it represented, particularly as her father did serve in France, as a Private in the Army Service Corps. In December 1928 she married Samuel Frederick French at Christ Church in Frome, and they had one son, who today is the proud possessor of the egg, a remarkable survivor of the war which offers an unusual insight into life on the Home Front. Brian's mother never told him about the egg, and he only heard the story from his father after his mother had died in 1977.

The egg sent to France by Vida Sheppard, and returned to her by Private Devall. Her message is in black, and his reply is in blue.

Above: Landships, or tanks, under construction at Fosters Lincoln factory, where George Atkin worked. Right: Enamel badge worn by George Henry Atkin while working at Fosters, to prove he was employed on war service.

EMPLOYED ON WAR MATERIAL

ISSUED BY WILLIAM FOSTER & CO LTD

· 1915 ·

A LAD WHO DID HIS BIT BY BUILDING TANKS

GEORGE HENRY ATKIN
1900–1982

George Henry Atkin was born in October 1900 in Friesthorpe, a small village nine miles from Lincoln. His father was a farm labourer and he had six brothers and one sister. When war was declared in 1914, it seems that George went into Lincoln to try to enlist, but was turned away because he was too young. As is well known, many young men who were underage were able to enlist, either by lying about their age or because the recruiting office did not check properly. It is thought that the youngest soldier to fight in the British army in the First World War was just 12.

A while later George (bottom right of photograph) found work with William Foster and Company, a manufacturer of agricultural machinery. Founded in 1856, the company was well known for its threshing machines and for its portable steam engines, the first of which had been produced in 1858. Later production included traction engines, steam tractors and road locomotives.

In the early years of the 20th century, versions of caterpillar-tracked vehicles were developed and produced in several countries, largely for agricultural use. The military possibilities of such vehicles were explored and engineers in France, Austria and Australia designed experimental

'I can sum up my grandfather in three words, a lovely old gentleman. My biggest regret is that I didn't ask him more about his work with the tanks project but researching his life inspired me to become a historian and writer.'

RICHARD PULLEN, GRANDSON

armoured self-propelled guns, but the projects were abandoned. However, a Californian manufacturer, Benjamin Holt, produced the best caterpillar-driven cross-country tractor of this era, and these did go into service with the British army for the haulage of guns and supplies over rough terrain. By 1916 over 1000 Holt caterpillar tractors were in use on the Western Front, and these practical and efficient vehicles were part of the inspiration for the tank.

By 1915, the Allies were aware of the need for an armoured fighting vehicle that could cross trenches and destroy barbed wire, and considerable development work was carried out in France, with several experimental vehicles being produced, some of which were based on the Holt tractor. In Britain various schemes and experiments were tried out in 1915, and gradually the government and the Royal Navy began to back the idea of an armoured fighting landship.

From October 1915 the landships began to be referred to as tanks for security purposes – the machines being described in documents and on crates as 'water tanks', 'water carriers' or simply 'tanks'. Unwilling to describe themselves as the 'WC Committee' due to fears it was inappropriate, the government's Landship Committee, which had been driving the project from the start, accordingly changed its name to the Tank Committee.

Instead of using the Holt tractor, the government went to William Foster and Company and several experimental machines were made between July and December 1915, none of which were successful. The breakthrough came in February 1916 with the successful testing of the first rhomboidal design, known officially as His Majesty's Landship Centipede, and unofficially as Big Willie. Immediately, Fosters were commissioned to build 100, and a further 50 were ordered in April 1916. British tanks were first used in action on 15 September 1916, at the Battle of Flers–Courcelette.

George Atkin worked on the landship project from its early days, and was involved in long weeks of hard and dangerous work. Young, small-sized boys like him were essential for getting into the remote and inaccessible parts of the tank during its construction, such as the area under the massive radiator. Those who worked on the landship project during the First World War were told never to talk about it, and George never did, even later in his life.

After the war, George continued to work for Fosters but the company began to struggle and in the 1920s he was laid off. At that point, he turned his back on engineering and went into farming, the other great Lincolnshire area of employment, and enjoyed his new life. In 1924 George married Dorothy Wright, and they had 11 children. His tank secrets nearly died with him in 1982, but instead, the chance discovery after his death of an enamel Fosters badge brought George's story to light over 70 years later.

When conscription was introduced in 1916, George was still too young to serve. However, by then he was an important and well-trained member of the tank production team, and so would probably have qualified for a Reserved Occupation. The problem faced by him, and by many other young men in his position who were employed in important war work in Britain, was that they could be seen as shirkers or cowards because they were not in uniform. They were often abused in the street or even handed a white feather. To counter this, brass or

Women were employed in many industries linked to the war effort. Typical is the group posed in front of a Fosters tank.

enamel badges were produced that stated that the wearers were engaged in war work, or on war service. Some of these were officially produced, for example for civilians working for the Admiralty or the War Office and in munitions factories, but many more were issued independently by private companies, such as the railways. Fosters issued their own version, one of which George wore from 1915.

It was finding this badge that made his grandson Richard determined to explore both George's story, and the story of tank production at William Foster and Company. Thanks to his grandson, George has come to represent all those who worked hard on the Home Front to support the war.

CHAUFFEUR TO THE PRINCE OF WALES

JOHN HENRY BRENTON
1888–1969

John Henry Brenton, or Jack, was born in Shropshire in 1888. His father Jesse was a publican and by 1901 the family moved to Hampshire, to manage an inn. Jack developed an early interest in machinery and motor vehicles and by 1907 he had a full driving licence and was working in the motor trade in west London. In 1913 he was employed as a chauffeur and mechanic by a wealthy London family and the same year he married Eveline Alice Burley.

They had one daughter. By 1914 Jack was working at Buckingham Palace as a driver and mechanic, based in the Royal Mews. On the outbreak of war he enlisted in the Army Service Corps to enable him to drive the Prince of Wales on war-related visits and duties. This, later the Royal Army Service Corps, had been established in 1888 to look after the army's supply and transport needs.

Edward, the eldest son of King George V, had been born in 1894 and was invested as Prince of Wales when he was 16. In 1914 he enlisted in the Grenadier Guards. He wanted to fight on the Western Front, but both his father and Lord Kitchener refused to consider it, mainly because of the problems that would have arisen had he been captured. Edward served as a Staff Officer, but took every opportunity to visit France and the front lines, frequently putting himself, and his

'Both during and after the war my granddad had to look after the Prince's busy social life by taking him to various places and maintaining absolute discretion, whatever the hour. My mother remembers as a child sitting on the Prince's knee while he was in the Royal Mews, having a cup of tea and a glimpse of normal family life.'

WENDY WARD, GRANDDAUGHTER

attendants, in danger. On one occasion in 1915, just after Edward had got out of the royal car, it was hit by a German shell, which killed the chauffeur (not Jack this time). However, the Prince of Wales's very visible presence made him popular with the troops and in 1916 he was awarded the Military Cross.

During three visits to France, in 1915, 1916 and 1917, the Prince of Wales's regular chauffeur was Lance Corporal, and later Sergeant, Jack Brenton, whose job was to look after the Prince, his transport arrangements and the royal Daimler. His responsible position was underlined in 1916 when he was awarded the Royal Victoria Medal, a reward for personal service to the royal family. Jack was described in his discharge papers at the end of the war as 'a first class driver who has been driving the Prince of Wales since 1915'.

Jack enjoyed a close relationship with the Prince and was well trusted, and this continued after the war; his job title in 1920 was Head Driver Mechanic for HRH Prince of Wales. During the 1920s and 1930s the Prince of Wales maintained both a busy professional life, with 16 tours to various parts of the Empire between 1919 and 1935, and a frenetic social life, with many romances and affairs, often with married women. As his chauffeur, Jack's discretion was absolute. He remained in royal service until 1935.

Jack not only taught Edward to drive but also his brother, the Duke of York, and the Dukes of Kent and Gloucester. In an interview in 1960, Jack revealed that Edward was the better driver, while the Duke of York was a bit of a tearaway and the Duke of Gloucester more at home on a horse.

Today, documents and passes preserved by his family offer an insight both into Jack's unusual war, and the role played by the royal family in supporting the war.

The driving licence given to John Brenton by the Prince of Wales.

A SOLDIER WHO RECORDED HIS WAR IN PHOTOGRAPHS

HUGH BOURN FORTUNE GODFREY
1883–1963

Hugh Bourn Fortune Godfrey, usually known as Huborn, was born in Basingstoke in 1883. Little is known about his family background, and he only had a rudimentary education. At some point in 1915 he enlisted in the 121st Siege Battery, Royal Garrison Artillery (RGA).

The RGA had been formed in 1899 when the Royal Regiment of Artillery was divided into three sections: the RGA took over the coastal, mountain, siege and heavy guns, while the Royal Horse Artillery and the Royal Field Artillery looked after the lighter and more mobile guns, which were usually horse-drawn. The RGA comprised large numbers of Siege and Heavy Batteries, many of which had county or local connections, and the list was greatly increased by 'Service' Batteries for the New Army, formed from volunteers recruited by Lord Kitchener. The Heavy Batteries were usually equipped with 6-inch, or 60-pounder guns, and had some mobility, while the Siege Batteries had the larger, and far less mobile howitzers, designed

'Pompa, my grandfather, died when I was ten. He was kindly and gentle, sometimes stubborn, and notoriously forgetful.
I believe he was a happy man though he didn't talk about the war, and was reluctant to let me look at his photograph albums.
He once ticked me off for wasting my pocket money on a toy tank, which he could not see as a plaything.'

RICHARD HILLS, GRANDSON

Photograph from Huborn Godfrey's album, showing his chance
meeting with his brother Jim on the Somme.

to send shells on a high trajectory from positions well behind the lines.
Their main function was the destruction of enemy artillery, strongpoints
and stores. Most Siege Batteries were equipped with 6-inch, 8-inch and 9.2-
inch howitzers, although a few had the massive 12-inch guns which were
generally mounted on railway wagons. Howitzers required a large crew
and the larger ones required a substantial emplacement and so could not
be moved quickly. The 6-inch howitzers had limited mobility, and their
crews were equipped with caterpillar-tracked tractors. There were well over
200 Siege Batteries, attached to various regiments. The larger batteries
were organized into Heavy Artillery Brigades, or Groups.

Huborn arrived in France in July 1916 with the 121st Siege Battery and
at some point was promoted to Sergeant. It seems he also took a small
camera with him, and plenty of film. This, likely to have been a Kodak
Vest Pocket Camera, was a type first produced in about 1912, and designed
to use the new, smaller 127-roll film. In 1915 Kodak introduced the Vest
Pocket Autographic camera. This, popularly known as 'the soldier's
camera', had a feature that allowed notes to be written on the back of the
film while still in the camera. Nearly two million were sold between 1915
and the late 1920s.

Throughout his military career, Huborn regularly took photographs
and sent the exposed but undeveloped rolls of film back to his wife, hidden

in handkerchief pouches. She, not knowing what to do with them, put them all in a drawer to await her husband's return. Huborn survived the war, was duly demobilized and, when he went home, he found the films. He had them developed and printed and mounted the photographs in two albums, which his grandson Richard inherited when Huborn died in 1963. There are about 135 photographs, indicating that there must have been at least 17 rolls of film sent back to Britain. Strangely, Huborn assembled the photographs in his albums in a rather random way and so, even though every one is captioned and many dated, there is no obvious chronology. The period covered is from September 1916 to late 1917, or early 1918, and so, by putting them in order, it is possible to record Huborn's military career, and therefore the history of the 121st Siege Battery.

The 1916 photographs are on the Somme, and include early pictures of tanks before and after their first ever engagement in the battle of Flers–Courcelette on 15 September, along with other tank images taken in October and November 1916. There are also photographs of howitzers in action, mostly 9.2-inch and 60-pounders, and the caterpillar tractors that hauled them, along with destroyed guns, crashed aeroplanes, dead bodies and the desolation of the battlefield. The famous 'Leaning Virgin' on the top of Albert church is featured, along with less familiar images such as haymaking going on behind the lines, French soldiers on Christmas Day and the grave of Raymond Asquith, the Prime Minister's son killed on the Somme on 15 September 1916. More personal is a photograph showing Huborn with his brother Jim who had emigrated to Australia before the war. Their meeting on the Somme was by chance, and they never met again.

In 1917 the 121st Siege Battery, and Huborn, were mostly in the Ypres area, though some Somme scenes still occur and there is a picture of Canadian soldiers preparing for the attack on Vimy Ridge and another showing German prisoners after the Vimy attack in April 1917. Photographs showing the Officers' and Sergeants' Mess at Kelsey Manor and Northampton Hospital suggest that Huborn was wounded and sent back to England to recover. Another, entitled 'God Bless the Nurses', underlines this. He was in Messines in June 1917, photographing the mine craters and the tanks used in that battle, and in Ypres in time to catch a French general viewing the ruins of the Cloth Hall.

Somme Offensive
Tank going into action at
Flers. Oct 1916.

Photograph from Huborn Godfrey's album, showing tanks at
the battle of Flers–Courcelette in 1916.

After the war, Huborn married Nellie Fulker and they had one daughter, born in 1923. He worked for the Great Western Railway and lived with his wife in the Reading area. Apart from during his war service, he never left Britain.

Altogether, the photographs are a very unusual and highly personal collection. Informal views of the war, taken by amateur photographers, are not uncommon and it seems that many soldiers, particularly officers, carried cameras in their pockets. In later life Huborn told his grandson that he had to hide the camera and take photographs secretly but, judging by the kind of scenes, their viewpoint and the other people in many of them, he must have taken some photographs quite openly. Certainly, after 1914, the carrying of cameras was not encouraged and in some areas actually banned, for fear that images could either give a damaging view of the war if seen back in Britain, or reveal secrets to the Germans if captured. However, amateur photography while on active service does not seem to have been generally regarded as a serious and punishable offence. The practical difficulties were often considerable, and Sergeant Huborn Godfrey's legacy is a remarkable insight into the life and experiences of an ordinary soldier fighting with the artillery on the Western Front in 1916 and 1917.

1916

ON THE WESTERN FRONT 1916 WAS DEFINED BY TWO major and long-lasting battles, the German attack on the French army at Verdun, and the Allied campaign on the Somme. Both were hugely expensive in men and materials and both failed to achieve the attacker's objectives. Despite being driven to the brink of mutiny, the French held on at Verdun, while on the Somme, where the British death toll on the first day was 20,000, the flower of the German army was gradually destroyed over several weeks and months. A war of attrition was the new strategy. The Somme was Britain's last great citizens' battle, fought largely by volunteers who, in many cases, had close social, geographical or professional bonds. Britain's new army was egalitarian, with all levels of society and all professions represented, including writers and artists. Imperial Forces from the colonies greatly strengthened Britain's fighting soldiers, in both quantity and quality, with volunteers flocking to the aid of the mother country. On the Somme, tanks were used for the first time, aviation tactics and communications improved and lessons began to be learned, notably that a reliance on long artillery barrages and heavy frontal attacks on strongly defended trenches would rarely achieve a breakthrough.

Lord Kitchener had created Britain's New Armies but he did not see much of them in the field as he was lost in the sinking of HMS *Hampshire* on the way to Russia for a diplomatic trip. A few days before, the Royal Navy had faced the German High Seas Fleet at the Battle of Jutland, the largest naval engagement since Trafalgar. The result was inconclusive, but the German fleet never ventured out again.

Increased fighting against the Turks in Mesopotamia and Palestine drew many troops to these new sectors, and broadened the war away from the Western Front. At first, things went badly, leading to the surrender of thousands of British troops at Kut, but by the end of the year a much improved and enlarged Allied army was starting to overcome the Turks.

On the Home Front Lloyd George took over from Asquith as Prime Minister. The civilian population was drawn increasingly into the war. London and other cities were bombed by Zeppelins and other airships, in random attacks to which there was at first no adequate response. Shortages of food and other supplies were being caused by the German submarine blockade. In Dublin, the Easter Rising reawakened the prospect of an Irish civil war and soldiers were diverted from other fronts to keep the peace there. With the passing of the Bill to introduce conscription, Conscientious Objectors and anti-war campaigners became more apparent, along with the public reaction to them.

Stories in this chapter document many of these campaigns and events, notably aspects of the Somme. They also offer an insight into the minds of those soldiers and their habits, the way families dealt with the unprecedented scale of death and injury, and the social and psychological problems faced by those who survived.

A SAILOR KILLED
IN AN ACCIDENT AT SEA

THOMAS GROVES
1896–1916

Born Thomas Groves in March 1896 in Tutshill, Gloucestershire, Tom was the fifth child, and second son, in a family of 13 children. His father, Albert, was a sailor from a long line of sailors, and Tom and all but one of his brothers became sailors too. His uncle had rigged either the *Terra Nova* or the *Discovery*, ships used by Captain Scott on his expeditions to Antarctica. His father had sailed the world, but when Tom was born he was working on sailing trows based on the river Severn. At the age of 15 Tom was an apprentice sheet iron roller but he soon left this and went to sea, probably influenced by his brother who had sailed round Cape Horn. Tom's first ships, small coastal schooners and barquetines, were mostly in the china clay trade, sailing from Cornish clay ports such as Charleston and Fowey to European destinations.

'Tom's death affected the whole family, and all anyone could remember was the grief. They said he was jolly and nice to everyone, and at all the funerals of his brothers and sisters they played Tom Bowling, the traditional folk song.'

SUZANNE HORNE, NIECE

The schooner *David Morris*, painted by an Italian artist in the early 1900s. Tom Groves was one of her crew in April 1916.

On 10 April 1916 Tom sailed from Oporto as one of the crew of a schooner called *David Morris*. On the outward voyage she may have been laden with clay, but her cargo on the return voyage to Britain is not known. The *David Morris* was one of a class of three-masted topsail coastal trading schooners associated with Porthmadog in North Wales, known as Western Ocean Yachts. She had been built in David Jones's yard in Porthmadog in 1897, a compact 162-ton ship designed to be sailed by a small crew and sturdily built, originally for the slate trade.

Soon after sailing from Oporto the *David Morris* ran into rough weather in the Bay of Biscay, and Tom and three other crew members went up the foremast to bring in the topsail. What happened next is described in a letter from Captain William Griffiths to Tom's family:

> Tommy, poor chap, was up with three others, and somehow he lost his hold, fell on deck and was killed instantly ... I put the vessel about to try to reach Oporto; but unfortunately the wind increased to a heavy gale ... and we were driven away from it. I kept his body on board for two days in the hope of the weather abating, but it kept blowing for 36 hours and I was compelled to bury him at sea. He was sewn up in canvas and weighted to sink, and I read the burial chapter, all the crew attending the funeral. I can assure you I did my utmost for him ... He was such a splendid chap and greatly respected by everyone. May the Lord give you strength in your great tribulation, and accept my sincere sympathy in your bereavement. I often heard him talk of his mother and family, and I gather he was greatly loved by all.

Throughout the First World War large numbers of sailing vessels were still in use, engaged in the regular coastal and European trading that continued in spite of the war. Many also carried vital food and war supplies to Britain, a traffic that became more essential as the effects of the German submarine blockade increased. This meant that small vessels like the *David Morris* were regularly attacked and sunk by gunfire by enemy submarines. Six vessels from the small fleet of Porthmadog-built Western Ocean Yachts were lost this way, so these voyages were hazardous beyond the normal dangers of sea and weather. Tom's death is also a reminder of the daily risks faced by those earning their living at sea as merchant seamen, even when they were not involved directly in wartime activities.

Tom's brother Will served through the war in the Royal Navy, and survived. In September 1914 he was attached to HMS *Patia*, an armed merchant cruiser based at Avonmouth, and later he was on HMS *Soar*, a Bristol-based minesweeper. The *David Morris* also survived the war, was sold in 1919 and then went overseas in 1923. She was subsequently lost.

Tom was a regular sender of postcards, to his mother and his sisters, and some of these survive in the family, giving clues to the routes he was sailing and the places he was visiting. For a long time his mother kept one in a frame, perhaps his last, and no one was ever allowed to touch it. Many years later, Suzanne, Tom's niece, managed to track down a painting of the *David Morris*, apparently painted by one of the many Italian artists who specialized in ship portraits in the late 19th and early 20th centuries. This had given her a tangible link to her uncle, whose death is still remembered within the family.

AN ARCHITECT AND ARTIST KILLED IN KUT

GILBERT MARSHALL MACKENZIE
1890–1916

Gilbert Marshall Mackenzie was the youngest son of the well-known Scottish architect Alexander Marshall Mackenzie, whose work includes Australia House and the Waldorf Hotel in London. Born in 1890, he grew up in a privileged environment that combined the artistic heritage of his father with the military experience of his mother's family, which stretched

from Robert the Bruce to the Napoleonic Wars. Having studied at Cambridge, Gilbert became an Associate member of the Royal Institute of British Architects in 1913, working with his father and elder brother Alexander George Robertson Mackenzie. After the war, Gilbert's father and his brother together designed the Aberdeen War Memorial.

While at Cambridge, Gilbert enrolled with the Officers' Training Corps and trained with the Seaforth Highlanders. On the outbreak of war, he was mobilized as a 2nd Lieutenant in the Seaforths' 2nd Battalion. This historic Scottish regiment had been formed in 1881 by the merging of two Highland foot regiments, the 72nd and the 78th. The 2nd Battalion landed in France on 23 August 1914 and was in action within days. From the moment he landed on French soil, Gilbert kept a diary. This very detailed and well-written document tells the story of an officer's life

'It is the warmth with which he was loved, and the memories of his cartoons and paintings that have echoed down the family, and which we, his great and great-great nephews and nieces, all share.'

JOHN SMITHELLS, GREAT-NEPHEW

Watercolour by Gilbert Mackenzie, showing a scene in Mesopotamia.

but also offers an insight into the varied nature of the First World War. He fought at Le Cateau and captures the desperation of those days of fighting a retreat which ended at the Marne: 'We were so much on the move that for days one thought of absolutely nothing except fighting and marching.' Next came the Aisne, the First Battle of Ypres and the fighting that led to the trench-line stalemate established at the end of 1914. Gilbert witnessed one of the many unofficial Christmas truces, which he described as 'a regular Mothers' Meeting'. Soon after, on New Year's Day 1915, Gilbert married Marjorie Osmond while on leave in London. Three days later they both went to France: 'We crossed the Channel together but parted at Boulogne, she on a train back to her hospital in Paris and me in a motor bus to Belgium and those damnable trenches.'

Gilbert's diaries are full of descriptions of the trenches:

'There is something very unpleasant about standing blear eyed in a soaking trench just awoken, at one o'clock in the morning. Everything seems to be pitch black ... the sides of the trench are all so horridly muddy and slimy, my elbows are soon soaking right through by touching them.'

Particularly evocative are entries about night patrols out into No Man's Land, always one of the most frightening and dangerous events in regular trench life:

> The Corporal and I still go on getting nearer the enemy at every step. Occasionally a rifle cracks out and the spurt from the muzzle is so painfully visible to us. We pass on, sometimes crawling, sometimes squirming, sometimes sitting up. There are dreadful moments when a flare goes up, and we lie absolutely flat out and absolutely and entirely still. It seems almost impossible that they could not help seeing us. We wait so very anxiously for the rattle of bullets as the flare dies out. We are now very close to the enemy's lines ... the return journey is quicker ... we move back quickly to our wire, we hurry through and drop into our own, our very own trenches. I hate these patrols ...

Gilbert also sketched continuously, noting all the details of military life, including drawing caricatures and cartoons, and the landscapes in which he found himself.

The 2nd Battalion fought through 1915, including at the Second Battle of Ypres. Gilbert was wounded in the leg and was sent back to Britain to recover. In July 1915 he was promoted to Captain. In 1916 the 2nd Battalion moved south to the Somme and then fought on the Western Front until the end of the war. However, in February 1916 Gilbert's regular battalion life changed, for he was then attached to a draft of Seaforth Highlanders being sent to Mesopotamia. They sailed from Devonport on 17 February, and arrived in Basra on 23 March 1916. They were to take part in the final British attempt to relieve the besieged city of Kut el Amara.

Trench drawing by Gilbert Mackenzie.

The siege at Kut had started in December 1915 when the retreating 6th Division of the Indian Army, commanded by Major-

General Charles Townshend, had been trapped in Kut by the German-led Ottoman forces. During January and March 1916 the British made several attempts to relieve the garrison in Kut, all of which were costly failures. Meanwhile, food and supplies within the garrison were running short. The final attempt, by a force of around 30,000 British and Imperial troops, was launched on 5 April. Advances were made, again at a high cost in casualties, but the attack stalled. Even though the Royal Flying Corps carried out the world's first air supply operation, dropping food and ammunition into the garrison, the situation in Kut became desperate and on 29 April 1916, after failed negotiations, General Townshend surrendered unconditionally. Around 13,000 troops went into captivity, over 50 per cent of whom were to die as prisoners.

The whole Kut disaster resulted in about 30,000 British and Indian casualties. Among them was Captain Gilbert Mackenzie who, despite the gravity of the situation, had found time to paint some watercolours in Basra which he sent back to his father. With his Seaforth Highlanders he had reached the front-line trenches on 17 April. From here, on 21 April, he wrote his last letter to his wife: 'I'm feeling extraordinary fit, so cheer up. The thirst quenchers from Mother very much appreciated – please send various kinds. It takes the taste from this beastly water.' At 07.30 on 22 April 1916, Gilbert's company led the final British charge, during which he was wounded and then killed. A fellow officer described the scene in one of the many letters of condolence sent to his wife: 'About 10 minutes after the attack started he joined me up at the front line of the Turkish trenches and from then onwards I was with him until he was killed. Although he was wounded four times he still managed to carry on directing his men in a most calm and heroic manner ... When I got back and saw them (his men) lying everywhere, some severely wounded, the first question they asked me was for news of Gilbert, and when I told them what had happened to him their eyes filled with tears, and they turned their faces to the earth and sobbed.'

Gilbert's body was never recovered, and no memorial commemorates the men who lost their lives during the Kut campaign, apart from the Kut Military Cemetery where 420 British soldiers are buried. In fact, it is widely believed that the British government drew a veil as quickly as possible over the whole disastrous episode.

Above: The cruiser HMS *Hampshire*, on board which Jack Buckenham served from 1913 until it was sunk in 1916.
Left: The Admiralty letter to Jack Buckenham's father, informing him of his son's death in the sinking of the *Hampshire*.

A SAILOR LOST
WITH LORD KITCHENER ON
HMS HAMPSHIRE

JOHN THOMAS BUCKENHAM
1878–1916

Born in Shouldham, Norfolk, in November 1878, John Thomas Buckenham, usually known as Jack, was one of six children. There were also half-brothers and a half-sister from a previous marriage. His father Richard was a forester on a private estate and after leaving school Jack also worked as a forester, probably with his father. The family story is that, aged 18, he was caught poaching and was given the choice of joining the army, or coming up before the magistrate and facing a prison sentence. So, having been given an unusual chance to redeem himself, on 6 February 1896 Jack enlisted in the 4th Battalion of the Norfolk Regiment. This famous county regiment had been formed in 1881 from the long-established 9th (East Norfolk) Regiment

of Foot. The 4th was one of the regiment's volunteer battalions. At the end of 1896 Jack was discharged from the Norfolk Regiment and transferred to the Royal Marine Light Infantry and was based at Portsmouth from January to June 1897.

'When I was small I used to sleep with my grandmother, John's only sister. She had a photograph of HMS Hampshire on the bedroom wall. I know she was very fond of John and treasured all the things he had brought home from his travels with the navy.'

MARGARET BAILEY, GREAT-NIECE

The idea of ship-based naval infantry goes back to the 17th century, and various marine regiments were raised in the 18th century. During the Napoleonic Wars, all naval ships carried Royal Marines and there were over 30,000 Marines in service at that time, some of whom were trained to fight on land, as raiding parties. From these came the idea of Royal Marines Light Infantry, and the name was formalized in 1855 (and tweaked to Royal Marine Light Infantry slightly later), to distinguish them from the Royal Marine Artillery.

Jack was attached to or served on a long list of ships, starting with HMS *Victory*, then in use as a school for naval telegraphy. Others include the battleship HMS *Camperdown*, the cruisers HMS *Fox* and HMS *Cressy*, as well as HMS *Hazard*, a torpedo gunboat, and HMS *Cormorant*, an elderly screw sloop launched in 1877. In the course of his pre-war service, Jack travelled the world, visiting the Mediterranean, the Middle East, China, the Far East and Russia, and he sent many postcards home on his travels. In the years before the First World War he was on the cruiser HMS *Europa*, and then his final posting in 1913 was to a *Devonshire*-class cruiser, HMS *Hampshire*. At this point, he sent a postcard home, a picture of HMS *Hampshire*, with the message: 'this is a photo of the ship I am going to we shall be on the way between Gibraltar and Malta on xmas day.' Jack was on the *Hampshire* for some time. In 1914 she was on the China Station, and in 1915 she returned to Scapa Flow, on patrol duties. On 31 May 1916, HMS *Hampshire* was at the Battle of Jutland, though not in the thick of the action. Surprisingly, Jack does not seem to have written any letters mentioning his presence at this, the greatest naval battle since Trafalgar.

Immediately after Jutland, HMS *Hampshire* was selected to take Lord Kitchener on a diplomatic visit to Russia, the exact purpose of which has never been made clear. Kitchener's party included engineers and diplomats and so the visit may have been partly to encourage Russian pressure on the Eastern Front in the run-up to the Battle of the Somme. Famously, HMS *Hampshire* was equipped with special safes for the secure transport of gold. However, as there is no evidence the ship was carrying gold from Britain, they may have been installed to bring Russian gold back to Britain for safekeeping.

On 5 June 1916, Lord Kitchener and his party sailed from Scrabster to Scapa Flow on HMS *Oak*. There, they transferred to HMS *Hampshire* and at

16.45 she set off into a force nine gale towards Archangel. The destroyers ordered to escort HMS *Hampshire* for the first part of the journey could not keep up because of the weather, and so Captain Herbert Savill, the *Hampshire*'s captain, sent them back to port, believing that enemy submarines could not operate in such conditions. That evening at about 19.40, when the ship was just over a mile off Marwick Head on the Orkney coast, an explosion tore a hole in the side of HMS *Hampshire* between the bow and the bridge. The ship immediately listed to starboard and sank about 15 minutes later.

There was immediate speculation about the sinking of the *Hampshire* and Lord Kitchener's death, and conspiracy theories have abounded ever since. The most popular was that the sinking was caused by a bomb inside the ship, placed by the IRA or some other organization. It was, after all, only a couple of months after the Easter Rising in Dublin. However, the truth, confirmed by subsequent investigations of the wreck, is that the *Hampshire* hit a mine, one of a group laid by the German submarine *U-75* on 28 May 1916 with the intention of impeding the movement of ships from Scapa Flow before and during the Battle of Jutland.

HMS *Hampshire* carried a complement of 655 officers and men, of which 643 were lost. There were 12 survivors, rescued from two Carley floats. Of the seven or so members of Lord Kitchener's party – the exact number is uncertain – none survived. About 100 bodies were subsequently recovered and these were buried in the Lyness Royal Naval Cemetery on Hoy. On 9 June 1916 the Admiralty informed Jack's father and his sister that Private John T. Buckenham had been lost on the *Hampshire*.

Historically, the story of the loss of HMS *Hampshire* has always been dominated by the death of Lord Kitchener. The story of Jack Buckenham is a chance to redress the balance, as he can stand for all the sailors who went down with their ship.

Memorial certificate for James Gardiner, issued by the
Tyneside Irish Brigade Committee.

A TYNESIDER KILLED
ON THE FIRST DAY OF THE SOMME

JAMES GARDINER
1886–1916

James Gardiner (on right of photograph) was born in County Durham in 1886 and lived his early life in Tanfield. After school, he went to work as a miner in one of the local collieries. In April 1910 he married Ann Moat and they lived with her parents in The Teams, Gateshead. Their first child, Joseph, died in 1911, aged six months, and their second, Catherine, died in 1913, aged five months.

In October 1914 James joined the army and was attached initially to the 4th Battalion of the Northumberland Fusiliers. At this point he was listed as James Gardner, and that misspelling of his name was continued throughout his army career. Soon, he was part of the 24th (Service) Battalion, Northumberland Fusiliers, popularly known as the 1st Tyneside Irish. This local battalion had been formed in November 1914 by the Lord Mayor and City of Newcastle and was supported by the city, like so many of the New Army Service battalions. Early training

'My grandfather died in 1916 and his son, my dad,
who was born in 1915, never knew him or his brother and sister.
I think this always distressed him and so he rarely talked about
his father, though he always looked after the papers and
memorabilia he had inherited from his mother.'

PHILIP GARDINER, GRANDSON

was on Newcastle Town Moor. In August 1915 the battalion was taken over by the War Office, becoming part of the establishment of the regular army and based for a time near Salisbury. In January 1916 the 24th Battalion arrived in France, and began training for what was to be its first action, the opening day of the Battle of the Somme.

The Somme campaign, the first great Allied offensive of 1916, had two main aims: first, to achieve the much hoped-for breakthrough of the German lines, and thus end the war, and second, to relieve the pressure on the French army facing the German onslaught at Verdun. The British attack, comprising 11 divisions, was to be along a 16-mile front stretching from Serre in the north to Maricourt in the south, supported by a simultaneous French attack of six divisions below Maricourt and spanning the Somme valley. There were months of preparations, including the training of a fighting force largely made up from Territorial battalions and the Service battalions of Kitchener's New Army. The latter included the famous Pals battalions comprising men who were friends and colleagues drawn from particular areas or professions. In all about 120,000 British soldiers fought on the first day. The attack was preceded by the longest and most violent artillery barrage in history, designed to annihilate all the German defences. However, on what had been a relatively quiet front since 1915, the Germans had had ample opportunity to fortify their lines and create deep underground shelters and strongpoints, little of which was destroyed by the British artillery. At 07.30 on 1 July 1916 the Allied armies climbed from their trenches and advanced into No Man's Land, expecting little or no resistance. Instead, they were met and destroyed by German machine guns and artillery. From the south of the British sector and all through the French sector gains were made, but for most of the British army the day was a disaster, with 60,000 casualties, of which 20,000 were dead, and little ground gained. However, this was not the end of the battle, and the Somme campaign was to continue for another 141 days, until it was brought to an end in mid-November by rain, mud and cold. By then, the Allies had advanced up to seven miles into German territory, and much of the German army had been broken. In the end, the British casualties on the Somme in 1916 were around 400,000, French casualties around 200,000, and German around 550,000.

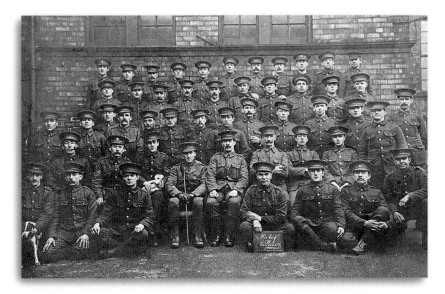

Private James Gardiner is 4th from the right in the second
row of this group of Tyneside Irish, many of
whom were to die on 1 July 1916.

One of those British casualties was Private James Gardiner. He was killed soon after he had left his trench on that summer's morning in July to march in lines across the cornfields, along with many of his friends and companions that made up the 24th Battalion, the 1st Tyneside Irish. All along the front line of the battle were battalions, companies and platoons made up of men who had grown up together, worked together, enlisted and trained together and were destined to die together. All over Britain, families, villages, towns and streets were devastated by the impact of 1 July 1916. Back in Gateshead, Ann Gardiner was left on her own to bring up a tiny baby, for whom his father would only be a name.

No one knows how James died, and his body was never found. His name, still spelled Gardner, is listed on the Memorial to the Missing of the Somme at Thiepval, along with 513 others who served with the Tyneside Irish. The high number of missing from this area may be explained by a local tradition. Tyneside miners working underground often attached their brass identity tokens to their braces. Out of habit, therefore, many wore their army name tags on their braces rather than round their necks, which was the usual place. When bodies were found with nothing round the neck, sometimes no one looked any further, and they were buried as 'unknowns'.

A CONSCIENTIOUS OBJECTOR WHO WON A DISTINGUISHED CONDUCT MEDAL FOR BRAVERY

JOHN POWIS
1892–1951

When war was declared in August 1914, there were many in Britain who, while keen to serve their country, felt unable to fight for religious or social reasons. Born in 1892 into a large family living to the south of Wolverhampton, John Powis was such a man. In the 19th century the

family owned and worked a coal mine in that area, and this remained the family business until the early 1920s when the mine was exhausted. Indeed, John's profession was listed as 'coal hewer' on his marriage certificate. The family were staunch Methodists, and this determined John's decision to be a Conscientious Objector.

Conscientious Objectors were faced with difficult choices. There was initially no conscription and so they could stay at home and run the risk of being regarded as cowards and abused by the public. Those that chose to register their beliefs could work in the mines, enlist and serve in the Royal Army Medical Corps or, later, join the Non-Combatant Corps. The last two choices involved an acceptance of army discipline, but without the obligation to carry arms. The refusal to take

'I have no memory of my grandfather who never really recovered from the gassings he sustained on several occasions. Conscientious Objectors were often called cowards but he was quite the opposite and I wear his wedding ring with pride.'

CHRIS POWIS, GRANDSON

any of these options could result in prison. The army tended to regard Conscientious Objectors as cowards in any case, and often treated them as expendable.

John, probably having registered as a Conscientious Objector, volunteered to join the 137th Staffordshire Brigade of the 46th North Midland Division of the Territorial Force, which had been established in 1908. The 137th Brigade, which was made up from battalions from the South Staffordshire Regiment, the North Staffordshire Regiment, the King's (Liverpool) Regiment, the Seaforth Highlanders and the London Regiment, was mobilized on 5 August 1914, along with the rest of the Territorial Force, and the 46th North Midland Division was in France by March 1915.

The 46th North Midland Division was sent to the Ypres sector in May 1915 and took part in the Battle of Hooge and the attack on the Hohenzollern Redoubt during the Battle of Loos. In late December 1915 the division was ordered to Egypt, arriving there in mid-January 1916. Orders were then changed, and the division was shipped back to France, arriving in time to take part in the attack at Gommecourt on 1 July 1916, the start of the Battle of the Somme. For the rest of the war the division remained on the Western Front, taking part in a number of important battles and engagements., notably the daylight crossing of the St Quentin Canal at Riqueval in 1918. Demobilization began in January 1919.

John was attached to the division's 3rd North Midland Field Ambulance, primarily to work as a stretcher-bearer, a dangerous and demanding occupation with a short life expectancy, and thus deemed suitable for Conscientious Objectors. Despite this, he survived, and served with his unit from 1915 until the end of the war. There is no detailed record of where he served, beyond the documented history of the 46th North Midland Division, or what he experienced. Like so many others, he never discussed his army life with the family. However, John was present at Gommecourt in 1916 and family legend has it that he went with his commanding officer, by chance the Powis family doctor, into No Man's Land during a gas attack on the night of 1 July to recover wounded survivors from the battle.

The Battle of the Somme started at 07.30 on 1 July 1916 with an attack over a long front that stretched from near Serre in the north to south of the river Somme. The attack at Gommecourt was planned as part of the

Somme offensive, even though the village was a couple of miles north of Serre, and detached from the main front line. It was both a diversionary attack, to tie down German forces that could otherwise have been used as reinforcements further south, and to eliminate a German salient, a fortified area projecting out towards the opposing trenches. It was also an attempt to secure the northern flank to protect the advancing British armies along the main battle line. In the event, there was no advance at all from the Serre area. The aim was to capture Gommecourt village but this was set behind a wood, which had been heavily defended by the Germans, and so the focus of the attack was the wood. It was a two-pronged attack, from the northwest by the 46th North Midland Division and from the southwest by the 56th London Division and orders had been issued to make the preparations for the attack obvious, to make sure German troops were not withdrawn to support other areas. An ineffective artillery barrage had failed to cut the barbed wire or destroy the German machine-gun posts which were, as a result, able to tear the attack apart. The 56th Division were quite successful at first but the 46th Division made no progress and the whole attack was a failure from the start. No gains had been made, yet, despite the slaughter, the reserve troops were sent in. By the end of the day the surviving soldiers were all back at their start line. Major-General Stuart Wortley, the General Officer Commanding (GOC) of the 46th Division, having watched the steady devastation of his battalions, eventually refused to send any more men to their deaths. For this he was relieved of his command by Field Marshal Haig, for displaying 'a lack of offensive spirit'. The British suffered over 6700 casualties at Gommecourt. It was in the aftermath of this slaughter that John Powis and other Royal Army Medical Corps soldiers struggled to save the wounded, as they must have done at other battles fought later by the 46th North Midland Division.

On 13 February 1917, the *London Gazette* reported the award of the Distinguished Conduct Medal to Sergeant John Powis, 'For conspicuous gallantry and devotion to

Opposite: Distinguished Conduct Medal awarded to John Powis.
Above: Discharge Certificate for John Powis, showing
his Honourable Discharge.

duty. He has performed consistent good work throughout, and has on many occasions shown great courage and coolness under fire.' This was an exceptional achievement for a Conscientious Objector.

John was discharged on 7 April 1919 and returned home to Wolverhampton. Later that year he married Emma Naomi Northall, a local girl, and they had two children. His wife's two brothers also fought in the war. The eldest, Bill, was permanently disabled by a shell blast in October 1915 that killed his younger brother, Charlie, who was advancing in line near him. Today, John's grandson Chris treasures his memory and looks after his medal and his discharge certificate, which for years had been forgotten by the family, along with much of his remarkable story.

A SOLDIER WHO SAVED HIS COMMANDING OFFICER

MAJOR PHILLIPS
1884–1917

Major (his first name, not his rank) Phillips was born in October 1884 in Monmouth, South Wales. His father George was employed as a railway packer, and Major was the sixth of seven children. After leaving school he worked in a coal mine and then in 1915 he enlisted in the 11th Battalion of the South Wales Borderers. This regiment has a long history going back to

the 17th century but it was not called the South Wales Borderers until 1881. Earlier, as the 24th Regiment of Foot, it was present during the Indian Mutiny, and fought in 1879 in the disastrous Battle of Isandlhwana during the Zulu War. The regiment's New Army 11th (Service) Battalion was raised at Brecon in October 1914 and was sent to France in early December 1915. In due course it became part of the 115th Brigade in the 38th Welsh Division.

In early July 1916 the Battle of the Somme moved into its second phase, an important element of which was the advance from Fricourt into the series of woods that had to be captured. Their names – Mametz, Bazentin, Trones, Delville and Forceaux (High Wood) – are famous today for heavy fighting and the huge losses involved in their

'As young children we were often told that our grandfather was a hero who had saved the life of his wounded Commanding Officer by carrying him across No Man's Land to safety.'

SHIRLEY SPANN AND BRIAN PHILLIPS, GRANDCHILDREN

capture. Mametz, the first, was attacked on 7 July 1916 by the 38th Welsh Division. The wood had been turned into a fortress by the Germans, and that attack failed.

A second attack went in on 10 July and, after several days of desperate fighting, Mametz was finally cleared and captured on 14 July. The conditions were dreadful. Days of shelling by artillery had cut the woods to pieces and the fallen trees and branches had formed an impenetrable tangle that hid the defenders and hindered the attackers. Much of the fighting was vicious and hand-to-hand but in the end the 38th Division, which included Lance Corporal Phillips and the 11th Battalion, triumphed. It was a famous Welsh triumph, but the cost was massive, with over 5000 casualties, and it took a long time to rebuild the regiments that had borne the brunt of the fighting. The scars of Mametz are still carried by the Welsh nation, and South Wales in particular.

In the course of this battle, on 11 July 1916, Major's Commanding Officer, Lieutenant Raymond Barrington-Parry, was gravely injured and would certainly have died had Major not rescued him and carried him to safety across the dangerous wilderness of No Man's Land. The very same day, Major's brother, Richard George, serving as a Private with the 19th Battalion (The Glamorgan Pioneers) of the Welsh Regiment, was killed in action. The 19th Battalion was also part of the 38th Division, and so it is possible that Richard George was killed fighting in the same battle as his brother.

Raymond reached the casualty clearing station, and survived the long journey back to the base hospital, where he recovered, although he continued to suffer from the effects of his injuries for the rest of his life. He resigned his commission in April 1918 and subsequently married and raised a family, finally dying in 1963.

Raymond Barrington-Parry never forgot Major Phillips. Soon after he had recovered, Raymond gave him a silver cigarette case, engraved with the message: 'Given to M.Phillips as a Token of Deep Appreciation and Everlasting Gratitude by R.B.Parry upon the Occasion of 11th July 1916 in Mametz Wood'. He also sent Major's mother a Christmas hamper every year until she remarried. The story has been passed down the generations of both the Phillips and the Barrington-Parry families.

Lance Corporal Major Phillips served on with the 11th Battalion through the rest of 1916 and part of 1917. He was killed in action on 31 July 1917, during the early phase of the Third Battle of Ypres. He has no known grave and he is listed among the Names of the Missing on the Menin Gate Memorial in Ypres. Major Phillips had married Florence Wakefield in January 1905, and they had five children. The youngest, Kenneth, was born on 26 May 1916, and it seems likely that Major never saw this son.

His grandson Brian remembers being taken to France when he was about 12 by his father, Major's son, to try to find his father's grave. When told there was no grave, but just a name listed on the Menin Gate Memorial, he broke down in tears at the thought that his father's body had never been found.

Silver cigarette case presented to Major Phillips by Raymond Barrington-Parry, with the inscription indicating his gratitude.

TWO BROTHERS KILLED ON THE SOMME TWO MONTHS APART

DONALD RYAN LEATHERDALE
1896–1916
ALAN RICHARD LEATHERDALE
1897–1916

Donald (top) and Alan (bottom) were the two younger sons of George and Mabel Leatherdale, who had married in 1885 and lived in south London. Donald Ryan Leatherdale, born in February 1896, worked for the Royal Exchange Assurance prior to the First World War. In January 1914 he enlisted in the 28th (County of London) Battalion of the London Regiment, better known as the Artists' Rifles. This corps of rifle volunteers was set up in 1859. Later, it served with distinction in South Africa. When the London Regiment was formed in 1908 as a Territorial Force to bring together the various volunteer battalions that had been set up around London, it absorbed the Artists' Rifles, which became the 28th Battalion. Later, when most Territorial units were merged with County Regiments, the London Regiment, with its 28 battalions, retained its independence.

'My father kept photographs of his cousins Donald and Alan on the piano. Their family had no direct descendents and his concern was that their sacrifice might be forgotten. My father was only five years younger than Donald, and I think he almost saw them as brothers. The two families had always been close.'

JOHN LEATHERDALE, NEPHEW

Postcard showing members of No. 4 Section of B Company, 28th Battalion, London Regiment. This was sent by Donald to his mother in September 1914, before he was stationed guarding German prisoners at the Olympia exhibition centre in London.

In October 1914 the London Regiment's 28th Battalion arrived in France, where it operated as an Officers' Training Corps, first in Bailleul and later in St Omer. A rare relic from this period is the menu for the Christmas dinner enjoyed by B Company of the Artists' Rifles, probably at Bailleul. This entertaining and light-hearted document, capturing the high spirits in an Officers' Training Corps at this early stage in the war, is covered with the signatures of young men who, like Donald, would soon be receiving commissions and joining various regiments. Precious few of those who celebrated that Christmas were destined to survive the war.

In June 1915 Donald was commissioned as a 2nd Lieutenant in the 1st Battalion of the Queen's Own Royal West Kent Regiment. This had been in France since 13 August 1914 and had fought in many of the early battles of the war, including Mons, Le Cateau, Neuve Chapelle and Hill 60. On 15 July 1916, soon after Donald joined them, the 1st Battalion arrived on the

Somme. Despite the disaster of 1 July 1916, the first day of the Somme, the offensive continued, with advances being made day by day along sections of the front line. The major barrier was a series of woods, Mametz, Bazentin, Trones, Delville and Forcaux (better known as High Wood), all of which had to be captured to allow the advance to continue, and all of which were heavily defended. After a great struggle, and huge losses, Mametz, Bazentin and Delville were captured, but High Wood remained a major obstacle. The first attack, on 14 July, involved a cavalry charge and was quite successful, but without support the troops who had gained part of the wood had to withdraw. The German defences were strengthened and a subsequent series of attacks all failed. On 22 July Donald's battalion was involved in a preliminary night attack on High Wood, a preparation for the main assault in the early morning of 23 July. The aim was to capture Wood Lane trench and Switch trench, major German strongpoints to the southeast of High Wood. The attack was unsuccessful, mainly because an inadequate artillery barrage had left German machine-gun posts intact. The 28th Battalion suffered 421 casualties, including Donald Leatherdale. A private from his Company reported seeing '2Lt Leatherdale wounded and lying in a shell hole at High Wood', but he was not seen again and his body was never found. A fellow officer wrote later that Donald 'went into action like a brave Britisher and a gentleman, with not the slightest fear of death'.

On 28 July his mother received a telegram reporting him as missing but this went on to say: 'This does not necessarily mean he is either killed or wounded. Further reports sent immediately if received.' A letter written by Donald's Colonel was also cautiously hopeful, suggesting that Donald might have been wounded and taken prisoner. No further reports were received but it was not until 1 April 1917 that Donald was finally presumed killed, in a letter sent to his mother: 'The Army Council are regretfully constrained to conclude that this officer died on or since 22 July 1916 and I am to express their sympathy with you in your bereavement.'

The position of dreadful uncertainty and false hope in which the recently widowed Mabel Leatherdale found herself was a common experience for families all over Britain and in other countries, owing to the hundreds of thousands of soldiers listed as missing. Many of these were never found, having, in effect, vanished into thin air.

The battle for High Wood continued, and the losses mounted steadily until 15 September, when it was finally captured. High Wood has re-grown but has never been cleared and today it is still the last resting places for thousands of soldiers, British and German. The Somme offensive continued until mid-November 1916. The Queen's Own Royal West Kent's 1st Battalion famously fought on the Western Front throughout the First World War.

Alan Richard Leatherdale (pictured on page 162, bottom) was born in May 1897. After leaving school he worked in a bank. In May 1915 he attempted to join the Inns of Court Officers' Training Corps but was rejected on medical grounds, probably because of his eyesight. He then enlisted in the 26th (Service) Battalion (Bankers) of the Royal Fusiliers (City of London Regiment). Formed in 1881 from the 7th Regiment of Foot, the Royal Fusiliers could claim an impressive history stretching back to the 17th century. In the First World War the Royal Fusiliers raised 76 battalions and served with distinction in every theatre of the war. Many of these were New Army battalions and some were linked to particular professions and interests, such as the Stock Exchange and banking, or sportsmen. Alan's battalion, the 26th, was sent to France in May 1916, as part of the 41st Division, and their first important action was the Battle of Flers–Courcelette which was launched on 15 September 1916. The 26th Battalion was heavily involved, suffering 264 casualties on that day. On 16 September they were withdrawn to the support line and two days later were at Dernancourt, near Albert, well behind the line. Corporal Alan Leatherdale was killed on 18 September, when most of the fighting was over. Nothing is known about the nature of his death and it has to be assumed that he was unlucky enough to be caught by a random shell. His body was never found. A friend from the battalion wrote later that Alan 'was the youngest corporal in his battalion but could handle his men as well as any of them, one of the truest and bravest chums I have ever known'.

Donald and Alan Leatherdale were born 15 months apart. Two months and a few miles separate their deaths on the Somme, a battle that started on 1 July 1916 and continued until mid-November. Both have no known grave and both are listed among the 72,000 names commemorated on the Memorial to the Missing of the Somme at Thiepval.

The menu for the 1914 Christmas dinner enjoyed by
B Company of the Artists' Rifles, signed by all the young men
in the Officers' Training Corps who attended.

Army Form W. 3195.

NOTICE PAPER to be sent to each man who has been attested and transferred to the Army Reserve under the provisions of the Royal Warrant of the 20th October, 1915.

[This Notice Paper should be despatched so that it will reach the addressee at least 14 clear days before he is required to present himself at the appointed place.

In accordance with the provisions of Section 24 (2) of the Reserve Forces Act, 1882, "evidence of the delivery at the last registered place of abode of a man belonging to the Army Reserve of a notice, or of a letter addressed to such man and containing a notice, shall be evidence that such notice was brought to the knowledge of such man."]

Surname *Walford*

Christian Name *Richard*

Number as shown on the Card, Army Form W. 3194 *3152*

Address *63a Common R*

Group Number *5*

Batley

You are hereby warned that you will be required to rejoin for service with the Colours on the *28th Jany* 191*6*.

You should therefore present yourself at *Recruiting Office Town Hall Dewsbury* on the above date, not later than *10a* o'clock, bringing this paper with you.

*This will be struck out if the man resides within 5 miles of the place at which he is required to present himself.

A Railway Warrant is enclosed herewith

Signature. *Fred. M. Newsome*
M.AJOR.

14 . 1 . 16 Date.

Recruiting Officer, 51st Sub. Dist. R.A.

Dewsbury Place.

Dewsbury
Appointment.

N.B.—Particular attention is called to Section 15 of the Reserve Forces Act, 1882, which provides that where a man belonging to the Army Reserve is called out on Permanent service, and such man, without leave lawfully granted or such sickness or other reasonable excuse as may be allowed in the prescribed manner, fails to appear at any time and place at which he is required on such calling out to attend, he shall be guilty, according to the circumstances, of deserting within the meaning of Section 12, or of absenting himself without leave within the meaning of Section 15 of the Army Act, 1881.

(3759) Wt. 13452—4194 700,000 12/15 McA & W Ltd.

Standard attestation papers sent to Richard Walford in 1916. The suitcase in which this was found contained numerous documents painting a picture of everyday life in the army during the war.

A SOLDIER'S LIFE FOUND IN A SUITCASE

RICHARD WALFORD

1893–1916

Richard Walford was born into a large Catholic family in May 1893 in Heckmondwike, near Batley in Yorkshire. His father was a powerloom carpet weaver and when Richard left school, he joined his father in the carpet mill. As a young man, Richard spent his time with the church and the Temperance Institute and was captain of the local Healey football team.

In January 1916 Richard enlisted in the King's Own Yorkshire Light Infantry and all his training was completed with that regiment. However, when he landed in France on 7 July 1916, he was attached to the 1/7th Battalion of the Duke of Wellington's (West Riding) Regiment, a Territorial Force battalion that had arrived in France in 1915. Richard was part of a draft used to fill the battalion's ranks which had been depleted by recent actions.

The Duke of Wellington's (West Riding) Regiment, popularly known as the Duke's, had a long and distinguished history. Its origins were in the 18th century, as the 33rd Regiment of Foot. It fought with the Duke of Marlborough and in the American War of Independence, at Waterloo, in the Crimea, in Abyssinia and in South Africa.

'When I was small my father took me sometimes to visit my aunts, old ladies to me. There was a photograph of Uncle Richard on the sideboard and that's how I first heard about him. Not that they said much; years later his death was still a tragic occurrence in their lives.'

BERNARD WALFORD, NEPHEW

The regiment's 2nd Battalion came to France in August 1914 with the first wave of the British Expeditionary Force (BEF) and made its name at Mons and at Le Cateau, where the rapid and accurate rifle fire by the battalion's regular army soldiers halted the German advance, and probably helped to save the BEF from defeat. The regiment's Territorial Force and New Army Service battalions joined the BEF through 1915 and 1916, with several, including the 1/7th, joining the 147th (2nd West Riding) Brigade in the 49th (West Riding) Division.

By mid-July 1916 the Battle of the Somme had moved into its second phase, with the steady, but costly, advance through the sequence of woods. However, further north along the battle line of 1 July there had been little or no advance, notably in the Serre area, along the Ancre valley and at Thiepval. The latter, heavily defended, supported by the Schwaben redoubt and commanding a vital ridge, resisted all attacks though July, August and early September. A well-planned and coordinated series of attacks launched from 22 September captured Thiepval and the surrounding area, allowing the Allies finally to control the Ancre valley. These attacks were famous for their use of new tactics, which included a rolling artillery barrage, night assaults, better use of gas and machine guns, and better tank and infantry coordination. The Royal Flying Corps also provided better air cover. As a result, September 1916 was the worst month of the Somme campaign for the German army, which suffered 135,000 casualties.

However, Richard was to see none of this, for as a member of a Lewis gun team, he had been killed in Thiepval Wood on 3 September 1916. In that engagement the battalion lost 15 killed and 99 wounded or missing.

Unusually, Richard's life in the army is very well documented. When the last of his aunts died a few years ago, Bernard Walford, Richard's nephew, inherited an old suitcase, which he had neither seen nor heard of before. When opened, it was found to contain a full record of Richard's career as a soldier, from his enlistment in January 1916 to his death nine months later, told in letters, postcards, photographs, official papers and documents. Assembled presumably by his mother, the archive must have passed from her to Richard's sisters, one by one, until the last one died. It contains all his letters home, to his mother and his sisters, along with many he

The suitcase, inherited by Bernard Walford, that contained
the story of his uncle Richard Walford's war record from enlistment in
January 1916 to his death nine months later.

received and so it is possible to track his route over those nine months
and find out where and when he was in line, where he fought, and when
he was resting out of the line or in reserve. Thanks to modern technology,
Bernard, his nephew, has taken this further, by relating internet mapping
to the route indicated by the letters, thus recreating a virtual picture of
Richard's life on the Somme.

The letters are unremarkable, dealing with day-to-day life and domestic details such as food parcels and the predictable events of his army existence. As is usual in such letters from the front, there are no detailed descriptions of places or events, for the censor's blue pencil was always poised. However, the letters and cards are full of interesting and personal details. One describes him receiving his first pay, 30 francs, and the good evening out that followed. Another reveals that Richard had a girlfriend called Clara, whom he addressed as his sweetheart. She replied to 'My friend Dick' and so he cannot have been that surprised when his mother told him she had married someone else. His last letter, sent on 29 August 1916, seems to contain a premonition of death. He wrote that he had been to a mass before going into battle, and then he signed the letter Good Night and God Bless. Every other letter from him was signed Good Night and Good Luck. The presence of letters received by Richard is unusual for someone who was killed in action. The assumption has to be that all his papers were in his pack and the Battalion War Diary reveals that packs were left in Aveluy Wood, in the Ancre valley, before the attack on 3 September. Documents indicate that the papers were found after his death and returned to his mother in January 1917.

Inevitably, the letters and documents received by Richard's mother after his death are both moving and revealing. There are the formal notifications of death and details about pension arrangements, along with a cutting about his death from the local paper. This must have been the way some families first heard about the deaths of their sons, brothers and fathers. There are messages of condolence, including one from the Secretary of the local Temperance Institute, who wrote: 'We knew him as a good member and comrade, very sociable and friendly towards his fellow members.' Another was from one of Richard's friends: 'He was always well liked by his pals and I'm sure those who are lucky enough to come home again will miss him. I'm sure you have my deepest sympathy in your sad bereavement but thousands have died and still more will have to pay the sacrifice that he paid for his country. But you will always know he died a true soldier.' Particularly revealing is the letter from Richard's Captain, written on 4 September. This starts in the usual way: 'I deeply regret to have to inform you ...' and then ends by saying: 'He will be buried just behind the firing line and a suitable inscription will be placed above his grave.' Today, Richard Walford has no known grave, and his name is listed on the Memorial to the Missing of the Somme at Thiepval. Yet, at the time of his death he had a marked grave, one of many thousands destroyed during later fighting in the area.

Every night throughout the war, and on every front and battle area, officers and senior NCOs were writing similar letters to families who dreaded their arrival. All are handwritten and, while inevitably a little formulaic, each one is an individual and personal statement.

Richard's younger brother Cyril, born in 1897, also enlisted. He went to the Dardanelles with the Northumberland Fusiliers, suffered from severe frostbite and was invalided out to Egypt, and thence back to Britain. The ship carrying Cyril back to England was crossing the Channel at exactly the same moment as a ship from Southampton was taking Richard out to France. Had they known, the two brothers could have waved to each other.

Richard Walford's last letter to his mother before his death in September 1916. The final line, 'Good Night and God Bless', was a change from his usual signature of 'Good Night and Good Luck' and seemed to be a tragic premonition of his death.

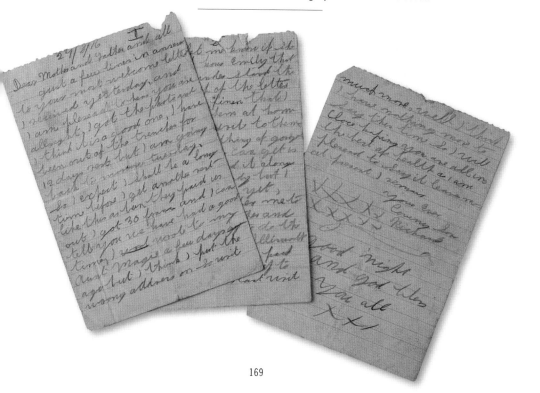

William Alexander Stanhope Forbes, painted by his father, Stanhope Forbes, from memory in 1916 after hearing of his son's death.

A FAMOUS ARTIST
PAINTS HIS LOST SON

WILLIAM ALEXANDER STANHOPE FORBES
1893–1916

The death toll in the First World War was enormous and it did not discriminate. Families at all levels of society, from the richest to the poorest, lost fathers and sons, brothers and uncles, husbands and lovers. Many famous families had to endure the loss of loved ones. Herbert Asquith, Prime Minister during the first two years of the war, lost his son Raymond in 1916. The writer Rudyard Kipling lost his son John in 1915.

William Alexander Stanhope Forbes was born in May 1893, the only son of the painter Stanhope Forbes and his wife Elizabeth, who had married in 1889. Famous for pioneering the artistic appeal of Cornwall and for setting up the Newlyn School of painters, Stanhope Forbes had been born in Dublin, educated in London and had studied art at the Royal Academy and in Paris. In 1881 he first started to paint in the open air in Brittany, developing a way of working that he maintained for the rest of his life. Moving to Newlyn in Cornwall in 1884, he rapidly found himself at the centre of a new and exciting artistic colony, and a painter with a growing reputation for contemporary genre and landscape scenes that helped to bring Impressionism to Britain. He and his wife founded the Newlyn School in 1899. They were doting parents and Alexander, or Alec as he was always known, grew up in the artistic environment of west Cornwall, and soon learned to draw. After attending Bedales School, Alec enrolled at the Architectural Association, quickly becoming a promising student. In

'My grandmother, who was Juliet Forbes, was given the painting and it has been in the family ever since. But my grandparents never talked about it, or about Alec, and so we know very little about him. But I do remember it as a child.'

ROWLAND MACDONALD STEPHENSON, GREAT-NEPHEW

1912, during Alec's second year, his mother Elizabeth died, an event that devastated both his and his father's life for a while.

When war broke out, Alec, like so many young men of that time, felt that he had to do his duty. Some (unknown) medical problems he had should have exempted him from military service but, determined to join the army, he secured a commission as a Railway Transport Officer in the Railway Operating Division which had been founded in 1915 to manage all the army's complex transport and supply activities that were railway-based. Alec was soon in France but, unhappy, as he put it, at spending his time walking round railway yards with a clipboard, he managed to secure a transfer to a front-line regiment, the Duke of Cornwall's Light Infantry (DCLI).

Formed in 1881 by the merger of earlier Regiments of Foot, the DCLI fought in South Africa and saw service in Ireland, India, Gibraltar and Hong Kong. During the First World War the regiment was greatly expanded by the creation of many new battalions, and it fought in every sector of the war, but notably on the Western Front, where the 1st and 2nd battalions and the Service battalions formed by Kitchener's New Army were heavily engaged. After training in England, Alec returned to France in mid-August 1916 to join the DCLI's 1st Battalion and was involved almost immediately in the fighting to capture the village of Guillemont, at the southern end of the Somme front line. Advances had been made in this area at the start of the battle, and the fighting continued through July 1916 as the line was pushed slowly eastwards. The capture of Guillemont, a well-fortified German strongpoint, was an essential stage in this battle. Attempts were made through July and August but all failed, at a considerable cost in casualties. On 3 September a better co-ordinated Anglo-French attack was launched and eventually Guillemont was captured. It had been an expensive and wasteful exercise. Gains overall were quite limited. Between mid-July and mid-September 1916, 32 British divisions were engaged on the Somme. The British attacked continuously, but in a series of independent actions on narrow fronts that were easily counter-attacked and broken up by German artillery, and the result was 126,000 casualties.

Among these was 2nd Lieutenant Alec Forbes, killed with three other young officers while leading an attack on Guillemont at the start of the battle, on 3 September 1916. Alec carried into battle some jewellery belonging to his mother. His father, who had remarried in 1915, responded to the death of his only son by painting his portrait from memory. The result is a moving testament to paternal love, in which every brush stroke must have reflected the painter's grief as he tried to capture the fading image and character of his son. The portrait is an enduring record of one lost son that, by its nature, can represent all those lost sons.

There are two versions of the painting, one in the family, and the other in Bodmin Castle, the home of Cornwall's Regimental Museum. It is not known which was painted first, though both are signed by Stanhope Forbes and dated 1916. Later, Forbes designed a memorial to Alec for Sancreed Church, near Newlyn, a bas-relief bronze plaque based on the painting.

Alec Forbes is buried in Guillemont Road Military Cemetery, close to where he died. This, originally a small battlefield and field ambulance cemetery with 121 burials, was greatly expanded after the war and now contains 2263 soldiers, of which 1523 remain unknown.

The painter Stanhope Forbes at home with his second wife, after his son Alec's death.

Two babies that escaped the baby killers, although they lived within 50 yards from where the Zeppelin fell.

(News I.

CUFFLEY ZEPPELIN FRAGMENTS

1916
(WORLD WAR I)

A. HAWES,
Optician,
49, NEW CAVENDISH STREET, W.,
— AND —
70, LEADENHALL STREET, E.C.,
LONDON.

(Molly
Hughes
given to MC
via JM Gray
1976)

Top: The newspaper photograph showing Joan and Jack Gray sitting on the wreckage of the German airship, *SL-11*, shot down over Cuffley, Hertfordshire on 3 September 1916. Centre and bottom: Box of fragments from the airship, collected by Maude Gray's family.

A NARROW ESCAPE FROM
A GERMAN AIRSHIP

FLORENCE MAUDE GRAY
1883–1975

A new chapter in warfare started on 31 May 1915 when a German Zeppelin airship bombed London. For the next two years these random attacks became an unpleasant feature of city life, with over 500 civilians being killed and more than a thousand injured. Most attacks were directed at London, but Midland and Northern cities were also targeted, along with some European cities. Throughout 1915 and much of 1916 the high-flying airships were impervious to attack by either aircraft or anti-aircraft guns and could bomb almost at will and so the word Zeppelin soon became synonymous with a new kind of terror weapon. Everything changed, however, on the morning of 3 September 1916 when Lieutenant William Leefe Robinson, flying a BE2c, managed to shoot down a German airship over Cuffley, in Hertfordshire. This event, for which Robinson was awarded a Victoria Cross, attracted huge public interest. It also marked the end of the airship's status as a terror weapon for, from this point, they became increasingly vulnerable. Out of the 115 used by the Germans to attack civilian and military targets, 77 were destroyed or damaged beyond repair, and from 1917 the airship's role as an attack weapon was taken over by conventional bombers.

Florence Maude Bliss was born in 1883. After her marriage to Herbert Gray, the couple lived in Enfield but soon moved to the country in order to keep animals. They rented Hill Farm, a traditional and rather basic cottage in Cuffley, in the heart of rural Hertfordshire. Herbert commuted by train to his work in Lloyds Bank in the City of London, and Maude came to terms

'My grandmother chose a tranquil country life for her family in rural Hertfordshire. When a German airship crash transformed it into bedlam, she wasn't happy.'

MICHAEL CLARK, GRANDSON

with a life dependent upon local farms for supplies and upon the local well for fresh water. She looked after the livestock, the vegetable garden and her two small children, Joan, born in 1911, and Jack, born in 1913.

On the night of 2/3 September 1916, a fleet of 16 German airships set off to attack London. The majority were Zeppelins but also included was the lesser-known Schütte-Lanz, an airship developed from 1909 as a rival to the Zeppelin. This featured a composite wood and metal construction, as opposed to the all-metal Zeppelin. Damp could affect the structural stability of the Schütte-Lanz airships and so those in service were operated by the German army, whereas Zeppelins were operated by the navy. Included in the fleet that set off for Britain on 2 September was *SL*-11, a Schütte-Lanz airship that had been in service for one month. Arriving over London ahead of the rest of the fleet, it was soon spotted by searchlights and several British aircraft were scrambled to intercept it, including the BE2c flown by the Royal Flying Corps' Lieutenant Robinson. He found the airship over north London, pursued it out towards Hertfordshire and finally attacked it over Cuffley. Robinson fired two drums of conventional ammunition at the airship, with no effect. He then fired a drum of newly developed incendiary ammunition and the airship caught fire. What happened next was described by Maude Gray:

> We are awakened in the early hours by a terrible noise and glare of light. Herbert looked out of the window and gave a yell as he grabbed Joan from her bed. I ran and gathered Jack up from his cot and we rushed downstairs as the air was filled with explosions and bangs from a falling Zeppelin.
>
> Bullets had fallen down the chimney and exploded in the smouldering fire left in the grate. It was really appalling, as we had hidden under the kitchen table and thought this was the safest place! The noise and glare as the wrecked airship passed over the house filled the kitchen and it crashed in flames behind the Plough across the road from us …
>
> When I got up the following morning to see what damage had been done by the falling debris, I could hardly believe my eyes. There was one solid mass of vehicles as far as I could see … I found out later that the roads were jammed for two miles in either direction.

Two officers were immediately billeted on us and everyone demanded food … I served them for as long as I could, but we soon ran out of all my reserves … My sister travelled from Enfield to see how we were and said that the train was packed out, with people even sitting on the engine.

In fact, for several days, Cuffley was filled with visitors and souvenir hunters. The destruction of *SL-11*, and the death of its crew of 16, provoked massive rejoicing, not just locally, but throughout the nation, proving as it did that the dreaded airships were no longer invincible. From this point on, German airships were regularly destroyed by aircraft or anti-aircraft guns, but it was *SL-11*, the first to be destroyed, that caught the public imagination. Although the Admiralty knew at the time that Lieutenant Robinson had shot down a Schütte-Lanz airship, they let the popular view that it was a Zeppelin prevail, in order to demolish the nation's widely held view that the Zeppelin was an invincible terror weapon. The press coverage was massive, with Robinson becoming a national hero. He also became the subject of many popular postcards, along with views of the crash site and the wreckage of the airship. However, it was this press interest that finally broke Maude Gray's patience. First, she found a newspaper article 'half made up with things I did not say' and then, when the *Daily News* published a photograph of her two children sitting on the coiled wreckage of *SL-11*, with the caption, 'Two babies that escaped the baby killers', she decided enough was enough and never allowed that newspaper, or that picture, into her house.

While some of the wreckage of *SL-11* was picked over by souvenir hunters, much of it was carefully guarded, notably the coils of wire. In due course these were cut up into short lengths and sold as official souvenirs by the Red Cross in specially printed envelopes as a fundraising exercise. Today, bits of the wreckage of *SL-11* are owned by collectors all over the world, as well as by Maude Gray's family, as a reminder of the role played by that family in what was, at the time, an event of great national importance.

AN ARTIST WITH
THE LONDON IRISH RIFLES

RUDOLPH ALFRED TANNER
1895–1978

Rudolph Alfred Tanner (in centre of photograph) was born in 1895, one of seven children in a family, with a Swiss father and an English mother, living in Chelsea, London. At 14 Rudolph won a scholarship to the Central

School of Arts and Crafts, and fell immediately under the influence of teachers such as W. R. Lethaby, A. S. Hartrick and Alfred Turner. The teaching at the Central was broad-based and Rudolph developed a variety of skills, including drawing, modelling and calligraphy. Many friendships made at the Central with both teachers and fellow students were to last a lifetime.

In August 1914 Rudolph volunteered for service, and joined the 1st Battalion of the London Irish Rifles. Formed in 1859 as a Volunteer Regiment, the London Irish Rifles first saw action during the South African War. During the First World War the regiment raised three battalions, two of which saw service in France

'My father was a perfectionist and very self absorbed as artists often are. He'd spend hours in contemplative silence but on a good day he could be the most delightful company. He could also erupt in frustration at the pressures of bringing up a family on limited means when he was quite old. My aunts and uncles all said his personality was changed by the war.'

VAL PEATMAN, ELDER DAUGHTER

and the Middle East. The 1st Battalion fought at Festubert, Loos, Somme, Messines, the Third Battle of Ypres, Cambrai, St Quentin and Albert. The most famous of these battles is probably Loos, mainly because of Rifleman Frank Edwards who kicked his football at the head of the attack. The London Irish Rifles distinguished themselves at Loos, although they lost well over 200 men. The battle started at 06.30 on the morning of 25 September 1915. Despite an inadequate preliminary artillery barrage and the uneven results of a gas attack, the British were initially successful, capturing Loos and the infamous Hill 70. However, poor communications and the lack of support from the reserves meant that the early promise of a breakthough could not be exploited or sustained and by the end of the battle on 28 September most of the British were back at their starting points. A British officer at Loos wrote later that 'the real tragedy of that battle was its nearness to complete success'. There were over 59,000 British casualties and the reasons behind its failure were to be repeated in subsequent battles. Loos also brought the active career of Sir John French to an end, with General Haig taking over as Commander of the British Expeditionary Force in December 1915.

It was during the Battle of Loos that Rudolph sustained a head wound, and a period of convalescence followed. But later, writing in 1916, Rudolph described Loos as 'a classical demonstration compared with the present conflict'. When he returned to the regiment in 1916, Rudolph took part in various Somme battles. In September the 1st Battalion fought at Flers–Courcelette, a battle famous for the first use of tanks by the British army. After the battle ended Rudolph wrote a letter on 25 September to his mother about his experiences:

> It is utterly impossible to describe the scenes ... of course I saw the ponderous and almost fabulous engines of war of which you will have read. These were to be employed the next morning when our regiment was to attack. When I got back to the transport, almost bewildered with what I had seen (the vast activity, men working like so many millions of ants and the huge guns roaring on every side), I felt somewhat of the stupendous effort which is being put forth ... I cannot properly convey what emotion all this great day produced, the flash of a great victory! But little by little we learned what it had cost.

Opposite: Chalk carving by Rudolph Tanner, inspired
by the story of Jacob and Rachel, and (above) the Boots tin
in which he sent it to his mother.

With the letter, Rudolph sent to his mother a chalk carving he had
made, carefully packed in a Boots tin. This bas-relief sculpture, made in
meticulous detail in a traditional style, depicts the love of Jacob for Rachel,
the Bible's greatest love story. He refers to this obliquely in the same letter:
'I received a letter and parcel from you. Oh, how good you have been to
me, can I ever forget all your love, so consistent, it seems to me a type of
greater love.'

Flers–Courcelette, which started on 15 September 1916, was one of the
many more local battles that had steadily pushed the British front line
eastwards since the start of the Somme campaign on 1 July 1916. The aim
of the battle was, as ever, to achieve a breakthrough. On the first day of
the Flers–Courcelette battle, advances were made by British, Canadian and
New Zealand troops and the villages of Courcelette, Martinpuich and Flers
were captured, along with High Wood. Flers will always be associated with
the tank. The development of the landship, better known as the tank, had
started in the summer of 1915 and the first prototype was ready for testing
in January 1916. General Haig, a great believer in the tank, had wanted to
use them on 1 July but they were not ready. By September, 49 were available

and Haig resolved to use them at Flers. There was strong opposition, with many in both the British and French armies believing they should remain a secret until enough were available to mount a major attack, and thus achieve a breakthrough. However, Haig held firm and the tanks attacked at Flers. The combination of mechanical failure and the difficulties posed by the terrain meant that of the 49 tanks that left the front line, only 27 reached the German lines and just 19 suceeded in reaching their first objectives. Nonetheless, the impact on the Germans, both physical and psychological, was considerable and there is a famous Royal Flying Corps account of a tank at Flers: 'a tank is walking up the High Street of Flers with the British Army cheering behind'.

In November 1916, while serving with the regiment at Ypres, Rudolph was wounded a second time. He was sent back to Britain to recover. Once again he returned to the regiment but no longer as a fighting soldier and, after a few months in support, he was registered as physically unfit and given an Honourable Discharge in January 1918.

After the war, Rudolph lived with his parents in Sussex, becoming involved with the artistic community around Ditchling. He resurrected his life as an artist, notably as a designer of stained glass. Rudolph rejoined the army in the Second World War, serving with anti-aircraft units. His parents moved to Atwood in Surrey and there, in 1942, he met and married the daughter of a local mill owner. They had four children, the youngest born when Rudolph was 58.

There are windows designed by Rudolph in St Colman's Church, Dunmurry, Northern Ireland, and some in St Catharine's Church, Nottingham, celebrating the life of Alice Maud Sargent, for many years the church cleaner. He also worked on the restoration of medieval glass in Tewkesbury Abbey. He returned to the Central School of Art, as a student and part-time instructor, and trained as a silversmith and jeweller, encouraged by H. G. Murphy, the Central's charismatic Principal and the leading British silversmith of that era.

A VOLUNTEER FROM BERMUDA WHO DIED IN FRANCE

NATHANIEL BENJAMIN HARRIOTT
1897–1916

Nathaniel Benjamin Harriott (usually known as Dick) was born in Bermuda in October 1897. He was the youngest of five children in a family that had been in Bermuda since the 17th century. The family tree records a succession of farmers, clerks and grocers, with the occasional shipbuilder

and sea captain. Bermuda, a subtropical island of about 20 square miles, had been a British colony since 1707. At the time of Dick's birth it had a population of about 12,000 black people and around 6500 white people.

In April 1913, when he was 15, Dick was allowed to join the Bermuda Volunteer Rifle Corps (BVRC). This had been formed in 1894 to serve as an all-white reserve force for the Bermuda Garrison, which was maintained by the regular army. Membership was usually limited to white males between 17 and 50, all of whom had to belong to a rifle club. The regulations were much the same as contemporary British Volunteer Corps, and the original uniform was the same green colour as other Rifle Corps, although this was changed to khaki in 1898. When war broke out, the BVRC was put to work guarding

'Great-uncle Dick's photograph was kept in a family Bible in my grandparents' living room but I never asked about him. Maybe questions weren't asked and we were certainly a family of least said, soonest mended.'

MARGIE HARRIOTT, GREAT-NIECE

the island's coastline and protecting the Royal Naval dockyard on Ireland Island. In December 1914 the BVRC began to assemble a detachment for service overseas. In March 1915 Dick, then aged 17 though he claimed to be 18, signed an attestation for Short Service, which meant for the duration of the war. After training, this detachment, which consisted of Captain Richard Tucker, the detachment's Commanding Officer, and 88 Non-Commissioned Officers (NCOs) and men, left Bermuda on 1 May 1915. Another army officer described the departure: 'Awaiting us to say farewell was a crowd such as Hamilton has never seen. The mothers and sweethearts were frantic.' After stopping in Quebec, the detachment sailed on to Britain as part of a large Canadian draft. On arrival they were attached initially to the 3rd Battalion of the Lincolnshire Regiment and were stationed at the regiment's Grimsby depot. As was often the case with small detachments there was an attempt to break them up and absorb them as replacements into Lincolnshire battalions, but a letter from the War Office stated they had to stay as one unit, wearing their own badge. They sailed for France from Southampton in late June or early July 1915, and on arrival were attached to the Lincolnshire Regiment's 1st Battalion as an extra company.

The progress of the BVRC was unremarkable during the remaining months of 1915. In November 1915 Dick became ill with pneumonia and was in due course transferred to a military hospital in Cambridge. This must have been a lonely time for the young Bermudan, cut off from both his family back home and his friends in France. Eventually he recovered, and was then sent to the Lincolnshire's depot in Grimsby to train new recruits, which may have included some of the men who were to form a second BVRC detachment. Dick returned to France on 16 June 1916 and was reunited with the other Bermudans. He must have written regularly to his mother but only one letter survives which doesn't say much at all, just a typical teenager's quick note to his mum.

On 25 September 1916 the BVRC went into action for the first time at Gueudecourt. Following the British advances achieved during the Battle of Flers–Courcelette, which had started on 15 September 1916, the village of Gueudecourt became within reach of the attacking forces, although it was heavily defended by German trench lines. The first attack on Gueudecourt

Nathaniel Harriott's 1914–15 Star,
inscribed with his name on the back.

on 25 September, part of the Battle of Morval, was mounted by battalions from the King's Own Yorkshire Light Infantry, the East Yorks, the Leicesters and the Lincolns, with the Bermudans. Most of the attack was stopped by artillery and machine-gun fire. Another attack was mounted the next morning, assisted by a tank, the second time a tank had ever been used, and this was more successful, with the village in British hands by that evening.

A few days later, their Commanding Officer, Captain Tucker, wrote in his diary: 'Since my last entry the battalion has been through hard times.

It went into action on the afternoon of Sept 25th and the Bermudas had heavy casualties.' A month later the *Bermuda Colonist and Daily News* carried a more detailed report: 'I'm sorry to say a few more of the boys have gone under and quite a lot wounded. We were in an attack a few days ago, we went in thirty strong and came out with eleven. It was certainly a warm corner. We had to advance quite a long way across the open, and Fritz did not forget to let us know he was there ... The boys certainly went over well, they walked across as if they were out for a walk up Front Street [the main street in Hamilton, Bermuda]. Lots of the boys were cracking jokes with one another.'

Among the dead from that first day of fighting at Gueudecourt was Dick Harriott, although, as his body was not found, he was initially listed as missing. The report in the *Bermuda Colonist* maintained this, but implied that he had probably 'gone under'. It is not known how the news of Dick's death reached his family in Bermuda, despite extensive research carried out by Margie Harriott, his great-niece.

The survivors of the first BVRC detachment were merged with the second, comprising one officer and 36 other ranks, which had recently arrived in France. By the end of the war 40 Bermudans had been killed and 34 were discharged as medically unfit having been wounded – in total around 75 per cent of their combined strength – while 16 men were commissioned, and six were awarded military medals.

Bermuda also supplied two separate detachments of black soldiers to the British Army, about 300 officers and men in total. The first left for France on 31 May 1916 and on arrival became the Bermuda Contingent of the Royal Garrison Artillery. The second left Bermuda on 6 May 1917 and on arrival was merged with the first. In 1916 the first detachment served on the Somme from June to December 1916, working in the supply and transport of ammunition to batteries at the front. Later, they worked in the docks, with the Canadians at Vimy Ridge and at Ypres from June to October 1917, again in ammunition supply.

Dick Harriott's body was never found, and his name is listed on the Memorial to the Missing of the Somme at Thiepval. All that remains today of a young man who left a small and remote island to fight for his mother country is a name, a photograph, a medal and a letter.

THE RECRUITING SERGEANT AND THE CONSCIENCE BATON

ARCHIBALD FREDERICK ASHTON

1878–1958

The Military Service Act, which introduced conscription in 1916, brought Conscientious Objectors into the spotlight as they now had to fight for their beliefs in front of tribunals. Many applicants were turned down, and sent back to their local recruiting office for their fate to be decided. For those prepared to wear uniform, this could be an attachment to the medical services or to the Non-Combatant Corps. Others could be put to work on the Home Front to support the war effort.

Archibald Frederick Ashton, generally known as Archie, was the Recruiting Sergeant at the Queen Street office in Cardiff in 1916. A well-known figure in Cardiff's commercial life, Archie ran a fish and poultry shop in the market, a family business with roots stretching back to the early 19th century. Chairman of the local fishmongers' association, he was a married man with four children and, as a fishmonger, he had a Reserved Occupation. With no previous army experience, he must have volunteered for the part-time post of Recruiting Sergeant, or been given the job through local connections. Either way, he probably enjoyed the status that came with it.

The introduction of conscription provoked a varied response in different parts of Britain. In Wales by the end of 1916 there was quite a strong feeling that the Principality had already carried more than its share of the burden of the war, and that conscription was likely to be, for the Welsh, a step too far. At the start of the war, Welsh men had volunteered

'Archie was never a soft touch and enjoyed his position in Cardiff society. He wasn't too worried about reaping the rewards of others' hard work, notably my great-grandmother's. He probably enjoyed the status and power that came with being a Recruiting Sergeant.'

NIGEL ASHTON, GREAT-GRANDSON

Top: Sergeant Ashton (centre) outside the Cardiff Recruiting
Headquarters. Bottom: The truncheon presented to Archie Ashton
by a man known only as D.V.D., which has remained
a family heirloom ever since.

Gold watch presented to Ivor Davies by his local chapel to celebrate his safe return to Wales, after his time in a prisoner-of-war camp.

A WELSHMAN CAPTURED ON THE SOMME

RICHARD IVOR DAVIES
1899–1976

Richard Davies was a well-known sheep farmer and judge of Welsh sheep in agricultural shows in the valleys of South Wales. He had a large family,

but only two sons and several sisters survived into adulthood. One of the sons, Richard Ivor Davies, always known as Ivor, was born in 1899. After school he worked on the family farm but, in 1915, he enlisted in the 10th Battalion of the Royal Welch Fusiliers.

This famous regiment had a long history dating back to the 17th century, and had earned its 'Royal' title in 1713. This explained the archaic spelling of 'Welch' which continued through the 19th century; it was officially changed to 'Welsh' before the First World War and then returned to 'Welch' in 1920. The 10th (Service) Battalion was formed in Wrexham in September 1914 as part of the New Army, arrived in France on 7 September 1915, then fought on the Western Front throughout the war.

'I have fond memories of him as a favourite uncle. He never talked about his war experiences though a cousin told me he would never eat cabbage because that was all they had in the prisoner-of-war camp. He enjoyed life, was sometimes a bit of a rascal, and drank and smoked quite heavily.'

GWEN GODFREY, GREAT-NIECE

Ivor's early service history is rather vague and it seems that at first he was serving with a regular army battalion. In July 1915 he sent his father a rather strongly worded letter from Liverpool, where he was stationed, expressing his great surprise at being asked to come home to help with the harvest. For Ivor, his father's request must have been a stark reminder about how little people in country areas actually knew about the war.

> With regard to that haymaking proposition of yours, I am afraid that you must dismiss it from your mind as impossible. Remember, I am in the regular army, not in Kitcheners where men may be spared for outside work … There are men in this battalion almost as old as you are, with large families, who have all their sons in the army, think of their example & then think of yours.
>
> I believe you think more of your hay than of your country, you grudge her even the one son who could most easily be spared. I enlisted for three years or for the duration of the war & until then nothing will induce me to leave the army. This is final.
>
> Your Surprised Son

In October 1915 he was sent to Gallipoli, where he must have been attached to another Royal Welch Fusiliers battalion. Perhaps he was sent with reinforcements to the 5th, 6th, 7th or 8th battalions, all of which served in the Dardanelles. However, suffering from frostbite, Ivor was hospitalized and then brought back to Europe. He probably then joined the 10th Battalion, in time for the later phases of the Battle of the Somme in 1916. He was with the battalion in the July attacks on Delville Wood, fought on through August, September and October, and then took part in the final stages of the Battle of the Ancre. On 11 November 1916 the preliminary artillery bombardment started that launched the final, and much delayed, attempt to capture Serre, a strongly defended village to the north of the Somme front that had resisted all attacks since 1 July. On 13 November the 10th Battalion attacked. Initially they did quite well but, without adequate support and with unprotected flanks, they were forced to withdraw. The battle ended with no gains having been made, and the battle of the Somme ground to a halt a few days later in the freezing cold and mud that made winter a common enemy for both sides.

TELEGRAMME POSTES ET TÉLÉGRAPHES.

= L CORP B PRICE DAVIES 144522

2 15 ARMY TROOPS R E CO FRANCE

+ YSTRADMYNACH 1615 21/20 5 11-35 M

= IVOR MISSING SINCE NOVEMBER 10- TH = ANNIE DAVIES

The telegram sent to Ivor Davies's family,
announcing that he was missing.

During the chaos of the night attack on 13 November Ivor was injured and then captured, along with a number of colleagues from the 10th Battalion's E Company. He was listed as missing, but it was soon established that he was a prisoner of war. Ivor spent the rest of the war in Limburg an der Lahn camp, near Koblenz, a large prisoner-of-war centre used both as a resident camp and a major processing centre for prisoners. It was also an important centre for the prisoner-of-war postal service. It is not known when Ivor was released but he was finally demobilized on 27 March 1919.

Ivor went back to the family farm at Ystrad Mynach, and the local Welsh chapel presented him with a gold watch to celebrate his safe return. He never married but was always well looked after by the family because they were so glad to have him. All in all, he seems to have had a good life. He hunted with the Gelligaer, went regularly to the Smithfield show in London, staying at the Strand Palace Hotel, and enjoyed outings, including a trip to Ostend. He claimed his medals, but never wore them as after his death they were found still in the box they had been sent in, and with their ribbons unattached.

A CHRISTMAS PRESENT FOR HIS MOTHER ARRIVED AFTER HIS DEATH

WILLIAM SANDERS
1893–1916

The eldest of six children, William Sanders was born in October 1893 in Abram, near Wigan in Lancashire. Like most people in this small mining village, his father James worked in a local pit. When he left school, William also became a coal miner, along with his sister Isabella, who was a pit brow girl, a surface worker at a coal mine. The family always lived in the same road in Abram.

On 14 October 1914, the 8th Battalion of the King's Own (Royal Lancaster Regiment) was formed in Lancaster. This regiment, whose origins stretched back to the 17th century, was established in 1881. During the First World War the regiment raised 17 battalions, seven of which, including the 8th, were New Army Service battalions. A week later, on 20 October 1914, William enlisted in the 8th Battalion, along with his friend Billy Holland, who was his sister Isabella's fiancé. After training the battalion landed in France on 27 September 1915, becoming part of the 3rd Division in October. William was then with the battalion for much of the Somme campaign, which ended in mid-November 1916. The whole sector was then quiet, apart from shelling, trench raids and other local activities. In December 1916, while the 8th Battalion was out of the line, William purchased a decorative handkerchief case and handkerchief set as a Christmas present for his mother and posted it back to Abram, with a note saying he had been promoted to Corporal. On 17 December the 8th Battalion went back into the front line near John Copse, relieving the 1st Battalion, the Gordon Highlanders. John Copse was one of four similar copses, named Matthew,

'My grandparents were devoted to their children and very patriotic.
They had a flagpole and flew the Union flag on important days.
That's why William enlisted at the start of the war.'

ANN GREGORY, NIECE

Mark, Luke and John, just to the north of Serre. It was from these copses that many of the Pals battalions had launched their attacks on 1 July 1916, and had been largely obliterated. Subsequent attacks in this area had all failed and, at the end of the Somme campaign, the British front line was exactly where it had been on 1 July. On 19 or 20 December 1916, William was killed, along with two of his comrades, when a German shell hit their part of the trench. Even when the front line was quiet, soldiers on both sides were being killed every day by this kind of random shelling and snipers.

When William's mother received the Christmas present he had sent her, she already knew her son was dead. For the rest of her life she treasured it, with his note, and kept it, still wrapped in the original brown paper, in the bottom of a chest. She also kept his letters, since lost, in a Nuttall's Mintoes tin on a shelf and every Sunday she would take them out and read them aloud. There was a photograph of William on the piano, since lost. William's friend Billy Holland was also killed, and Isabella remained unmarried until 1941, when she was 49.

Corporal William Sanders is buried in Euston Road Cemetery, Colincamps, near where he died. His parents James and Ann were never able to see their son's grave.

The Christmas present and note that William Sanders sent his mother
shortly before he died. She received it after news of her son's death.

Amos Finn's injury label, giving details of his
gunshot wound (GSW face, neck and left leg), from
the 10th Stationary Hospital, St Omer.

A MAN WHOSE LIFE WAS DESTROYE
BY WARTIME INJURIES

AMOS FINN
1894–1935

Amos Finn, sometimes known as Mike, was born in Sydenham, south London, in 1894, the youngest of four children whose father worked in the local gas works. A year after the outbreak of war Amos enlisted in the 8th Battalion, the Royal West Kent Regiment, on 21 August 1915.

The Queen's Own (Royal West Kent Regiment) had been established in 1881. Kent was one of only four English counties to have two or more regiments at this time, the others being Surrey, Yorkshire and Lancashire. The regiment served in the Sudan and South Africa and, on the outbreak of war in 1914, its 1st Battalion was one of the first to be sent to France with the British Expeditionary Force. The 8th, a New Army Service battalion, was raised in Maidstone in September 1914 and, after training, was in France by the end of August 1915. Their first action, on 26 September, was at the Battle  of Loos, where they suffered heavy losses. In 1916 the battalion moved south to the Somme, and it was probably there that Private Amos Finn joined them. He fought at the Battle of Delville Wood and took part in

'I am glad to have found out so much about my great-uncle and his unhappy life. He was always a casualty of the war. Now I can lay this old soldier to rest, knowing he won't be forgotten.'

PAT ROBERTS, GREAT-NIECE

the unsuccessful attack on High Wood at the end of July. Next, in early September came the Battle of Guillemont, which opened the way for subsequent success at Flers–Courcelette and the final capture of High Wood on 15 September 1916.

Having lost many men through this period, the 8th Battalion was withdrawn northwards to Philosophe, between Béthune and Lens. Here, they rested and received reinforcements and then, on the morning of 24 December 1916, the battalion went back into the front line, to be greeted by a vicious German artillery barrage. It was probably during this that Amos was wounded in the leg and then severely in the neck, with part of the right side of his face destroyed. Treated initially in the field, he was then passed to a casualty clearing station, and was finally received at the 10th Stationary Hospital, St Omer on New Year's Eve.

Amos's injury label dates from this period. A rare survivor from the hundreds of thousands that must have been used, it offers an insight into the way casualties were treated and their injuries documented. On one side is Amos's name and regiment. On the other are details of the injury, GSW (gun shot wound) face, neck and left leg, along with a list of options to describe the severity of the injury, from severe to slight, to be crossed out as required. Details of treatment given were also recorded, such as antitetanus and eusol (a basic form of wound care). Finally, the label is signed by a doctor, in this case a Lieutenant from the Royal Army Medical Corps. In the chaos and confusion of a casualty clearing station during a battle the use of such labels was essential, tied to the soldier's uniform or around the wrist.

From St Omer, Amos was transported back to Britain, for full treatment and convalescence. During this time he would have worn his blue hospital uniform, introduced so that the general public would recognize those wearing them as convalescing soldiers, rather than shirkers avoiding military service. It is likely that Amos's face was permanently damaged but he was not selected for plastic surgery. All photographs from this date show only the left side of his face. Making no allowance for his mental state, the army decided that Amos was fit for limited military service, passing him category C1 or C2, that is eligible for labour and menial work, and he later served in the Royal Flying Corps and the Labour Corps before being eventually demobilized.

In June 1919 Amos was present at his sister Harriet's wedding but shortly afterwards had a disagreement with his father, probably about his inability, or reluctance, to get a job. He left home and was never seen again. His sister Harriet, or Doris as she was better known, organized searches, placed missing person advertisements and issued postcards with an artist's impression of him, all to no avail. The family concluded that he had probably died in the Spanish influenza epidemic after living rough, or had committed suicide, unable to live with his memories and his damaged face.

After Doris's death in 1982, Amos's great-niece, Pat Roberts, inherited the documents and memorabilia Doris had treasured for so long and decided to try to reconstruct Amos's life, a process made much easier by the internet. The truth finally came out. Through remote relatives she found records of a Finn who had died in Camberwell, south London, in 1935, and this turned out to be Amos. On 22 December 1935, he had died following an operation to remove a blot clot from his brain. Aged 41, he was described as a labourer of no fixed abode and his place of death was the poor house in Camberwell.

Amos Finn was one of the many thousands of men permanently scarred, both physically and mentally, by the injuries they had suffered during the First World War, the psychological impact of which was rarely understood at the time.

AN ARTIST WHO CONTINUED TO SCULPT WHILE FIGHTING WITH THE ARTILLERY

ALEXANDER CARRICK
1882–1966

Alexander Carrick was born in 1882 in Musselburgh, where his father was an edge tool maker. In 1897 he was apprenticed as a stonemason to the sculptor Birnie Rhind. During this time he enrolled as a student at Edinburgh School of Art and later went on to spend two years in London

at the South Kensington School of Art, studying under the influential sculptor Professor Edouard Lanteri. Alexander then returned to Edinburgh and set up his own yard and began to make his name as a sculptor. He exhibited regularly at the Royal Scottish Academy, and became known for his monumental and architectural work. In 1914 he began to teach at the Edinburgh School of Art, and the same year he married Janet MacGregor, a fellow student from Greenock.

By 1916 Alexander had enlisted as a Gunner in the Royal Garrison Artillery and joined the 8th Siege Battery, which had arrived in France in October 1914 and then served throughout the rest of the war in Belgium, in the Ypres area. Though never injured, he was left in a state of shock after the

'My grandfather was a quiet man, who loved his family.
He made me appreciate art, but he didn't encourage me to be an
artist as he wanted the family to get on and do more.'

JOHN SCOTT, GRANDSON

Alexander Carrick's bronze
of a Gunner carrying a shell,
modelled in 1916.

premature explosion of a shell in one of the guns in his battery, something that was not uncommon. He had a period of convalescence with a Belgian family but never fully recovered, and suffered from a form of shell shock for the rest of his life. Throughout his military career Alexander sketched continuously, depicting his comrades, guns in action, the daily details of battery life and the war-ravaged landscape, many drawn in a free and modern style. He also continued to model, using the raw clay from the trenches. In 1916 he modelled in clay a large and powerful figure of a Gunner carrying a shell towards his gun. This is a striking and dramatic figure that manages to combine the influence of Michelangelo and Rodin with the modernism of Jacob Epstein and Frank Dobson. Remarkably, in his war-torn environment, Alexander found a Belgian sculptor, Leopold Beun, who helped him cast the figure in plaster. Even more remarkably, Alexander managed to arrange for several copies of the plaster to be shipped back to Britain and one, tinted bronze, was exhibited in Edinburgh. A bronze version of *The Gunner* was shown at the annual Royal Scottish Academy exhibition in Edinburgh in 1918, which was open from April to August that year. Alexander was still in Belgium, and before the war was over he was made an Associate of the Royal Scottish Academy.

After he was demobilized in March 1919, Alexander returned to Edinburgh and re-established his sculpture workshop. He continued to exhibit, including a series of soldier figures, but more important was his involvement in the war memorial movement. The early 1920s was a good time to be a sculptor, with many cities, towns, villages, institutions, companies and private individuals wanting war memorials to commemorate the Fallen. Many were simple, symbolic forms such as crosses and obelisks, but the more ambitious ones often required figurative sculpture. The result was a rich period of sculptural creativity in both Britain and France, with both well-established and young contemporary sculptors becoming involved. Alexander's first commission was a soldier figure for Lochawe and others carved in stone soon followed, for Killin, Oban, St Margaret's Hope in Orkney (his mother's home village), Kinghorn, Newburgh and Auchtermuchty. For the memorials for Dornoch, Forres, Blairgowrie, Walkerburn, Berwick-upon-Tweed and Fraserburgh, he created figures in bronze. Small-scale versions were made of some of these.

Trench drawing by Alexander Carrick.

Alexander also modelled the bas-relief panels commemorating the Royal Engineers and the Royal Artillery for the Scottish National War Memorial in Edinburgh Castle. There is no doubt that Alexander Carrick's career as a sculptor was hugely influenced by his experiences on the Western Front. Some of his figures can stand alongside the work of Charles Sergeant Jagger, the best British sculptor of the war, and another man radically changed by his experience as a fighting infantryman in Gallipoli and on the Western Front.

Alexander Carrick continued to work through the later 1920s and 1930s, on architectural commissions and on smaller-scale pieces. He maintained a long friendship with the Beun family, who had helped him cast his 1916 figure, in Belgium. In 1928 he became Head of Sculpture at Edinburgh School of Art, and remained an influential teacher over a long period. He last exhibited in 1954 and died in 1966, having enjoyed a long retirement with his wife in the Scottish Borders.

A bronze version of *The Gunner* has always been in the family and this may be the one exhibited in Edinburgh in 1918. It has been passed down the family, along with Alexander's sketchbooks, drawings and letters, including one sent from Belgium enclosing heather picked on the battlefield at Hellfire Corner. There is also another bronze soldier, a small version of the figure Alexander created for the Killin war memorial. One other version of *The Gunner* has been recorded and was sold at auction some years ago.

THE SOLDIER WHO RESCUED RATTY

MAURICE WELLS
1888–1916

Born in 1888, Maurice Wells was one of a family of six. His grandfather was James Hayllar, a noted portrait and genre painter of the late Victorian and Edwardian eras, and his grandmother was Ellen Cavell, Edith Cavell's aunt. Four of James Hayllar's daughters also became noted artists and one of these, Mary, married Henry Wells. Their six children included two boys, Maurice and Guy, both remembered as being good-looking.

Before the war, Maurice enlisted as a volunteer for the Territorial Force and at the outbreak of war he joined the 4th Battalion of the Royal Berkshire Regiment. The battalion landed in France at the end of March 1915, as part of the South Midland Brigade. In 1916 the battalion fought through the early weeks of the Somme campaign, starting with the attack on 1 July 1916 on the German strongpoint the Heidenkopf (the Quadrilateral), where they suffered heavy casualties. Later they were involved in the battles of Bazentin and Pozières. In 1917 the battalion moved north and took part in the Third Battle of Ypres, and then in November 1917 it was sent to Italy, to support the Italian armies in Asiago and Vittoria Veneto.

'I have struggled to find out anything about my uncle
Maurice and now no other family members remain
with any connection to that era. But I would like Ratty
to be remembered, that's the least I can do.'

DAVID LILLEY, NEPHEW

At some point Maurice, by then a Lieutenant, found a tree rat, or a kind of squirrel, lying on the ground unconscious near his trench. He decided it was suffering from shell shock and took it back to his quarters, where it made a full recovery. By now named Ratty, it became a pet and personal mascot. In 1916, Maurice transferred to the Royal Flying Corps, joining 11 Squadron. On 15 September he was killed. Ratty was then looked after by Maurice's batman and then by a brother officer and friend of Maurice's who, having been wounded, was repatriated back to England. Somehow he managed to bring Ratty back with him and handed him over to Maurice's family. Maurice's youngest sister, Beatrice, took care of Ratty until his death a few weeks later, when she persuaded her father to take him to a taxidermist to be preserved and mounted. Married to a naval officer, Beatrice took Ratty in his glass case around the world, and he now lives with Beatrice's son (and Maurice's nephew), David. He has become an important member of the family.

Lieutenant Wells is buried in the Canadian No. 2 Military Cemetery at Neuville St Vaast, near Arras.

Ratty, the tree rat rescued and kept as a pet by Maurice Wells on the Western Front. After Maurice's death, his friend brought the rat back home to England to give to Maurice's sister, Beatrice.

A SOLDIER WHO MADE HIS OWN MASCOT

ARTHUR HICKMAN
1897–1961

Superstition was always strong among soldiers, and many carried mascots to protect them. These could take many forms but were usually either things that had been found, or things given to them by friends or loved

ones. It was rare for soldiers to make their own mascots, but Arthur Hickman, who was born in Manchester in December 1897, did. His father Luther was a cabinet-maker who had trained in Birmingham and, after leaving school, Arthur worked with his father in the furniture trade in Manchester. In 1916 he joined the army, although it is not known whether he volunteered with a group of friends, or was conscripted.

Little is known about Arthur's military service. He seems to have joined the Seaforth Highlanders first and then been transferred to another famous Scottish regiment, the Argyll and Sutherland Highlanders. It seems odd that a lad from Manchester ended up in Scottish regiments but batches of recruits were sometimes used to bring back up to strength battalions that had been weakened by heavy losses in combat. In any case, Arthur spent the rest of the war with the Highlanders.

'Sadly, I was born after my grandfather's death, but he was often talked about when I was a child, along with his "little man" mascot. He was a quiet and loving man, very generous, and always with his pipe. I wish I had been able to meet him and talk to him.'

DONNA OWEN, GRANDDAUGHTER

Arthur had been an amateur embroiderer before the war and shortly after he joined the regiment, he made a little figure from scraps of tartan cut from his uniform, as a keepsake for his sweetheart, and as a mascot to protect him. It worked, as he survived unharmed, and from that point the 'little man' never left his sweetheart's handbag for at least 50 years. He and Eva Williams had met at Sunday School in about 1911 but they did not marry until March 1929. They had one son.

After the war Arthur worked as an oil engineer, collected antique porcelain, was a keen rose grower and loved animals, often going out with his little dog or a couple of kittens in his pockets. He also enjoyed the Isle of Man motorcycle TT, something he loved almost as much as his wife, Eva.

Donna, Arthur's granddaughter, who had known the 'little man' as a child, rediscovered it after her grandmother's death, along with Arthur's mouth organ, his Argyll and Sutherland Highlanders cap badge and a photograph of him in his kilt. For her, the 'little man' is not only a link to her grandfather, but also something to remember him and all the other young men like him who went to fight in foreign fields.

Arthur Hickman's Argyll and Sutherland Highlanders cap badge (above) and 'little man' mascot (left).

A fragment of stained glass from Rheims cathedral,
acquired by Albert Pullin, possibly when the
cathedral was used as a casualty dressing station.

A SOLDIER WHO FOUGHT WITH THE INTELLIGENCE SECTION

ALBERT VICTOR PULLIN
1887–1966

Albert Victor Pullin was born in Thornbury, Gloucestershire, in 1887, the youngest of three children. His father James was Head Gamekeeper for the Earl of Berkeley and died in a riding accident in 1911. After school, Albert worked as a gardener on the Berkeley Castle estate. When war broke out, Albert enlisted in the 8th (Service) Battalion of the Gloucestershire Regiment. Formed in Bristol in 1914, this battalion was one of 11 formed by

the Gloucestershire Regiment as part of Kitchener's New Army. This famous regiment, known as The Glorious Glosters, was formed in 1881 by the merging of old foot regiments whose history goes back to the 17th century. Over its long history, the Glosters earned more battle honours than any other British line regiment. During the First World War the Gloucestershire Regiment raised 25 battalions and fought on the Western Front, in Gallipoli, in Macedonia, in the Middle East and in Italy.

After training, the 8th Battalion went to France in July 1915 as part of the 57th Brigade of the 19th Division, following an inspection by King George V on 23 June. Albert's first action with the battalion was at the

'I remember a quiet, considerate and caring man.
My grandfather never learnt to drive and was the most contented
person I have ever known. Time spent with my grandparents
was special and left an indelible impression on me.'

DAVID PULLIN, GRANDSON

1917

IN 1917 THE WAR ENTERED A WIDER, MORE GLOBAL PHASE.
On the Western Front the stalemate of trench warfare continued.
In spring the Germans, finding their front line too stretched,
withdrew to the shorter, and much stronger, Hindenburg Line.
Despite the lessons of 1916, both the British and the French
launched major attacks. For France, the so-called Nivelle
Offensive was a disaster, leading directly to a large-scale mutiny
in the French army. The British had more success at the Battle
of Arras, thanks to new tactics, including better use of tanks.
Few significant gains were made, apart from the capture of Vimy
Ridge by the Canadians. Soon after Arras came the Third Battle
of Ypres, which ultimately ground to a halt in the winter mud
and destructive chaos of Passchendaele. The massive losses in
these campaigns were felt both by the experienced volunteers
and the new generation of conscripts.

On the Eastern Front Russia's military success was stopped
in its tracks by the Bolshevik Revolution, which swept the Tzar
from power. At the end of the year a peace treaty took Russia out
of the war, and sent German armies back to the Western Front.
The Italian army was defeated by the Austro-Hungarians at the
Battle of Caporetto but the collapse of Italy was averted by large
numbers of Allied troops fighting there to restore the balance
of power. In the Middle East, the Allies continued the successful
campaign launched in 1916, and Jerusalem fell at the end of the
year. The reversal of Turkish fortunes had been helped by the
irregular Arab forces under the command of T. E. Lawrence. Until

the Revolution, Russian troops were also defeating Turkish forces in the Caucasus.

The most significant event of the year was the declaration of war in April against Germany by the United States. The immediate impact was more psychological than practical, with few American troops in Europe before the end of the year. By 1918 the United States planned to bring 10,000 troops a month to Europe, although they aimed to keep their armies independent from the collective actions of the Allies. More immediate was help to the Allied navies, in the form of ships and equipment.

At sea, Germany returned to a policy of unrestricted submarine warfare, and increasing losses to Allied merchant shipping brought suffering to Britain's civilian population. In response the British introduced a convoy system with warship escorts, and the number of ships lost each month began to decline. At the same time, Allied attacks on German submarines were becoming more successful, thanks to depth charges and other new technology. However, for sailors in the Merchant Services, having their ship sunk by torpedo or gunfire was a common experience.

This chapter's stories highlight some of these aspects of the war, seen often through the eyes of the ordinary front-line soldier or his family. A surprising number of lives were saved by hard objects in uniform pockets. While many soldiers had been brutalized by years of fighting, others continued to risk their lives to save their friends and colleagues.

———————

A SAILOR CAPTURED
BY A COMMERCE RAIDER

STANLEY ORRITT
1880–1965

Before the introduction of the convoy system in 1917, British and Allied merchant ships sailed the oceans of the world on their own, often

following well-known trade routes. They were, therefore, easy victims of German submarines patrolling the same routes. There was also the risk of mines but a much greater threat was posed by German commerce raiders. These were heavily armed merchant vessels sent to prowl the seas in search of Allied shipping. The idea of commerce raiding was not new, and can be traced back to the privateers of the Napoleonic era. However, the first use of commerce raiding as a part of government policy and under naval control was during the American Civil War. By the First World War the idea was well established, with Germany launching a Handelskreig, or

trade war, against the Allies. The Germans used a number of commerce raiders and one of the most successful was the SMS *Moewe* (Seagull), as many British Merchant Service sailors found to their cost.

'My great-uncle had a dry sense of humour and liked telling jokes.
He was a determined man, and prepared to make the most
of whatever came his way. His diary, a very detailed document,
allowed us to share his adventures.'

DAVID ORRITT, GREAT-NEPHEW

One of a family of 11 children, Stanley, or Stan, Orritt, was born in Burscough, Lancashire, in August 1880. His father was a paviour (a person who lays paving), who later became Surveyor of Roads for Ormskirk Council. After Ormskirk Grammar School, Stan went to the Liverpool School of Science and then trained as a mechanical engineer. In about 1905 he joined the Merchant Service as a ship's engineer and then he travelled the world pursuing this career.

On Christmas Day 1914 the SS *Potaro* left Liverpool bound for Montevideo. Stan was Second Engineer on this 4400-ton ship operated by the Royal Mail Steam Packet line. On 10 January 1915, when she was 450 miles east of Brazil, the *Potaro* was stopped by two shots fired across her bow by the German Auxiliary Cruiser, the SMS *Kronprinz Wilhelm*. This former liner had been in German naval service since 1914 and, until April 1915, when she was interned in the United States, she sank or captured over 56,000 tons of British shipping. The *Potaro* was boarded, and later scuttled by the Germans, and her passengers and crew were transferred to the *Kronprinz Wilhelm*, and held as prisoners. They were treated with courtesy and well looked after, as was the usual practice in these circumstances. Before he left the *Potaro*, Stan removed the engine-room clock and he managed to keep this souvenir through all his subsequent adventures. The *Kronprinz Wilhelm* continued her cruise, capturing three more British ships and taking their crews on board, making a total of 220 prisoners. After 33 days all the prisoners were transferred to a German tender, the SS *Holgar*, and put ashore in Buenos Aires. Stan returned to Britain via Montreal, finally arriving in Plymouth on 15 November 1916.

Stan's next ship was the SS *Brecknockshire*, another Royal Mail Steam Packet line vessel. Newly built, she sailed from Belfast on 11 January 1917 on her maiden voyage, with Stan as her Second Engineer, bound for Rio de Janeiro. On 15 February, when east of Brazil, she was ordered to stop by an approaching ship and, when her captain ignored the order, eight shells were fired at her. At this, Captain Mackenzie stopped and surrendered his ship. His captor was the SMS *Moewe*. The *Brecknockshire*'s crew were taken on board the *Moewe* and then they watched as she was sunk by the *Moewe*'s guns.

Built as a cargo ship in 1914, the *Pungo*, as she was then, was taken over by the German navy in 1915, converted into an armed minelayer and

renamed the *Moewe*. While retaining her cargo ship appearance, *Moewe* had two 6-inch guns and considerable smaller armament. Like all commerce raiders, she was designed to look like a neutral cargo vessel to enable her to get close to her prey unsuspected. On 29 December 1915, she sailed on her first voyage, first laying mines in the Pentland Firth, one of which sank the British battleship *King Edward VII*, and then cruising the south Atlantic where, over the next three months, she captured or sank 15 ships.

On 23 November 1916, *Moewe* set sail on her second voyage into the Atlantic and, over the next four months, she captured or sank 25 ships, including the *Brecknockshire*. Unlike the large *Kronprinz Wilhelm* the *Moewe* was a small ship, and so there was little space for prisoners. Stan found himself sharing a 14ft by 15ft cabin with other junior officers and, as the *Moewe* continued to capture other ships, so the number steadily increased, reaching 35 by the end. They lived, ate and slept in this space, with only 20 minutes' exercise allowed each day on deck in groups of 50. For ordinary seamen, the conditions were even more crowded. Food was scarce, and the rations diminished as the voyage went on. Washing facilities were very limited and lice flourished. In addition, there were men with injuries and others with illnesses such as tuberculosis. Commerce raiders in the First World War tended not to abandon or kill crews of captured vessels, and their crews were generally well behaved towards prisoners. There was no cruelty, just a severe shortage of space that got worse as the voyage progressed.

One of the last ships attacked by the *Moewe* was an armed New Zealand merchant ship called the *Otaki*. She fought back and, although outgunned and sunk in the battle, she damaged the *Moewe* enough to compel her to return to port. On 22 March 1917 the *Moewe* finally docked in Kiel and all the prisoners were taken ashore. It was the end of Germany's most successful commerce raiding venture, with 40 ships captured or sunk totalling 180,000 tons. *Moewe* did not go raiding again, later becoming a submarine tender in the Baltic.

Throughout his time on the *Moewe*, Stan kept a diary, documenting his daily life, which he filled with watercolour sketches. There are views of the *Moewe* and the *Brecknockshire*, scenes of other ships being sunk, and one of the battle with the *Otaki*. Once they were in Germany, all the captured British sailors were sent to prisoner-of-war camps. Stan went first to one near Heidelberg, then briefly to Beeskow, near the Polish border, before finishing the war near Hanover, in a prison hotel for Merchant Service officers. When the war ended, Stan was released and back in England in December 1918. He kept up his diary and continued to sketch all the time he was a prisoner of war.

The sinking of the S.S. "Esmeraldas." March 10th 1917.

Stan married in 1919 and then returned to sea with the Merchant Navy, as the Merchant Service was then called. During the rest of his career he served on at least 12 different ships and continued to travel the world as a ship's engineer. The engine-room clock from the SS *Potaro* held pride of place on his kitchen wall, and remained there until he died.

Opposite: A watercolour sketch by Stanley Orritt, showing the prisoners' kitchen in the camp at Beeskow. The individual cookers are made from biscuit tins.
Above: A sketch by Stanley Orritt, showing the sinking of the SS *Esmeraldas* by the commerce raider *Moewe*.

A SOLDIER ALWAYS LOVED BY HIS WIDOW

FREDERICK CHARLES SEWELL
1881–1917

There are many tales of young couples torn apart by the war. Typical is the sad story of Fred and Grace Sewell. Born in Cudham, Kent in April 1881, Frederick Charles Sewell was the youngest son of Richard and Fanny Sewell.

His father was a wine merchant and the family lived comfortably in a large house in the village. As they grew up Fred and his two older brothers went into the hotel business and by 1914 they owned one in Robertsbridge and two in Bexhill-on-Sea. By then Fred was 33, and so resisted the initial enthusiasm for the war. He lived a bachelor life with his dog Tinker in the Devonshire Hotel in Bexhill. In 1916 he decided to volunteer, partly as a response to the ever-increasing losses, and partly because he knew that conscription was on its way. On 4 May 1916 he enlisted in the 7th (Service) Battalion of the Bedfordshire Regiment. Formed in Bedford in September 1914, the 7th Battalion was part of the second phase of Kitchener's New Army, the result of his appeal for a further 100,000 volunteers. Attached initially while training to the 15th

> '*My indomitable grandmother played a large part in my life when I was a child. While she had had an interesting life, I knew she never forgot Fred, her first husband, and the love of her life. She used to say sometimes that we are not meant to be happy.*'

SYLVIA SILVESTER, GRANDDAUGHTER

Top: Grace Sewell, wearing her wedding ring. Grace married Fred Sewell on 3 May 1916, the day before he enlisted. Bottom: The engagement ring given to Grace by Fred Sewell.

A DOCTOR, AND AN ARTIST, WHO LOVED HORSES

HERBERT ARNOLD LAKE
1883–1969

Common to many who survived the First World War was a reluctance to talk about their experiences and their memories, which often remained deeply buried for the rest of their lives. Some found an escape from inner turmoil by writing, and their legacy is the remarkable literature of the war, which began to appear in the 1920s. For others, painting offered a different type

of escape. A soldier who took this route was Herbert Arnold Lake. Born in 1883, he trained initially as a vet but did not go into practice, having already decided to retrain as a doctor at University College Hospital, London. He qualified in 1915, worked briefly as a country doctor then enlisted into the Royal Army Medical Corps. However, a lasting legacy of his veterinary experience was a life-long passion for horses, which he had begun to draw as a young man, and for hunting. For most of his life, his sketchbook was never far from his hand and whenever possible he was in the saddle.

Herbert's war record seems to have underlined his attachment to horses as he served with several cavalry regiments, including the 4th

*'Grandfather Lake was a most amusing and kind man.
He taught me to ride, fish and paint. I never once heard
him speak of the war and my mother said it had been so horrific
it remained a buried subject for him. His paintings
said it all, so there was no need for words.'*

JULIA ROBERTS, GRANDDAUGHTER

(Queen's Own) Hussars, the 5th Royal Irish Lancers and the 16th The Queen's Lancers. No details of this service are known, except that he was mentioned in despatches in May 1917 and attained the rank of Major. However, he was certainly with one of the four Cavalry Field Ambulance units attached to the 3rd Cavalry Division during the Battle of the Scarpe in April 1917, part of the Arras offensive. A notable feature of this was the capture of the village of Monchy-le-Preux on 10 and 11 April 1917, an action that included one of the last British cavalry charges. Early in the morning of 11 April, a cold day with drifting snow, the 8th Cavalry Brigade, which included the 10th Hussars and the Royal Horse Guards, was ordered to attack. Watching soldiers, which included Herbert, saw the dramatic sight of the cavalry streaming down the hill towards the village, under ever-increasing German fire. Cavalry was not suited to fighting in narrow village streets and soon Monchy was filled with dead and dying men and horses, while the troopers still able to fight clung on to the village cellars. Fighting went on all day, without reinforcements or medical help able to get into Monchy. In the evening the surviving cavalry retreated back to Arras. In darkness a Field Ambulance entered the village but was unable to collect any wounded. Meanwhile, back at the division headquarters, there was no knowledge of the large number of wounded awaiting medical attention in Monchy and so nothing was done until the evening of 12 April, when accurate reports were finally received. For the next three nights medical teams struggled through the snow and German fire to bring out the surviving wounded from Monchy.

The battle for Monchy-le-Preux was a small part of a major campaign which included the capture by the Canadians of Vimy Ridge. Despite the huge losses, and the limited gains, the Battle of Arras was generally considered an Allied success. There were, of course, many disasters within that success, not least the pointless and wasteful cavalry charge at Monchy. No one knows exactly how many horses died there but, after the battle, the 8th Cavalry Brigade requested 800 replacement horses from the Remount Service.

Herbert Lake was deeply affected by all he witnessed at Monchy and put his feelings into a series of paintings depicting troopers and their horses before and after the battle. These are powerful images, filled with cold and

Left: Painting by Herbert Lake, showing the cavalry
waiting to attack in the early morning. Right: Sketch by
Herbert Lake of a horse-drawn ambulance.

the grey light of morning, and marked with the change from expectation
to despair as the attack failed. There is a sense of resignation, beneath the
snow, rain and mud. They were based on sketches done on the spot, hasty,
accurate, intense and full of the reality of military action. Despite his lack
of formal training, Herbert was a remarkable artist and his work is in a
number of collections, including the Imperial War Museum.

After the war Dr Herbert Lake married Stella Drysdale and they had
two children. He became a general practitioner in Beaminster in Dorset,
and famously continued to ride his horse to all his appointments until
his retirement. He was a well-known and much-loved local figure, as a
doctor, as a huntsman and horseman, and as an artist. His granddaughter
Julia knew him well and loved riding with him over the Downs around
Beaminster as he visited his patients. 'Thanks to him,' she says, 'I was
never short of a good pony or horse.'

A LADY WHO LOST HER SWEETHEART

MARION FORBES BAIRD
1894–1979

The daughter of a brickworks owner in Paisley, Marion Forbes Baird was born in November 1894. She and her two brothers had a comfortable childhood, and she was sent to finishing school in Switzerland. At some point, either just before the war or soon after the start of hostilities, she met and fell in love

with Arthur Henderson. It is likely they met in Paisley as his father George was a local magistrate and also involved in the building trade.

Arthur enlisted in the 4th (Militia) Battalion, the Argyll and Sutherland Highlanders and was later attached to the 2nd Battalion. This had landed in France with the British Expeditionary Force on 14 August, was quickly in action and was then on the Western Front throughout the war, taking part in most of the major campaigns and battles.

On 23 April 1917 Acting Captain Henderson was involved in heavy fighting near Fontaine-les-Croisilles, part of the on-going Battle of Arras, and during this engagement he won a Victoria Cross. The citation describes his action:

'My grandmother was a feisty lady, fun, often outrageous but she could never be persuaded to talk about Arthur at all. She never attended any Service of Remembrance as her memories were too painful, even 60 years later.'

MARIAN MORRISON, GRANDDAUGHTER

For most conspicuous bravery

During an attack on the enemy trenches this officer, although almost immediately wounded in the left arm, led his Company through the enemy front line until he gained his final objective.

He then proceeded to consolidate his position, which, owing to heavy gun and machine gun fire and bombing attacks was in danger of being isolated.

By his cheerful courage and coolness he was enabled to maintain the spirit of his men under most trying conditions.

Captain Henderson was killed after he had successfully accomplished his task.

Arthur had given Marion a regimental sweetheart brooch and, shortly before his death, he had sent her from France a gold necklace. This became at once her most treasured possession, though she never wore it, nor told anyone about it.

During the war Marion was for a while a volunteer ambulance driver but Arthur's death overshadowed her life. Her father also died in 1917 and Arthur's brother was killed in the war.

After the war, Marion and her brother tried unsuccessfully to run the family business and then in 1921 she married William Palmer, another

Argyll and Sutherland Highlander. They had three daughters but William had problems, having been damaged emotionally by the war, and he was a remote and isolated man. He may also have known about Marion's love for Arthur, which cannot have been easy for him. In the 1920s there was little general understanding of the psychological effects of the war and many, including William, struggled to cope with their memories of the war. The support systems now taken for granted simply did not exist then, and so William had a difficult relationship with Marion and barely knew his daughters.

When her granddaughter was 21, Marion gave her Arthur's gold necklace. No one in the family had ever seen it before, nor had they heard Arthur's story. Marian, the granddaughter, had always been close to her grandmother: 'She was younger in outlook than my parents, very modern and never judgemental. Definitely fun to be with and could be outrageous in her attitudes. She was calm, good at dealing with crises – and she had had plenty of those. I can see now that Arthur's death ruined her life and left a long shadow she did her best to hide.'

Captain Arthur Henderson is buried in the British cemetery at Saint-Martin-sur-Cojeul, near where he died. Marion never went to see her sweetheart's grave.

Opposite: A simple gold necklace, probably purchased from a local jewellers, which Arthur Henderson sent to Marion Baird shortly before his death.
Above: The regimental sweetheart brooch that Arthur also gave to Marion.

A SOLDIER KILLED THREE MONTHS BEFORE HIS SON'S BIRTH

ARTHUR TURNER
1886–1917

A coal miner who joined up with his friends, Arthur Turner was born in Kilburn, Derbyshire, in June 1886. His was a mining family, and he worked at New Hucknall Colliery after leaving school. In July 1908 he married Agnes Lee at St Mary's Church, Sutton-in-Ashfield, Nottinghamshire and they had three children.

On 7 September 1914, Arthur and a group of local friends went into Mansfield and enlisted in the Sherwood Foresters, a local regiment serving Derbyshire and Nottinghamshire that had been formed in 1881. A week later Arthur was transferred to the 1st Battalion, the Royal Marine Brigade. This was one of four battalions in the brigade formed at the outbreak of war with men from the Royal Marine Light Infantry and the Royal Marine Artillery. Almost immediately this was renamed the 63rd Royal Naval Division and expanded into eight battalions named after famous admirals: Nelson, Drake, Benbow, Hawke, Collingwood, Howe, Hood and Anson. Soldiers either came from the Royal Navy or, like Arthur, were volunteers or reservists. The division fought throughout the 1914 battles in France and Belgium, and then in April 1915 it was sent to Gallipoli. Here, Arthur was wounded and also caught enteric fever; he was sent back to Britain to recover. This took a long while, and he

'I don't know what Arthur was like and I don't know where the rest of his family are. I do remember my great-grandmother though, she had Arthur's picture on her bedroom wall and she left it to me when she died.'

ANITA ELLIOTT, GREAT-GRANDDAUGHTER

missed the Royal Naval Division's involvement in the later phases of the Battle of the Somme from September 1916.

Arthur was not passed fit for service until the early part of 1917 and he was then back with the battalion in March 1917. It must have been so hard for a couple in their situation, with young children, to come to terms with first the stress of the injury, then the increasing normality of the recovery period and finally the knowledge that a return to action was inevitable. Before leaving Britain, Arthur gave Agnes, pregnant with their fourth child, a beaded necklace. This was to be the last time they saw each other.

On 26 April 1917 Arthur was killed in action during the Battle of Arras, which had started on 9 April. In June Agnes sent her husband a postcard which said: 'To my dear husband on his 29th birthday.' This suggests that she did not know about, or believe, Arthur's death, two months after he had been killed. His fourth son, Sydney, was born on 18 July 1917, a day that would also have been Arthur and Agnes's ninth wedding anniversary.

According to family legend, Arthur had made Agnes promise never to marry again in the event of his death. She kept that promise, bringing up her four children on her own, and remaining a widow until she died in December 1977. All her life Agnes kept the postcards her husband had sent her, and on her bedroom wall was a photograph of Arthur, framed with a decorative Roll of Honour. Anita, her great-granddaughter, knew Agnes until she was 16 and, when Agnes asked her if there was any object she wanted after her death, Anita asked for Arthur's framed photograph.

Private Arthur Turner has no known grave but is listed among the 35,000 Names of the Missing on the Arras Memorial.

Opposite: A memorial locket containing a photograph of Arthur Turner.
Right: Typical wartime postcards, sent between Arthur Turner and his wife Agnes.

WOUNDED FOUR TIMES
AND SAVED BY HIS CAMERA

RALFE ALLEN FULLER WHISTLER
1895–1917

Ralfe Allen Fuller Whistler was born in Glasgow in July 1895. Both his parents were associated with the Highland Light Infantry. He was educated at King's School, Canterbury, where he was Captain of Games and an all-round athlete. He enrolled there in the Officers' Training Corps and went to Sandhurst in 1912. On passing out he was commissioned in March 1914 as a 2nd Lieutenant in the 2nd Battalion of the Highland Light Infantry. Formed in 1881 by the merging of two long-established Scottish

Regiments of Foot, the 71st and the 74th, the Highland Light Infantry had a notable career in the First World War, fighting on the Western Front, in the Dardanelles, in Mesopotamia and Palestine and in Russia.

The 2nd Battalion landed in France on 14 August 1914, as part of 5th Brigade, the 2nd Division, and Ralfe fought with them at Mons. On 12 September he was wounded in the head at the Battle of the Aisne. He returned to the battalion in November 1914, and was wounded again in May 1915 at Festubert. This time his recovery and recuperation took longer and he spent some time in hospital in Woolwich.

'I had some trousers altered in Hastings after World War Two, and the tailor remembered my uncle bringing in his bullet-riddled uniform for patching. He had a weekend leave and was going hunting with the East Sussex Foxhounds, then taking the Dieppe ferry on Monday morning back to the trenches.'

RALFE ASHTON WHISTLER, NEPHEW

The bullet-damaged camera that saved Ralfe Whistler's life in Mesopotamia.
Vest pocket cameras were increasingly popular during the 1910s and many
soldiers used them to record their experiences.

On his return to service Ralfe was promoted to Lieutenant and attached
to the Highland Light Infantry's 1st Battalion, then serving in Mesopotamia.
He arrived there in time to take part in the unsuccessful relief of Kut in April
1916, and was wounded for a third time. There were several bullet holes
in his uniform but the one aimed at his heart, which would have killed
him, was stopped by his camera in his breast pocket. After a spell in Basra
hospital he returned to the 1st Battalion but then contracted typhoid fever
and was evacuated, first to India and subsequently back to Britain.

On 22 March 1917 Ralfe, by now promoted to Captain, rejoined the 2nd
Battalion in France, in time to take part in the Battle of Arras. The Arras
offensive, launched on 9 April 1917, was concentrated on a narrow 11-mile
front and designed to achieve a major breakthrough of the German lines.
New tactics were used, including creeping barrages, flexibility in attack,
increased mining and tunnelling, tanks and improved air cover and
reconnaissance. Initially the attack was successful. Vimy Ridge was taken

SOUVENIR

In ✲ *Loving* ✲ *Memory*

OF THE

MEN, WOMEN AND CHILDREN

KILLED IN

The London Air Raid

ON WEDNESDAY, JUNE 13TH 1917,

The casualties include 120 children either killed or injured

"SUFFER LITTLE CHILDREN TO COME UNTO ME,
FOR OF SUCH IS THE KINGDOM OF HEAVEN."

These tiny school babes, our little ones,
Had ceased their tasks and were listening with bated breath,
For the blotting out of the glorious sun
By the broken thunder of the German Death.

"IN THE MIDST OF LIFE, WE ARE IN DEATH."

Opposite: Rose Tuffin's older brothers and sisters in about
1908. Clockwise from top, Susannah, George, Peter and Bill,
who was injured in the bombing. There is no known photograph
of Rose. Above: A commemorative handerkerchief printed on
tissue paper to remember the bombing raid of 13 June 1917.

A CHILD KILLED IN LONDON'S FIRST BLITZ

ROSE TUFFIN
1911–1917

Between 1915 and 1918 German airships launched about 55 bombing raids on London and other British targets. Many attacks were thwarted by weather and the bombing that occurred was largely random, although over 500 were killed, mostly civilians. From 1916 airships were increasingly

vulnerable to attacks from British aircraft and anti-aircraft guns, and so the raids became few and far between. However, the story of the Zeppelin menace had by then became a part of popular culture, and has remained so for the last century. As a result, it has tended to overshadow the story of London's first Blitz, the attacks on the city by German aircraft from 1917. Between May 1917 and the end of the war there were 22 raids on British targets by German Gotha G.IV and other heavy bombers, many of which were directed at London's civilian population. This, planned by the Germans in 1916 as Operation Türkenkreuz, was the world's first example of terror bombing from the air and resulted in hundreds of deaths and injuries, including 18 children in a school in Poplar, east London.

> 'My dad never mentioned his sister's death until my children were born so I grew up knowing nothing about how the family had been torn apart, and the impact the bombing had had on him. Finally, perhaps thinking of his grandchildren, he wrote about his memories.'

SALLY DENNIS, NIECE

Rose Tuffin was born in 1911, the fifth child of George and Susannah Tuffin. They were typical East End Londoners, he a carman and she a domestic servant. Along with two brothers and a sister Rose attended Upper North Street School, Poplar.

On 13 June 1917, the children were in their classes at the school, and all was proceeding normally. Early that morning, a squadron of 20 Gotha bombers had left their base in Belgium and set a course for London. This was the third planned daylight bombing raid on London, the other two, on 25 May and 5 June, having been switched to secondary targets in Kent because of bad weather. There were no such problems on 13 June, however, and the Gothas were soon flying at 15,000 feet towards London through cloudy sunshine. There were no specific targets and the aim of the raid was terror and destruction, against a city that was unprepared and inadequately defended. There was no effective air raid warning system, anti-aircraft gunners had difficulty in spotting the bombers against the sun, and the defending aircraft, generally older or obsolete types, struggled to reach the bombers' operational ceiling.

The Gothas flew in formation across Essex and towards central London, dropping bombs in and around the city. They then turned east, roughly following the Thames, and bombed the East End and the Docks indiscriminately. It was during this part of the raid that a bomb hit Upper North Street School, killing 18 children outright and injuring many others. Rose Tuffin was among the dead, and her brother Bill among the seriously injured.

Years later Peter, Rose's other brother at the school, and Sally's father, wrote about that day:

> Then it was 1914 and the war began. At first it didn't affect us much. We had Zeppelin raids ... when the anti-aircraft guns were loud we all sang louder to reassure the younger ones ... this rotten war ... was a shocking blight on our family ... one morning there was a daylight raid and they dropped a very large bomb on our school. Rose was killed and Bill injured.
>
> Our whole family life was pretty well destroyed. Ivy, who was just a year younger than Rose, was terribly affected by this tragedy, she became very ill and eventually died.

Although uninjured physically by the bombing, Peter bore the scars for the rest of his life, becoming insecure and having his confidence damaged through the heartbreak of seeing his family torn apart.

The bombing of the Upper North Street School caused horror and outrage throughout the country and reinforced the popular view, originally engendered by the Zeppelin raids, that the Germans were baby killers. In all, the raid on 13 June 1917 killed 170 and injured 432 but the nation focused on the 18 dead children. There was an impressive and moving mass funeral at All Saints' Church, Poplar, on 20 June, attended by thousands, followed by an inquest which included harrowing eye-witness accounts. A public appeal for a memorial quickly reached its target and this, listing all the children by name, was unveiled in Poplar Recreation Ground on 23 June 1918, one of the first memorials to the events of the First World War.

Children lay flowers at the memorial in Poplar Recreation Ground in 1919, to commemorate those killed in the Upper North Street School bombing.

There were further attacks on London by German bombers but more effective defences forced them to switch from daylight to night raids in September 1917. The last large-scale attack on London was in May 1918, after which the German bombers were switched to attacking military targets on the Western Front, in an attempt to hinder the progress of Allied advances. In total, Zeppelin raids killed 557 British people and injured 1358.

The real lesson of London's first Blitz, not lost on both politicians and military strategists, was that the nature of war had changed forever. From this point, civilians were in the front line, and terror bombing became an established weapon of modern warfare.

A MERCHANT SERVICE SAILOR TORPEDOED THREE TIMES AND SAVED BY HIS CANARY

WALTER EDWARD THORP
1897–1961

Walter Edward Thorp's first love was technology. Born in Canning Town, London, in 1897, the eldest of four brothers, he was apprenticed to his father, an undertaker, learning all kinds of carpentry, cabinet-making and woodworking skills.

However, Walter's real love was electricity and wireless and he taught himself everything he could about these new technologies, including the rapid transmission of Morse code. In 1914, Walter, aged 18 and caught up in the general excitement at the outbreak of war, joined the Merchant Service, perhaps wanting to travel and make use of his wireless skills.

Walter's first ships were operated by Ellerman Lines, a Liverpool-based company that had grown rapidly by mergers and acquisitions since it was founded in 1892. On every ship on which he served he was given the post of Wireless Operator, his skills ensuring that he was seldom without a job. Life in the Merchant Service

'Though very strict, my father was a wonderful man and an inspiration to me and he is still much missed by my sister and me. Sometimes I can't get my head round the idea that he is not here though if he were, he'd be 117. I know he would have loved computers and mobile phones.'

DAVID THORP, SON

could be precarious, with seamen unpaid when they were between ships. However, due to the serious losses being experienced by merchant ships at the time, largely because of the submarine menace, Walter rarely found himself in that position. In the course of the First World War Ellerman Lines and its subsidiaries lost 103 ships, totalling over 600,000 tons.

Over the whole war, 5000 Allied and neutral ships totalling over 12,850,000 tons were sunk by German submarines, resulting in the deaths of nearly 15,000 sailors. Attacks on merchant ships began in October 1914 but only 19 ships had been sunk by February 1915 when the German government introduced the policy of unrestricted submarine warfare, namely the decision to attack merchant vessels without warning. Immediately, the loss rate rose to around two ships per day. In November 1915 the unrestricted warfare policy was withdrawn, mainly because of pressure on Germany from the United States and other neutral governments whose ships had been sunk. Nevertheless, in 1916, 416 merchant ships were sunk by submarines. Early in 1917 the German government reintroduced unrestricted submarine warfare, with the declared intention of bringing Britain to its knees by sinking 600,000 tons' worth of ships per month. This target was met each month from February to June, with the largest losses, of 881,000 tons, in April. In January 1917, 49 ships had been lost, but come March the monthly figure had reached 147.

Britain responded by introducing the convoy system in April and from July 1917 monthly losses never exceeded 500,000 tons. At the same time, German submarine losses sharply increased, with 69 being sunk in 1918. These unsustainable losses, combined with seriously demoralized German crews, brought the submarine campaign to an end. In all, 178 German submarines were sunk, 50 per cent of the fleet in use during the First World War, and 5000 sailors died. As a result of the vital role played by merchant ships in supporting Britain through the war, George V announced shortly afterwards that the Merchant Service would in future be known as the Merchant Navy.

The names of all the ships on which Walter served are not recorded, though the list includes the SS *Cawdor Castle*, a Union Castle Line vessel used as a troopship in 1914 and wrecked in 1926, and the SS *Mesaba*, a small liner on the transatlantic service sunk by a submarine in September

The SS *City of Corinth* photographed as it sinks on 21 May 1917, taken from one of the ship's lifeboats.

1918. During the four war years he visited most corners of the world and sailed round the globe twice. He took part in two convoys to Russia in 1917, transporting horses to the Russian army, and described how the crew had to work in freezing conditions to remove ice from the masts and superstructure to stop the ship capsizing. He also described dead horses being lifted from the hold by the ship's cranes and dumped over the side. Luckily, his ship survived those voyages.

However, his luck ran out on three occasions when his ship was torpedoed. On the first occasion, Walter was in the crow's nest repairing some wiring when the torpedo struck. The ship was sinking quickly so he slid down a steel cable from the mast to the bow area, badly burning his forearms and hands in the process. As the ship was coal-fired there was no oil contamination in the sea but survivors did get very black from the coal dust floating on the surface. In this case, he found the healing properties of salt water were beneficial to his burns.

The second sinking was on the SS *City of Corinth*, an Ellerman Line ship, when she was torpedoed by *UB-31* off the Lizard peninsula in Cornwall, nearing the end of a voyage from Singapore on 21 May 1917. The ship was sinking slowly so Walter stayed in the wireless cabin sending SOS messages for as long as he could. Eventually he realized he was the only person left on board, the rest of the crew having got away safely in the lifeboats. He was about to jump overboard when he remembered his new pet canary was in his cabin. He went down below to his cabin in which the water was now chest high, grabbed the canary in its wooden cage, made his way back to the deck and stepped off into the sea. The bamboo cage with its broad base floated perfectly in the calm sea so he swam away from the ship, towing it behind him. He was in the water for over eight hours and got increasingly tired. However, every time he started to doze off, the canary woke him by singing loudly. He was eventually rescued by a British ship that took him to London, where he got a lift back to his parents' house in Chelsea. He installed the canary there and it lived for another 13 years. During that time the bird remained completely silent, except when it heard Walter coming along the street towards the house, at which point it would sing its heart out.

The third occasion was on the SS *City of Cambridge*, another Ellerman Line ship, sunk in July 1917 by *U-17* off the coast of Algeria. Several crewmen were killed and the survivors were in the water for several hours, with sharks circling nearby, before they were rescued by another merchant ship.

Walter met his future wife one night in Cardiff, where he had disembarked from a ship, and they were married in October 1921. Walter had left the sea in 1918 and took up civil engineering, becoming a Member of the Institute of Civil Engineers, and worked as a surveyor for Denbighshire County Council. In 1949 he was appointed County Surveyor for Denbigh. He and his wife had two children and lived in the same house in Ruthin from 1933 until 1961. During the Second World War Walter joined the local Home Guard, finishing as Captain in charge of the 9th Battalion, Denbighshire Home Guard (Royal Welsh Fusiliers). He died in 1961, soon after his retirement.

Above: Frank Parker's letter to his wife from his prisoner-of-war camp, telling her he was alive. Opposite: Henry Parker with his wife and four sons, in about 1902. Frank is seated in the front row, centre.

A SOLDIER CAPTURED WHILE SAVING A WOUNDED PAL

FRANK PARKER
1893–1965

One of four sons, Frank Parker was born in Shoreham, Sussex, in July 1893. From about 1901 his father Henry owned a butcher's shop in Carshalton, Surrey, where all the sons also worked. Frank was the delivery boy, driving his father's horse and cart around the grand houses of the area, and developing a lifelong love of horses. This may have encouraged Frank to enlist in 1912 in the Surrey Yeomanry, then part of the Territorial Force. The regiment had its origins in the 18th century but had been established in a modern form in 1901, when it became known as the Queen's Own Surrey Yeomanry. Frank was attached to C Squadron, which was based at West Croydon.

'Our grandfather was a lovely and affectionate family man who rarely spoke about his wartime experiences but they had a profound effect on him. We were told never to complain about being hungry as we had no idea what it meant to be really hungry.'

BARBARA READER, GRANDDAUGHTER

Patient logbooks from the Lakeside Unit, Rouen,
maintained by Arthur Boyce.

A PADRE WORKING WITH THE AMERICANS

ARTHUR E. BOYCE
1879–1968

Military chaplains, popularly known as Padres, played a crucial role in the war, offering comfort, solace and advice as well as Christian support. The majority were Anglicans, but there were also plenty of Catholics and Methodists. Padres had officer status, wore uniforms but never carried arms.

While much of their work went on behind the lines, many regularly risked their lives in the trenches and in No Man's Land giving help and succour to wounded and dying soldiers. While their role was primarily spiritual, Padres also helped with letter writing and other practical and pastoral care problems faced by soldiers away from home. Some started social clubs, available to all ranks, the most famous being Talbot House, or Toc H, set up by the Reverend Tubby Clayton in Poperinge, near Ypres.

Arthur Boyce, born in December 1879, was one of six children who grew up in the East End of London. His father was in the grocery business. After school, he worked as a commercial clerk until 1911 when he became a Methodist minister. His first appointment was at Stoke Bruerne, Northamptonshire, working with canal families.

In 1917, believing that he could help those fighting for their country, Arthur enlisted as a Chaplain, and was attached to the 19th (2nd Tyneside Pioneers)

'My grandfather was a wise and thoughtful man but he had great charisma and people were drawn to him. He was a great listener and easy to be with. When I was small, we watched Test matches on the TV together. But he never talked about the war.'

DAVID SWEETNAM, GRANDSON

A PHOTOGRAPHER WITH THE ROYAL FLYING CORPS

WILLIAM CHARLES CAMBRAY
1894–1976

At the start of the First World War the Royal Flying Corps had five squadrons and just over 2000 personnel. At the end of the war the Royal Air Force, which had taken over the Royal Flying Corps and the Royal Naval Air Service from 1 April 1918, had 150 squadrons, 4000 combat aircraft and

114,000 personnel. This exponential growth had been not just in scale, but also in experience. In the early years that experience had been hard won by officers and men drawn from army regiments with little or no flying knowledge, but prepared to learn on the job or die in the process.

William Charles Cambray was born in November 1894, one of four children in a family from south London. By 1912 he was working as an insurance clerk. When war broke out he enlisted in the 2nd (City of London) Battalion of the London Regiment. He was in France early in 1915 and fought through much of 1915 and 1916 as a 2nd Lieutenant, including action in the Somme. In later life he described a typical Somme engagement: 'Our Company did

'Grandpa was modest, charming and a stickler for manners.
He was reluctant to talk about the war, though he did once say
to me "War is a really terrible thing. Anyone who hasn't
been in one will never know how terrible. But if everything
else fails, you have to fight for what you believe in."'

NICK CAMBRAY, GRANDSON

NO 20 SQUADRON RFC
FE2D A6516.

POSITION FOR FIRING BACK GUN AT HUN ATTACKING FRO
THE REAR.   ARMAMENT 3 LEWIS GUNS
                    1000 ROUND AMMUNITION
                      TRACER BULLETS ONE IN TH
        AND EIGHT 25 LB COOPERS BOMBS

Above, left: William Cambray's Military Cross, awarded in September
1917. Below: FE2d of 20 Squadron. This was the type of aircraft
William Cambray would have flown in as an observer, and shows the
observer's exposed position when firing to the rear.

one show where we went in with five officers and 160 men. In two days I brought out 31 men and myself. What a waste.'

Later in 1916 William transferred to the Royal Flying Corps (RFC) and qualified as an Observer/Gunner in June 1917. At this point many of the RFC front-line aircraft were two-seaters, underlining the traditional military view of the aeroplane as a reconnaissance and observation machine. He joined 20 Squadron, which was based at St Marie Capelle, near Cassel. This, one of the RFC's highest scoring squadrons, was then equipped with the FE2d, the latest in a family of two-seater aircraft first developed by the Royal Aircraft Factory from 1911. Thanks to the rear-mounted pusher propeller configuration, the observer in the front seat had an uninterrupted view and field of fire. The FE2d was well armed with forward- and rear-mounted machine guns, and it often did well in dogfights with German single-seater scouts and fighters. However, success – and survival – depended upon close cooperation between pilot and observer. William was lucky with his pilots. He first flew with Donald Cunnell, a pilot who became an ace before being killed in July 1917. On 31 May 1917 William had his first success, when he and Donald Cunnell destroyed an Albatros D.III. Five more followed by September 1917, with William flying with another ace pilot, Frank Stevens. His last came from the Observer's back seat in a Bristol Fighter. At a time when life expectancy was short, William and his pilots rode their luck, sometimes limping back to base in aircraft almost wrecked in dogfights. Later, he wrote: 'The life of a pilot and observer was one dogfight. If you came back from one, you were good for two more. If you still came back you were probably experienced enough to last six months, and be sent home to train others.' This is what happened, with William being sent back to England on 9 October 1917 to serve as an instructor. He did not return to combat and finally left the RAF in April 1919, with the rank of Lieutenant.

On 17 September 1917 William was awarded a Military Cross, 'For conspicuous gallantry and devotion to duty whilst acting as observer to offensive patrols. On four occasions, at least, he has shot down enemy scouts and has also had numerous indecisive combats, in all of which he has displayed the greatest gallantry.'

From an early point in his life, William was an enthusiastic photographer. He took photographs while in the army and continued in the RFC,

FRANCE 1915.

CLOUDS { } CLOUDS

GAS → ← GAS

13TH OCTOBER 1915. A REAL SOUVENIR PHOTO.
THE FIRST TIME THE BRITISH ARMY USED CHLORINE
GAS THE GAS IS BEING BLOWN TOWARDS THE
HUN LINES. WHITE CLOUDS ABOVE THE GAS

William's photograph of the first British use of chlorine gas,
showing the darker clouds of gas, below the white clouds,
being blown towards enemy lines.

although that was part of his job as an observer. The FE2d was equipped with a camera, and many of his missions will have been for reconnaissance purposes. However, he made the most of the high-quality cameras that he had access to, and amassed a large collection of official and unofficial photographs taken by him and many others. These date from 1915 onwards and, apart from capturing RFC life, they depict trench lines, mine craters, ruined villages and, in one case, the first use of gas by the British, seen from the air. When he left the RAF, William managed to hang on to his photographs and he later mounted them in albums, preserving what had become by then a collection of considerable historical interest, so much so that the RAF Museum copied them all in the 1970s.

After the war William married Gladys and they had two sons. In the Second World War he rejoined the army for a while, was discharged and then worked as an Air Raid Warden. Following a period with a building company, William emigrated to Queensland, Australia, where he died in 1976.

A SOLDIER SAVED BY HIS BIBLE

WILFRID NORMAN BUSH
1884–1960

Wilfrid Norman Bush was born into a large family in the St Philips area of Bristol in August 1884. His father was a policeman who later worked as a sanitary inspector. He went to school in Bedminster, then went to work at the Golden Valley paper mills in Bitton, where he was to remain, war service apart, for 44 years. In 1909, after a five-year courtship, he married

Mary Ann Sanders, a local girl he had met at church, and they had two children. Early in 1917 Wilfrid received his call-up papers and enlisted as a Private in the 7th Battalion of the Somerset Light Infantry.

With a history stretching back to the 17th century, the regiment, which acquired its Somerset attachment in the late 18th century, had taken part in many important campaigns and battles, including the Napoleonic Wars, the First Afghan War, the Crimea and South Africa. It also had a long association with India. In 1912 the regiment's name was changed to Prince Albert's (Somerset Light Infantry). During the First World War the regiment was greatly expanded, and its battalions fought on the Western Front, in Mesopotamia and in Palestine. Wilfrid's battalion, the 7th, was a Service battalion for the New Army, formed in September 1914. It landed in France in July 1915.

Wilfrid went to France in March 1917, initially to Etaples for training, and he was with the battalion on the Somme in June 1917. After a brief

'My grandfather died when I was 11. He was a quiet man who loved his garden, always good to me, but the war had changed him. I know he thought about his pals who never made it.'

DAVID BUSH, GRANDSON

period of leave, he was back with the battalion in time for its move north to the Ypres area, as part of the preparations for the Third Battle of Ypres.

By September 1917, a continuing sequence of separate battles had turned Ypres into a desolate wasteland of mud and broken trees, scattered with flooded shell holes, and every day the conditions worsened, as the battle continued to rage. By October and November, this had become the dreadful setting for the Passchendaele battles.

A religious man, Wilfrid always carried a bible in his breast pocket. One day that September, Wilfrid was hit in the chest by two bullets, which knocked him off the duckboard and into a water-filled shell hole, where he nearly drowned. He was rescued that night, under cover of darkness, unconscious but still alive, because both bullets had hit the bible in his pocket. One was stopped by it, and the other, deflected, passed through his collarbone. Wilfrid was carried back to a dressing station, and from there he went to a base hospital where in due course he made a full recovery. He was then declared too old, at 33, for front-line service and so was returned to Britain, to spend the rest of the war guarding German prisoners of war at Bovingdon camp in Dorset.

For the rest of his life, Wilfrid felt that he had been more than lucky, often saying that the Lord had looked after him that day. He was a big man, 16 stone and over 6 feet tall, a talented amateur musician who played the organ in several Bristol churches, including St Mary Redcliffe, and he was also a very keen gardener and an enthusiastic motorcyclist. He liked his pipe and, while in the army, had learned the trick of sleeping anywhere, at any time. After the war, he returned to the paper mill and worked there until his retirement in 1947. He died in March 1960. David, his grandson, remembers him saying, more than once, 'anyone who takes part in a war is a casualty'.

The bullet-damaged bible that saved Wilfrid Bush's life in September 1917 at Ypres.

A SOLDIER SAVED BY A WHISTLE

JOSEPH THOMAS CLUCAS
1895–1917

In November 1895, Joseph Thomas Clucas, generally known as Joe, was born in the Toxteth area of Liverpool, the eldest of five children. His father John was a policeman who became an 'Inspector of Nuisances' (what would

now be an environmental health officer). Joe was a bright lad, winning a prize in a national essay competition organized by the RSPCA, and a gold medal for four years' unbroken attendance at school. He was musical and played the concertina.

In about 1908 his father joined the 3rd West Lancashire Brigade of the newly formed Territorial Force, and it seems Joe did too. His father became a Quartermaster Sergeant and served until 1916 but did not go overseas. Joe seems to have left the army for a while and then re-enlisted in 1913, by which time his brigade was part of

the Royal Field Artillery. He was in France in time to take part in some of the battles of 1914, earning himself in the process the 1914, or Mons, Star. His military record is incomplete but he was mentioned in dispatches.

In 1915, while taking part in an attack, he was struck by a bullet which was deflected by his whistle. The damaged whistle, which clearly saved Joe's life,

'For the family he was always Our Joe, a nice lad who
did well at school, always there for everyone, the apple of
his father's eye, and loved by his girl. For me,
he has become a real person, someone to be proud of.'

FLO CLUCAS, NIECE BY MARRIAGE

is treasured today by his family. By 1916 he had been promoted to Corporal, though he was briefly demoted to Gunner following a disciplinary offence. A Corporal once again, he served in the Ypres area in 1916, sending home postcards which mention Givenchy and La Bassée, famous names from earlier battles. In 1917 Joe, by then engaged to Hilda Burgess, was with the Ammunition Column of the 57th Division. He took part in the later part of the Third Battle of Ypres, or Passchendaele as it is better known. This battle, notorious for its longevity, high number of casualties and the dreadful fighting conditions caused by mud and rain, had started in the summer of 1917. The decision to mount a major offensive in Ypres in that latter part of 1917 was contentious at the time, and has always remained so. By late October, the conditions were at their worst and it was then, on 21 October 1917, that Corporal Joseph Clucas was wounded while he struggled to get ammunition to the guns, as part of the preparations for the final battle of Passchendaele, which started on 26 October 1917. As he was being taken to a dressing station, a shell killed him and his stretcher-bearers. In a letter to his family, Joe's Commanding Officer said that he 'was one of the finest young men in the brigade'. His body was never found and his name is listed on the Memorial to the Missing at Tyne Cot cemetery in Belgium.

Joe's mother never recovered from his death, and died herself soon after. In 1928 John Clucas visited Tyne Cot, to see his son's name. More recently, Flo Clucas and her husband took their two grandchildren, aged nine and eleven, on a tour of Ypres sites, which ended at Tyne Cot. They were shocked to see Joe's name but said that having a relative there 'was quite something'.

The bullet-damaged whistle that saved
Joseph Clucas's life.

Willie Hancock. His brother, George, was with him when he died on 26 August 1915. They were both serving as rangefinders in the Machine Gun Corps.

A SOLDIER WHO WAS WITH HIS BROTHER WHEN HE WAS KILLED

GEORGE TREVOR HANCOCK
1896–1978

A Welsh boy who joined up alongside his brother and some friends, George Trevor Hancock was born in Pontypridd, South Wales, in October 1896. His father Charles was Clerk to the County Court in Porth, in the Rhondda, and had four children. After attending the Pontypridd Boys Intermediate School, later the Grammar School, George and his older brother Willie, together with a group of friends, joined the 1/5th Battalion of the Welch Regiment, part of the Territorial Force. This battalion had been formed in Pontypridd in August 1914. After training and local defence duties, the 1/5th Battalion joined the 1/4th, and together they left Devonport on 15 July 1915, en route to the Dardanelles, and landed at Suvla Bay on 9 August. The brothers had already been allocated to the Machine Gun Corps attached to the Welch Regiment, and trained as rangefinders, whose job was to identify targets for the machine-gun team

and establish the correct range. They were immediately in action, joining an offensive that aimed to break through the Turkish lines via a flanking operation near Chocolate Hill. This was unsuccessful but the fighting

'After the war my uncle and aunt led a comfortable life.
They had no children and so we, his four nephews, were indulged
at times. My uncle suffered from periods of melancholy and
so it was difficult talking about his war experiences.
But he bore no animosity to his old enemies.'

DAVID HANCOCK, NEPHEW

continued through August 1915 as the Allies tried to break the stalemate of trench warfare.

On 26 August 1915 Willie, while carrying out an order to find the range of a target, was shot in the head by a sniper and killed. George, just a few yards away, knew his brother had died.

Although a regular writer of long and detailed letters home, George did not mention his brother's death, and his feelings of devastation, for another six weeks and then only because his mother, having received the official notification of her son's death, wanted more details:

> He (Willie) went round a traverse in the trench to take the range. He was only about fifteen yards away. About three minutes after he had gone, he came back. I can see him now in his khaki shirt sleeves smiling as he nearly always was and said 'that was a near shave'. I asked him what had happened and he said one of those snipers had spotted him and had blown up a cloud of dust in front of his eyes. I tried to persuade him from going back to that spot but he wouldn't listen although I knew quite well he knew how dangerous it was. He just said 'it will be alright, I will be back in a minute' and went again to finish the task. He had hardly gone a minute when a shot cracked very near and then I heard the Sergeant shout 'stretcher'. Something told me immediately that it was Willie so I ran round the traverse but I was too late to say anything to him. The bullet had penetrated his brain and death was instantaneous ... The grave was dug in front of the firing line ... I was very sorry that we could not get hold of a Chaplain to read the burial service ... but you can rest assured he was buried very reverently.

Meanwhile, the fighting continued until the whole campaign ground to a halt in December 1915. George, by then the only survivor of the group of friends who had joined up together, was evacuated to Egypt on 12 December 1915. He was to remain in Egypt until October 1916, by which time he had been promoted to Quartermaster.

In April 1917 George was selected for officer training and was commissioned as a 2nd Lieutenant into the Heavy Section of the Machine Gun Corps. Little understood by the British army at the start of the war, the importance of the machine gun was soon appreciated and the Machine

Gun Corps came into being in October 1915, with Infantry, Cavalry and Motor Sections. In March 1916 the Heavy Section, associated with large and armoured vehicles, was set up and it was men from this section who crewed the first tanks to go into action in September 1916. Following the rapid growth in the use of tanks, the Heavy Section was detached from the Machine Gun Corps in July 1917 to become the Tank Corps, later the Royal Tank Regiment. When George arrived in France in August 1917 he was, therefore, one of the first generation of tank commanders in the newly formed Tank Corps.

In November George took part in the Battle of Cambrai. This offensive against the German Hindenburg Line exploited new artillery and infantry tactics, including large numbers of tanks, and was initially successful. However, effective German counter-attacks meant that progress was much slower after the first day and, when the battle ended on 7 December, Allied gains were quite limited. Tank tactics were still in their infancy, and many were lost or rendered inoperable by the nature of the terrain and firm German defence. However, lessons were learned, and from this point the tank became a much more effective attack and infantry support weapon.

George fought with his tank all the way through from Cambrai to the end of the war and was demobilized in 1919 with the rank of Lieutenant. He came back to Britain to take up accountancy, working for the same firm of accountants until his retirement in 1961. He married his childhood sweetheart, Doris Phillips, but they had no children.

Although reluctant to talk about the war, George did occasionally refer to his time as a Tanks Corps officer, perhaps aware of his nephew's interest in things mechanical. David remembers asking him why tanks carried a large bundle of sticks on top, and was told they were released into trenches to support the tank as it crossed over. George explained that the 5-ton bundles (called fascines) could only be released by one of the crew climbing on top of the tank, in full view of the enemy. He always carried out this dangerous chore himself because he did not want to ask his crew to take such a risk.

In 2008 David and two of his brothers went to the Gallipoli battlefields, where their uncle Willie had been killed, and visited his grave in Green Hill Cemetery, near Suvla Bay. They spread some soil from the garden of the family home in Pontypridd around the grave.

Geoffrey Carr's Will, written when he returned to active service, before the Third Battle of Gaza in November 1917.

A SOLDIER WHO DID MORE MARCHING THAN FIGHTING IN PALESTINE

GEOFFREY CARR
1886–1969

Geoffrey Carr was born in 1886 in west London. His father, John Baker Carr, was a stockbroker who drank and gambled away his wife's money. After leaving school Geoffrey worked for a firm of accountants. A keen sportsman, he won a silver medal for coxed fours in the rowing in the 1912 Olympic Games in Stockholm and was a member of a rifle club. Soon after this, in 1913, he married Maud and they went on to have three children. Geoffrey's interest in shooting may have led him towards the Territorial Forces, for on the outbreak of war he enlisted in the 5th Battalion of the Seaforth Highlanders. This had been formed in Golspie in August 1914. Later that year the 5th Battalion moved south to Bedford for training and then landed in France on 2 May 1915. A few days later it was attached to the

152nd Brigade in the 51st Highland Division, and was soon in action.

However, Private Geoffrey Carr was not with them. Shortly before the battalion's departure for France he had developed appendicitis, and was

'My grandfather didn't talk much about the war but he had plenty of amusing anecdotes. He always refused to eat oranges as they were never as good as the ones he had had in Palestine and he kept a piece of shrapnel that tore his shirt, but missed him.'

ANDY PROBYN, GRANDSON

sent back to the depot hospital in Golspie for a major operation. He was not fully recovered until the end of 1915. Meanwhile, he had followed his battalion's progress, and wrote in his diary: 'My old company had a horrible cutting up at Festubert [15 May to 25 May]. They left their trenches 140 strong and had 97 casualties in a few minutes. Only five of my platoon came back unwounded, and many of the good friends I made at Bedford are dead.' There is little doubt that the appendicitis saved Geoffrey's life.

After his recovery, Geoffrey was commissioned as a 2nd Lieutenant in the Isle of Wight Rifles. This, properly known as the 8th (Territorial) Battalion, the Hampshire Regiment, Princess Beatrice's Isle of Wight Rifles, had been formed out of various volunteer corps set up to protect the Isle of Wight from the risk of invasion from France. Mobilized in 1914, they were sent after training to the Dardanelles. When that campaign ended they were sent to Egypt. In February 1917 the battalion marched across the Sinai desert, covering 145 miles in 12 days. Next came the first two largely unsuccessful battles of Gaza.

Geoffrey arrived in time to take part in the successful Third Battle of Gaza early in November 1917, where he received a minor shrapnel wound, but fought on as Acting Captain when his Commanding Officer was wounded. The Allied armies, with significant Australian, New Zealand and Indian contingents, and under the command of General Allenby, advanced steadily across Palestine, fighting a continuous series of battles and engagements. However, Geoffrey commented that there was much more marching than fighting, with the whole campaign being fought on foot. The Allies won an important victory on 13 November 1917 at the Battle of Mughar Ridge, forcing the German and Turkish forces to retreat and thus opening the way to Jerusalem, which was finally captured by Allenby's forces on 30 December 1917. Geoffrey wrote entertainingly about the sights of Palestine: 'The women walk, carrying very large loads on their heads. There appears to be no limit to the load of a woman or a donkey. The men seldom carry anything.' He also noted that elders in the Jewish community complained about Allied soldiers wearing shorts as they did not want their young women to gaze upon so many masculine knees.

The capture of Beirut followed, leaving the British in control of Palestine and the French looking after Syria, following the terms of the Sykes–Picot

Geoffrey Carr (left) in Palestine around 1918.
The binoculars around his neck remain in the family today.

Agreement of May 1916. After the capture of Beirut and Damascus the Austrian and Turkish forces surrendered. However, the negotiations to settle the Armistice with Germany took longer and Geoffrey described the moment that Brigade Headquarters announced that it had been signed:

> Just before dinner Verey lights went up from Brigade HQ and it was taken up by all the camps around. Soon the air was full of Verey lights, red, white and green. The Machine Gunners took a lot of guns on the beach and opened fire out to sea. Soon the trench mortar battery joined in, they of course made the most noise. It was a mighty din! There was a rum ration for the men, headquarters mess produced a case of champagne and with that and other things we celebrated the end of the war in a becoming manner.

After demobilization, Geoffrey Carr returned to accountancy, becoming chartered in the early 1930s. He died in 1969.

Top: A letter sent to Thomas Preston by his sister Beatrice, which was returned with 'Killed in Action', confirming the family's knowledge of his death. Bottom: Gary Noden (kneeling, centre) and other members of the 8th Battallion, before they were sent to the front.

DEATH IN ACTION CONFIRMED BY A RETURNED LETTER

THOMAS PRESTON
1898–1917

The ninth of 11 children, Thomas Preston was born in March 1898 into a large family living in Winsford, Cheshire, where his father Joel worked in the local salt mines. Thomas went to the local school, and sang in the choir at St Chad's Church. After leaving school, he joined his father in the salt mines. In March 1916 he enlisted in the Cheshire Regiment, transferring at the end of August to the 8th Battalion of the King's Own (Royal Lancaster Regiment).

This famous regiment had a long history stretching back to the 17th century. It fought at Culloden, through the Napoleonic Wars, in the Crimea and in South Africa, taking part in the Relief of Ladysmith. The 8th Battalion was raised locally in October 1914 from volunteers responding to Lord Kitchener's appeal for 100,000 new soldiers, one of many Service battalions for this New Army. Arriving in France in September 1915, the 8th Battalion was then to fight on the Western Front for the rest of the war. First in action in March 1916, the battalion took part in the later phases of the Somme campaign, fighting at Delville Wood, Guillemont and Serre.

Thomas joined the battalion on 28 December 1916 and fought at the Battle of Arras in April 1917. Later that year, the 8th Battalion moved north, to the Ypres sector, as part of the preparations for the Third Battle of Ypres,

'I can't read his letters today, it is so upsetting, thinking what they had to go through. My great-uncle was a very, very quiet chap who had never left Cheshire until he went to France.'

GARY NODEN, GREAT-NEPHEW

which was launched at the end of July 1917. This infamous battle dragged on through the summer months and into the autumn of 1917 as the Allies struggled to gain ground from the Germans. There were several phases to the battle, which culminated in the mud and desolation of Passchendaele. By the latter part of September the focus was on Zonnebeke and Polygon Wood, and it was here, on 26 September 1917, that Private Thomas Preston was killed.

Throughout his time in the army, Thomas had written regularly to his sister Beatrice, to whom he was particularly close, and 20 of his letters are still with his great-nephew today. Though he didn't say much, they reveal that he was homesick and missing his family. He sent one of the standard army postcards pre-printed with statements for soldiers to tick on 19 September with the added message, 'I'm fairly well.' His last letter home was posted on 26 September. Beatrice also wrote regularly to him and her last letter, full of family news and containing three Woodbine cigarettes, was posted on 27 September. It is not certain when the family received notification of Thomas's death but there was a short article about him in the local paper on 17 October, which quoted a letter from his platoon Lieutenant: 'I deeply regret to inform you that your son was killed in action on the 26th September. It was whilst we were waiting for the signal to advance that a shell burst in the trench, causing many casualties in your son's platoon. His death was instantaneous. Your son was a staunch and brave lad and his loss is much felt by officers and men.' A couple of days later Beatrice's letter was returned to her, complete with the cigarettes, and with the envelope overwritten in red, Killed in Action, next of kin informed. It is all too easy to imagine the distress caused by the arrival of this letter back in Winsford.

Two of Thomas's brothers, Bill and Fred, fought with the Royal Artillery, but survived. Another brother, Labon, died in the Spanish influenza epidemic just after the war. Beatrice married after the war but died in childbirth in 1921. Her son, Gary Noden's father, survived and was brought up by Beatrice's sister.

Thomas Preston is buried in Perth Cemetery (China Wall) near Zillebeke, a couple of miles from Ypres town centre. A few years ago, Gary, his great-nephew, went to see the grave. 'I was probably the first member of the family to visit him,' he said. 'It was something I needed to do.'

POACHER TURNED GAMEKEEPER – FROM GERMAN INFANTRY TO BRITISH MEDICAL OFFICER

STEPHAN KURT WESTMANN
1893–1964

In July 1893 Stephan Kurt Westmann was born in Berlin, into a Jewish family with a long association with the medical world, although his father, Louis, owned a hat factory. Stephan was studying medicine at the University of Freiburg when he received his call-up papers for the German army early in 1914. The principle at that point was that medical students would serve as infantry for half the year and train as medical officers the other half, serving with a regiment based in or near a university town so studies could continue. All this changed with the outbreak of war and Stephan, serving with the Freiburg Infantry Regiment No. 113, found himself immediately in the thick of the action, initially in the Alsace-Lorraine region. He was with the infantry for the first year of the war, fighting largely against the French at various Western Front locations.

He soon became a non-commissioned officer (NCO) and, as a patrol leader, he was awarded an Iron Cross 2nd Class for an action near Baccarat, during the fierce fighting in Alsace. He was also sent briefly to the Eastern Front,

'My grandfather was one of life's high achievers. My father called his indomitable spirit and energy Churchillian. I can remember playing chess with my grandfather at his home, though he died when I was eight. He was a kindly man but he spoke English with a German accent one could cut with a knife.'

MICHAEL WESTMAN, GRANDSON

where the fighting and the conditions were often far worse than anything in the usual experience of soldiers on the Western Front. His memoires, published in the 1960s, reveal all the horrors of trench warfare, but from a German perspective.

After a year of fighting with the infantry, Stephan was given a commission as a medical officer. For the next three years, he was attached to various regiments and other units and took part in many of the major battles in various parts of the Western Front, including Ypres, along with the German Spring Offensive of March 1918. In 1917 he was given special training in the treatment of soldiers injured in gas attacks, and there are graphic accounts of his experiences in this field of warfare in his memoires.

> My advanced first-aid station near Hill 60 (which the Germans called the Kemmel) in the Ypres salient was in a small dug-out, reached through a deep valley. German and British casualties filled this valley which was suddenly bombarded with gas shells by the enemy ... the fumes started to drift in our direction and the gas alarm was given. After putting on our gas masks we found that most of the British had thrown theirs away. We had a few to spare but not nearly enough for all the British so we packed them like sardines in our dug-out and closed up the entrance with blankets and greatcoats. Several improvised tubes which we had fitted with gas filters were pushed into the space as breathing tubes. To seal the entrance we wetted it with the only liquid at our disposal, namely urine.
>
> After about half an hour, a breeze sprang up and drove the poisonous gas away. We removed the blankets and greatcoats with heavy hearts, fearing that our British guests would have suffocated, but they were all alive and none the worse for their incarceration.

Medical officers in all armies routinely looked after and treated all injured soldiers that came under their care, regardless of whether they were their own or enemy soldiers. The principles of medical practice were generally stronger than nationalism; however, as his memoires make clear, Stephan was a fervent supporter of the German cause, blaming the French, the Russians and the British for starting the war. Even so, he was aware of the sense of chivalry and respect that often existed between the fighting soldiers of rival armies whose defined task was to kill each other.

That same year, 1917, Stephan was awarded an Iron Cross 1st Class. He served with infantry battalions and artillery batteries on the front line, was attached to military hospitals, ran hospital trains and at one time was attached to the German Air Force, serving as medical officer to Manfred von Richthofen's squadron.

After the war, Stephan returned to Berlin and qualified as a doctor, specializing in gynaecology. He married Marianna Goldschmidt, a pioneering woman doctor, and they had three children. Later, he became Professor of Obstetrics at the Berlin Postgraduate Medical School, enjoying a reputation as a charismatic public speaker. However, as an outspoken anti-Nazi who refused to keep his mouth shut, he was soon in trouble and he received a tip-off from Marlene Dietrich, who was one of his clients, that he was about to be arrested. He fled to Britain in April 1933 with his second wife, their five-year-old son and the children from his first marriage, who adopted English names, Elizabeth, Anne and Tom, in order to fit into their new environment. He made his way to Edinburgh, where he trained again as a doctor in order to acquire British medical qualifications and then set up in practice in London's Harley Street, ultimately achieving eminence in his field. Living in Hampstead in north London, and craving an intellectual life amid an alien culture and language, he kept in touch with other leading Germans who had fled to Britain, including Albert Einstein, the architect Walter Gropius and the pianist Artur Schnabel. His son remembers, as a child, seeing Schnabel accompanying Stephan and some friends while they sang German drinking songs.

During the Second World War Stephan, who had by then changed his name to Stephen Westman and been baptized into the Church of England, ran an army hospital near Glasgow, with the honorary rank of Colonel. His three older children served in the RAF, with both girls involved in secret activities. Stephen died in October 1964 at his home in Chorleywood, Hertfordshire.

The Iron Cross 1st Class awarded to
Stephan Westmann in 1917.

1918

ON THE WESTERN FRONT, THE KEY EVENT OF THE YEAR WAS the German Spring Offensive. Launched in March, Operation Michael was designed to split the French and British armies. Planned by General Ludendorff, it was a desperate last attempt by Germany to win the war before overwhelming numbers of American troops arrived in action.

Thanks to new tactics, including the use of trained stormtroopers, the attacks were initially successful, driving the Allies back. However, a fierce fighting retreat by rapidly assembled reinforcements, including fresh Australian and Canadian forces, eventually stopped the German advance, which had already been slowed by its own lack of supplies. Further German offensives followed in the north, around Ypres, and in the south towards Paris but they were all stopped by the Allies. By July, the German offensive was over, and the German army had suffered irreplaceable losses.

From 8 August, the Allies, with around 350,000 troops and 532 tanks, attacked over a long front, using modern tactics learned from the Germans, and combining successfully for the first time ground and air forces. In what Ludendorff called 'the German army's blackest day' the Allies opened a nine-mile gap in the German line and forced the German armies into a retreat that was destined never to stop.

This was the start of the 100 days, a continuous, hard-fought and steadily advancing battle that ended with Germany's surrender on 11 November 1918. By then, the Allied and American armies were on the borders of Germany. Deprivation and hardship caused by years of the Royal Navy blockade of Germany had provoked civil and political turmoil and, by the time the Armistice had been signed, the German Emperor had fled the country.

The weeks that preceded the Armistice with Germany had seen a widespread collapse of the Central Powers. Separate peace settlements had taken Turkey, Austro-Hungary and Bulgaria out of the war, bringing to an end after centuries of power the Ottoman and Austro-Hungarian empires.

Stories in this chapter document both the German Spring Offensive and the Allied advance, along with campaigns in Mesopotamia and Palestine. At the same time, there are accounts of a meeting with an Official War Artist, the death of the Red Baron, the Zeebrugge Raid and the celebration of the Armistice. More personal are stories that show the effects, both immediate and enduring, of the experience of the war on soldiers and members of their families. Some of these make it all too clear why those that survived generally never talked about the things they had seen and experienced.

Telegrams:—" Navy Accounts, London."

In any further communication on this
subject, please quote
No. 9 N.P.
and address letter to—
The Accountant General of the Navy,
Admiralty,
London, S.W.

Admiralty,

19 January 1918

Madam,

I regret to have to inform you that *Ernest John Hunt, Petty Officer,*
Official Number *241909* , has lost his life on duty.

(2) For your confidential information I have to state that
the Submarine in which he was serving is reported as being
considerably overdue, and it is feared that there can be no
doubt that the vessel has sunk with all on board.

(3) It is of the utmost importance that the Enemy shall not
become aware of this loss at present, and I have therefore to
ask you to be so good as to assist in keeping the knowledge
of it from the Enemy by refraining from inserting any notice
in the Press, except in the following form:

> "Lost his life on duty while in one of
> H.M. Ships on War Service, *Ernest John
> Hunt, Petty Officer. Rn*"

(4) Any application which the next-of-kin or legal represe-
ntative may have to make in consequence of the foregoing
information should be made by letter addressed to the
Accountant-General of the Navy, Admiralty, S.W.1, *except
applications relative to pension which should be addressed
as directed in the attached leaflet.*
I am, Madam,
Your obedient Servant.

A.E. Bramie

Accountant-General
of the Navy.

*Mrs Harriet Hunt.
C/o Mr J. Mungean,
North Halling,
Rochester, Kent*

The Admiralty letter announcing the death of Ernest John Hunt, and
instructing his wife not to reveal that he had died on a submarine.

A SAILOR LOST IN A SUBMARINE HE SHOULD NOT HAVE BEEN ON

ERNEST JOHN HUNT
1886–1918

Ernest John Hunt was born in 1886 in south London. His father was a stonemason and his mother was in service, but little is known about the family, except that he had brothers, who also served in the First World War. In 1901 Ernest went into the Royal Navy, and trained on HMS *Impregnable* at Devonport. His first ships were the battlecruiser HMS *Lion* and the battleship HMS *Hannibal*, in 1902.

Over the next few years Ernest seems to have spent most of his time on shore in training establishments such as HMS *Pembroke* at Chatham and HMS *Vernon*, the torpedo training base set up in 1876. He spent little time at sea, serving only briefly on two cruisers, HMS *Shannon* in 1908 and HMS *St George* in 1910. The outbreak of war found Ernest, by now a Petty Officer, shore-based and this seems to have continued into 1915, when he was attached to HMS *Dolphin*, the submarine depot and training establishment at Gosport. His next posting was to HMS *Alecto*, the submarine depot ship based at Chatham and it seems that by 1916 or 1917 Ernest was serving on submarines.

Ernest married in 1915, and in December 1917 he was at home on leave with his wife Harriet when his daughter was born – something extremely

'He was lost so soon after the birth of his daughter, my mother, and I'm so sorry she didn't have him in her life. And I had no grandfather. He was a gentle man, he used to copy out poetry and the navy meant so much to him. I'm proud of him.'

ANGELA DEVLIN, GRANDDAUGHTER

unusual for men in the services at that time. Soon after, he returned to the depot, HMS *Alecto*, and on 6 January 1918 he sailed with the submarine HMS *H10* for a patrol off the Dutch coast.

In the First World War British submarines had numbers with a class prefix, but no names. HMS *H10* was one of a large class of submarine designed to be used for mine-laying in enemy waters and for attacking enemy submarines. They were small ships able to operate in coastal waters, and the class had been brought into service from 1915. The crew of 26 lived in a very small and cramped space, but the *H*-class submarines were efficient in operation and popular with their crews. They saw action all round Britain and in the Adriatic. The first ten of the class were built in Montreal, Canada and then brought across the Atlantic. The second batch of ten was built in the United States and the final batch of 23 was built in British yards. *H10* was the last of the first, Canadian-built batch, commissioned in June 1915: accompanied by five other *H*-class submarines and escorted by a cruiser, she set off from Halifax on 22 July and arrived at Devonport 13 days later. She then transferred to Great Yarmouth as part of HMS *Alecto*'s submarine flotilla and her first patrol was in September 1915. She was in action again in 1916, and carried out a patrol from 27 to 31 December 1917. It is possible that Ernest was serving on *H10* from late 1915 but little is known about his record at this point.

H10 sailed again on 6 January 1918 to cruise northwest of Vlieland. The scheduled return date for *H10* was 14 January 1918, but the submarine did not return from her patrol, and nothing was ever heard from her. By 19 January the Admiralty accepted that *H10* had been lost but the cause was never known. She might have hit a mine, or been sunk through an accident or mechanical problem. There were no enemy activities on her route and the Germans never claimed to have sunk the submarine.

H10's Captain was Lieutenant Martin Huntly Collier, a popular man well known for his sporting accomplishments, particularly in boxing. According to a contemporary report he was: 'a real, clean, Christian gentleman ... and the example he set of simple, manly religion greatly impressed the officers and men not only of his own crew but of the whole depot'. He died, along with the other 25 members of his crew, which included Ernest Hunt. However, Ernest was not even meant to be there. On 9 January 1918 a letter had been sent to Ernest by the Admiralty informing him that he was to be promoted to Gunner and Warrant Officer, and instructing him to proceed to the HMS *Acteon*, a shore establishment at Portsmouth linked to HMS *Vernon*. This letter arrived at his house after he had sailed on *H10*'s final patrol.

The next thing his wife heard was another letter from the Admiralty, dated 19 January 1918, informing her that Ernest had been lost: 'there can be no doubt that the vessel has sunk with all on board'. This letter also instructed her firmly that she was not to reveal in any way that her husband had been lost on a submarine, in case this knowledge reached the enemy. She was only to say that he had: 'Lost his life on

Ernest John Hunt in one of the many photographs of himself at sea that he sent to his wife during the war.

duty in one of HM Ships on War Service'. There was a memorial service but Harriet was unable to attend because of her new baby.

In June 1918 a final letter from the Admiralty informed her that, as her husband had been promoted with effect from 12 December 1917, she was entitled to a larger pension, as befitted his new rank. It is easy to forget that families not only had to come to terms with the loss of loved ones, but also had to deal with often quite complex paperwork relating to pensions, salary payments and even outstanding mess bills. Ernest Hunt's name is listed among the 8515 commemorated on the Chatham Naval Memorial.

Harriet Hunt moved to Kent with her two children and bought a small house, where she was to live for the rest of her life, supported by her husband's pensions. She never remarried, and lived until 1982 with the knowledge that her husband's death had been caused by the Admiralty not sending his promotion letter in time.

A DOCTOR'S PAINTING FROM MESOPOTAMIA

RICHARD WILLIAM MATHEWSON
1890–1976

Born in July 1890 into a Presbyterian family associated with the linen industry in Scotland, Richard William Mathewson, always known as Dick, attended medical school in Edinburgh. When he qualified in 1917, he

went straight into the Royal Army Medical Corps.

Dick was posted to Mesopotamia (now modern-day Iraq), and attached to field hospitals in the Basra area, Baghdad having been captured in March 1917. Promoted to Captain, he was very involved with the fighting in that region and on a number of occasions hospitals had to be packed up at short notice and moved with teams of mules.

In March 1918 Richard came across B. H. Wiles, an Official War Artist, at work painting a watercolour of the land bridge at Nineveh. Knowing the scene well, he bought the painting on the spot, and asked Wiles if he would post it to his parents in Edinburgh as a present. He omitted to tell his parents anything about this arrangement, however, so when the painting arrived at their house without any prior warning, they were understandably mystified and contacted the artist directly.

'I feel as though I know Dick as the family, who have always been proud of him, often talk about him. And I love the painting because it makes me feel so calm.'

CHRIS HYLAND, STEP-GRANDDAUGHTER

Watercolour of the land bridge at Nineveh, by B. H. Wiles (1918).
The painting remains in the care of Richard Mathewson's
step-granddaughter today.

Wiles duly wrote to them, in December 1919:

I am sorry no documentation was forthcoming about the watercolour sketch you received from me. Capt Mathewson RAMC asked me to do it for you and send it before Xmas as a present to you and the family. I met him in March last year when I was painting for the War Museum and this sketch is of the land bridge at Ninevah with the Kurdistan hills in the background. The middle distance being where Ninevah was. I heard from Captain Mathewson a few months ago, he seems to have been in the thick of it. I hope you like the sketch, it is very slight, the only way I found to treat the subject.

I should be obliged if you could inform Capt Mathewson that the picture has arrived safely.

After serving in Mesopotamia, Mathewson was posted to Kurdistan and then he became involved in the transport of sick and injured soldiers back to Britain. Later, he moved to India, fell in love with the country, became a medical missionary and then bought an eye practice in Delhi. In 1920 he moved back to Britain with his family, bringing with him an Indian nanny, whom he educated. He died in March 1976. His two brothers, George and Kenneth, were both killed in action in France.

The Allied campaign against the Ottoman forces in Mesopotamia started in November 1914 and officially ended on 30 October 1918 with the signing of the Treaty of Mudros, although the British army carried on fighting until Mosul fell in November. The British relied heavily on Indian troops, with Australian support, and over the four years of the war around 400,000 troops were drawn into Mesopotamia, of which 92,000 became casualties. British interests in western Asia were based on the Sykes–Picot Agreement of May 1916 by which the French controlled Syria and Lebanon, and the British Palestine and Mesopotamia, an arrangement, later ratified by the League of Nations, that established the modern countries and their borders in that region.

From 1918 the British were drawn into attempts by the Kurds to set up an independent Kurdish state. Between 1919 and 1924, there were several Kurdish revolts that brought the British army and, increasingly, the Royal

Air Force into action. In fact, the RAF was given the task of subduing the Kurds, and did so by frequent bombing and machine-gunning of tribes and villages deemed to be rebellious.

The war artists scheme, whereby the British government commissioned artists to depict many aspects of the war, was established in 1916. Initially under the umbrella of propaganda departments, it became part of the Department of Information from 1917. Early members of the scheme included Muirhead Bone, William Orpen, C. R. Nevinson and Paul Nash, but later it came to include hundreds of artists, from well-established figures such as John Singer Sargent and Sir John Lavery to unknowns straight from art school, in an effort to cover all campaign areas and services, industry and the Home Front. As such, it became a remarkable example of government sponsorship of the arts. Artists employed by the scheme were given nominal army ranks and enjoyed considerable freedom of movement and choice of subject, in order to depict all aspects of modern conflict. War artists were contractually obliged to offer their work first to their government employers before anything could be sold independently, and in Dr Mathewson's case, Wiles did a second version for the government. The Imperial War Museum, set up in 1917, was tasked by the government with looking after the collections of works produced by war artists. Over 350 artists who worked during the First World War are represented in the War Museum's collections, including many women. Similar schemes operated in Canada and Australia.

There are four watercolours by B. H. Wiles in the collection, including one entitled *The Mosul Bridge*, the second version of the painting bought by Captain Mathewson. Wiles worked largely in India and the Far East, and is best known for a series of genre and landscape scenes painted in Burma before 1914.

A FAMILY DESTROYED BY THE WAR

WILLIAM HUGH KING
1894–1918
JOHN HEADLY KING
1898–1918

In 1917 the King family were living in middle-class comfort in a large house in Colchester. The father, William Headly King, was a respected local businessman and he and his wife Hannah Sophia, always known as Annie, had four children. Their three sons were educated at Colchester Royal Grammar School and their daughter trained as a secretary and worked in

Paris before the First World War. This popular family faced a promising future but, within a year, it had been torn apart by the war.

The eldest son, William Hugh King (left), always known as Hugh, was born in May 1894. After leaving school, he had spent time in Germany improving his languages before joining Davey Paxman and Company, a local engineering business, to train as an engineer and fulfil his passion for all things mechanical. At some point he had enlisted in the Essex Regiment, serving in the 2/8th (Cyclist) Battalion. This New Army battalion had been formed in Colchester in September 1914 and, like many of the Cyclist battalions, spent much of the war engaged in coastal defence work. Later, he transferred to another battalion and went to France, working at first at the regiment's Headquarters as a translator. By

'When her two sons were killed Annie, their mother,
was inconsolable and never recovered. Their father died
the following year, perhaps from grief. Their daughter and
third son never married and lived isolated lives.'

STEVEN BROOK, GREAT-GREAT-NEPHEW

1917 he had risen to the rank of Lieutenant and, in November of that year, he transferred again, this time to the Royal Flying Corps (RFC).

Hugh returned to Britain for training as an observer and by March 1918 was back in France attached to 7 Squadron. This had been formed in May 1914 and was the last RFC squadron to be created before the outbreak of war. It was sent to France in 1915, flying RE5s primarily in observation and reconnaissance roles. In 1916 the squadron was re-equipped with BE2s but by the time Hugh arrived they were flying the two-seater RE8 and were based in the Ypres area. These aircraft could also carry a small bomb load, and were sometimes used for bombing enemy trenches and installations. Hugh must have been involved in this work, as the family received a letter from the squadron Chaplain describing Hugh's death on 11 April 1918:

> He had done his work over the line this morning & was returning to the aerodrome. When just about to land the machine was blown to pieces by one of the bombs which apparently had not been dropped on the enemy. Why or how the bomb exploded is a mystery, and it is useless to conjecture. By the time we reached the wreck your boy was dead. There is no doubt that he was killed instantly & can have never known what killed him. We laid him to rest this evening by the side of his pilot ... As soon as possible crosses made from the propeller will be erected to mark the last earthly resting place of two very gallant airmen.

Another part of this letter was quoted by the local paper in its report on Hugh's death: 'He wasn't with us very long, but long enough to prove that he was good all through – brave, conscientious and thorough in all he undertook, and a very loyal and charming comrade.'

Meanwhile, Hugh's younger brother John had enlisted straight from school into the 2nd Battalion of the Northamptonshire Regiment. This battalion, in Egypt when war broke out, had arrived in France in November 1914 and fought through the major battles of 1915 and 1916. John was with the battalion over Christmas 1917 and in April 1918, and probably involved in the fighting to stop the German Spring Offensive. On 23 or 24 April he was seriously wounded by a shell in the chest, thigh and arm, rescued from the battlefield and taken to the 47th General Hospital at Le Tréport. Here, his condition steadily deteriorated and he died on 28 April 1918.

Both Hugh and John were regular writers of letters home and some of these survive, with descriptions of the base and squadron life. John's last letter home, written on 18 April, tells his mother he is going back into the front line and asks about his brother: 'How is Hugh getting on I wrote to him the other day but have had no reply yet.' At this point, John (below) had not heard about his brother's death. The hospital matron had been in touch with John's family, and between 26 and 28 April wrote to his mother, first telling her that he was seriously ill and asking her to write to him, which she did, and then informing her of his death:

> Dear Mrs King
>
> … your son became gradually worse all yesterday & in spite of all we could do to save him he died quietly this morning at 5.15am … he was so young to die though his loss will be a very great one for you I am sure.

Reading this story today, it is hard to grasp two things. First, that despite the constantly changing front lines and the movements of regiments the postal system operated with such great efficiency throughout the war, making sure that letters were sent and received as quickly as possible. Second, despite being surrounded by serious injury and death, and the burden of her duties, the Matron at Le Tréport, E. M. Lang, somehow found

time to write almost daily to John's mother, and presumably to the families of other soldiers in her care.

Hugh and John's sister Gwen was also a great correspondent and she was particularly close to John. Letters from Gwen, neatly typed and full of lively and light-hearted news, must have entertained her brothers and reveal her outgoing nature.

However, everything was now to change. The boys' mother Annie, consumed by grief at losing two sons within 17 days, became something of a recluse. In August 1919 their father died, aged 59, and Annie then lived with her daughter Gwen until she died in 1937. Both women became isolated and reclusive, communing with birds and nature rather than human beings. After her mother's death Gwen moved to a remote bungalow in Devon, living alone until her death in 1979. Paul, the youngest son, virtually disappeared after the war and little was known about him until his solitary death in a flat in Wandsworth, south London in 1979.

Gwen had become the keeper of all the letters and other family papers and after her death her cousins – the grandparents of Steven Brook – who knew her well, cleared her bungalow. Shortage of time and space meant that much was burned. They found in the house a painting of a soldier hanging on a wall and, not knowing who it was, took it out to the bonfire. Both tried to put it on the fire but were overcome with a feeling of dread – the family story is that the sky clouded over as they approached the fire. So they took it back to the house, with some of the papers. Since then, the painting, which is a portrait of Hugh, has been carefully looked after and kept on display. It is said that things start to go wrong in the family if the painting is put away out of sight. Such stories, and experiences, are not uncommon among families with members who died in the First World War.

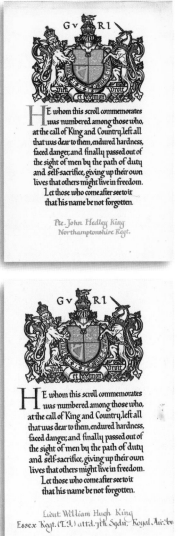

Official issue Commemorative Scrolls marking the deaths of William Hugh King and John Headly King.

A silver plate from the Machine Gun Corps' regimental silver, found
by Wilfrid Prew's granddaughter Judith. The inscription reads
'Presented by Lieut. Colonel J.Ancell. D.S.O. M.C. And the officers
of the eighth BATT. C.CORPS who were serving in Flanders on
Armistice Day 11th November 1918'.

A SOLDIER WHOSE DEATH LED, INDIRECTLY, TO A DISCOVERY OF REGIMENTAL SILVER

WILFRID ERNEST PREW
1887–1918

It is now increasingly common, and relatively easy, for families to research the stories of relatives who fought in the First World War. Sometimes this process is straightforward, confirming information already partially known, but on other occasions it can result in surprising journeys and the discovery of new, and not always expected, information.

Wilfrid Ernest Prew was born in April 1887, a likeable child who was a favourite among his ten brothers and sisters. His father was a cabinet-maker, but after leaving school Wilfrid trained as a butcher and at some point went to Wales with his brother Jesse looking for work. Eventually, he was employed as a manager of a butcher's shop in Cwmfelinfach, a newly developed and expanding mining community near Risca in the Welsh Valleys. Here Wilfrid met and married Sarah Lewis and they had two children: Tudor, born in 1913, and Anne, born in 1916. When conscription started in 1916 Wilfrid was too old to be considered but, as the war dragged on and the losses mounted, the upper age limit was raised, eventually reaching 51. Also, the initial exemption for married men was soon withdrawn. Sarah wanted him

'My grandfather was handsome, kind-natured, witty and outgoing and my grandmother never stopped loving him. After his death she had a diamond set into her wedding ring, a precious stone for a precious memory.'

JUDITH LAPPIN, GRANDDAUGHTER

to work underground as a miner and thus achieve Reserved Occupation status, but Wilfrid either couldn't or wouldn't. Instead he joined the Welsh Regiment at Cardiff and by late 1917 was in France, where his younger brother, Alfred William Prew, was also serving. Alfred was a Sergeant in the 8th Battalion of the Somerset Light Infantry, and on 4 October 1917 he was killed at Passchendaele and has no known grave.

Wilfrid was transferred to the Machine Gun Corps, becoming the No. 2 in a Vickers machine-gun team, either with the 57th Company, part of the 19th Division, or with the 51st Company, part of the 17th Division. The loss of his military records makes it hard to be certain. Soon after his arrival in France, Wilfrid was taken seriously ill, perhaps with rheumatic fever, and was sent back to Britain to recover. After convalescence, he returned to France early in 1918 and was with his company during the chaotic conditions that followed the German Spring Offensive in March 1918.

Germany's final attempt to break the stalemate and win the war had been launched by General Ludendorff on the Somme on 21 March, where a well-planned and wide-ranging attack had driven the Allies into retreat. The Germans tried to drive a wedge between the British and French armies but the line held, even though the retreating Allies lost much of the ground gained at huge cost in earlier Somme battles. At the behest of the Allied High Command, General Foch took over as Supreme Commander on the Western Front, ensuring better cooperation between the Allies, and by 5 April the German attack was over. A few days later, on 9 April, Ludendorff launched the offensive's second phase, a coordinated attack on the river Lys and the Ypres sector. Again, the Germans were initially very successful, driving through the sector held by the Portuguese and forcing the Allied armies into retreat. On 11 April, after the loss of Messines, Field Marshal Haig issued his famous order that was distributed to every soldier: 'With our backs to the wall and believing in the justice of our cause each of us must fight on to the end.' Despite a desperate situation and further losses, which included the Passchendaele Ridge and Mount Kemmel, the Allies stopped the attack and the German offensive was finally abandoned by Ludendorff on 29 April 1918. The losses at the Battle of the Lys, as the offensive came to be known, were huge, with both the Germans and the Allies suffering over 100,000 casualties. The Allies could fill the gaps, thanks to Imperial Forces from Canada, Australia, New Zealand, India and South Africa, along with the ever-increasing number of American soldiers, but for Germany the failure of the offensive was a disaster, causing critical damage to her army and making possible the Allied advance to victory that started in July 1918.

Among those casualties was Private Wilfrid Prew. He was shot by a sniper on 11 April 1918 and taken to a casualty clearing station at Lozinghem, near Béthune, where he died early on 15 April, having asked the Chaplain to return his family photograph to his wife. Sarah was informed of her husband's death on 23 April and was distraught with grief.

In the course of documenting her father's life, Judith Lappin found out about her grandfather Wilfrid, and decided to research his story. Helped by the Imperial War Museum, the Commonwealth War Graves Commission and the Machine Gun Corps Old Comrades' Association, she was able to discover many hitherto forgotten facts about Wilfrid's life and service, including the location of his grave, in Lapugnoy Military Cemetery. Her research also revealed that her father, traumatized by the loss of his father, Wilfrid, when only five years old, had had a very unhappy childhood.

Developing a good relationship with the Old Comrades, she became increasingly involved with the association and in 1996 took on the post of Honorary Secretary. Looking through the small amount of historical paperwork owned by the association, Judith found a reference to a safety deposit box in a bank in Victoria Street, London. In due course this was located and opened, and found to contain nine pieces of regimental silver belonging to the Machine Gun Corps.

A WITNESS TO
THE RED BARON'S DEATH

GLADSTONE ADAMS
1880–1966

The story of the Red Baron, Manfred Albrecht Freiherr von Richthofen, is one of the most familiar of the war. The greatest flying ace of the First World War and a national hero in Germany, the Red Baron was widely respected by the Allies. Credited with 80 victories, he brought a modern, scientific approach, combined with great personal bravery, to aerial combat. His death, on 21 April 1918, was immediately the subject of controversy, even though there were a large number of witnesses.

One of those was Gladstone Adams, sometimes known as Glady. Born in 1880 in Newcastle-upon-Tyne, Gladstone came from a large family, the youngest of ten children. After school he was apprenticed to a local photographer and then set up his own studio in Whitley Bay in about 1904. Fascinated by machinery and a habitual inventor, he quickly became well known as a photographer, making his name with a dramatic view of the newly completed *Mauretania* leaving the Tyne in 1907. A keen sportsman and local footballer, Gladstone had enlisted as a volunteer in the Northumberland Hussars Imperial Yeomanry, one of the many part-time forces created by the army in response to the failure of traditional regiments in the first phase of the South African conflict. Around 25,000 volunteers joined the Imperial Yeomanry movement in 1900 to 1901 with a view to fighting in

'I remember Gladstone visiting my grandparents when I was small. He was a kindly man, always jolly. Uncle Glady and his wife were creative people and they always encouraged me to do my best. I grew up surrounded by his photographs and that helped me to become an artist and photographer.'

KAREN MASTERS, GREAT-NIECE

South Africa, but the war ended before many could take part. Gladstone was probably one of those Yeomanry volunteers who never reached South Africa.

When the First World War broke out Gladstone, then aged 34, carried on with his busy life. However, with the introduction of conscription from 1916, things changed. In December 1917 Gladstone was called up. He joined the Royal Flying Corps as a 2nd Lieutenant, attached initially to 35 Squadron in France as a Technical Officer. This was the start of a career that was largely administrative and he ended the war as an Acting Captain.

The high point for Gladstone was 21 April 1918, when he was present at the death of Manfred von Richthofen. That morning the Red Baron was engaged in a dogfight over the British lines east of Amiens. During the course of this he was attacked by Captain Arthur Brown, flying a Sopwith Camel, and then seen to break off the fight, fly in a gentle arc away from the conflict and crash-land in a field beside a road near Vaux-sur-Somme. Having landed behind the British lines, von Richthofen's red Fokker triplane was quickly surrounded by Australian soldiers, who found the pilot gravely injured and on the point of death. The Fokker was rapidly torn apart by souvenir hunters. It later transpired that the fatal shot, a single .303 bullet,

had entered von Richthofen's body from below, and had therefore been fired by an Australian anti-aircraft Machine Gunner on the ground. Gladstone, who had seen the Red Baron's last moments, was ordered to take a photograph of the dead pilot. He confirmed later that he saw only one bullet wound on von Richthofen's body. Copies of the image were dropped over the German lines, to prove that the famous Red Baron was really dead.

A photograph of Baron von Richthofen's body. It is unconfirmed whether this is the photo taken by Gladstone Adams, but he was required to print numerous copies of the image of the dead Baron for dropping over enemy lines to demoralize the German forces.

The next day, Gladstone and another British officer were sent into Abbeville to buy wreaths, and von Richthofen was buried with full military honours at Bertangles, with six officers from 3 Squadron, Australian Flying Corps, acting as pall-bearers. The body was subsequently moved three times and the Red Baron now lies with his family in Wiesbaden, Germany.

Demobilized in the summer of 1919, Gladstone returned to the North East and to his life as a photographer, recording urban, industrial and landscape scenes and events and people of local importance. He married Laura Clark, the daughter of a local artist, in 1920 and they had one son. From the 1920s to the 1950s he was the official photographer for Newcastle United football club.

Gladstone Adams's standard issue kit bag, with his initials and RFC markings, is still preserved by his family today.

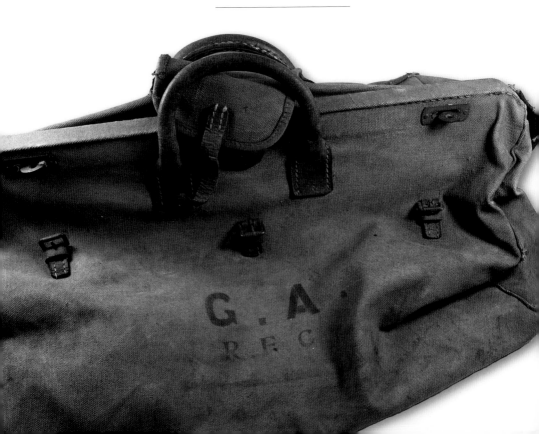

A SAILOR WHO TOOK PART IN THE ZEEBRUGGE RAID

JOHN JOSEPH CROWLEY
1885–1939

The Zeebrugge Raid of 23 April 1918 was one of the most dramatic naval actions of the war, and served as a blueprint for Commando actions in the Second World War. The aim was to block the former Belgian port of Zeebrugge and thus stop its use by German submarines as an important base giving them access to the English Channel and the North Sea. Plans

for an attack on Zeebrugge had been drawn up in 1915 but nothing was done until February 1918, when the raid, with revised plans, was given the go-ahead under the direction of Rear Admiral Sir Roger Keyes. The raid was led by the cruiser HMS *Vindictive* and consisted of three more old cruisers, HMS *Thetis*, HMS *Intrepid* and HMS *Iphigenia*, which were to be sunk as blockships in the harbour, as well as two former Mersey ferries, the *Daffodil* and the *Iris*, and two old submarines, loaded with explosives, to destroy the viaduct linking the harbour jetty to the land. There was a large accompanying fleet of support ships, and Royal Marines were to be landed to destroy German gun positions.

The first attempt was on 2 April 1918 but the raid was abandoned because of the weather, and the fleet returned to port. The second attempt was on

'*My father, who died when I was ten, was a kind and caring man who encouraged his children to learn. He was full of information but never talked about the war or his life in the navy.*'

PHYL BALLARD, DAUGHTER

23 April, and coincided with an attack on the port of Ostend. There have been many descriptions of the drama of the night, as the ships approached the harbour. HMS *Vindictive* fought her way alongside the mole, or harbour breakwater, to land the Marines, while the blockships and the submarines went at full speed for their targets. The German defences, on high alert once the raid had started, poured a continuous and heavy fire from the mainland, the jetties and the ships in the harbour. In the event, it was a partial success, with two blockships sunk in the narrow channel and the viaduct blown up. The movement of German submarines was seriously hindered for a while. However, in propaganda terms the Zeebrugge Raid was a triumph, and widely promoted as a British victory. It also helped to focus public attention away from the successes being achieved on the Western Front by the German Spring Offensive. Zeebrugge was a raid filled with many stories of exceptional and individual bravery, and eight Victoria Crosses were awarded. Over 200 British sailors and Royal Marines were killed.

John Joseph Crowley took part in the Zeebrugge Raid, as a member of the gun crew in HMS *Vindictive's* rear turret. Born in Bath in October 1885, he had three brothers and two sisters. His father, also called John Joseph, was a labourer, from a family that had emigrated from Ireland during the Great Famine in the 1840s. In 1902, John enlisted in the Royal Navy, starting as a Boy, 2nd Class, on the HMS *Northampton*, a former *Nelson*-class armoured cruiser used as a training ship. Then, after further training, he joined his first ship, HMS *Good Hope*, a *Drake*-class armoured cruiser launched in 1901. Next came another armoured cruiser, HMS *Duke of Edinburgh*, and then he went ashore for a further period of training. He returned to sea on HMS *Ariadne*, then joined the pre-Dreadnought battleship HMS *Albemarle*. During this long pre-war career, John sailed the world, visiting South America, the Caribbean, China and the Mediterranean.

When war broke out John was an Able Seaman and a Gunner. His war service is not well recorded, but he served on two cruisers, HMS *Attentive* and HMS *Amphitrite*. He also had a spell fighting as an infantryman with the Royal Naval Division, during which time he was gassed, in January 1918.

At some point John went back to sea, and HMS *Vindictive* was his last posting. During the raid, the rear turret was under the control of Lieutenant Commander Edward Hilton Young, a Naval Volunteer Reserve

Gold rank braid given to John Crowley by his Commanding Officer,
Lieutenant Commander Edward Hilton Young.

officer. Early in the action Hilton Young was severely wounded in the arm, but continued to direct the turret and encourage his men. When the raid was over and a very battered *Vindictive* had escaped from the mayhem of Zeebrugge, Hilton Young gave John the rank stripes from his uniform jacket sleeve, telling him to 'keep them to remember this day'. These zigzag Reserve officer stripes, in worn gold braid, have been kept by the family ever since.

After the war, the two men went their separate ways. Edward Hilton Young lost his arm, but this did not hinder his subsequent career as a Member of Parliament, representing Norwich. He became Financial Secretary to the Treasury and in 1922 a Privy Councillor. The same year he married Kathleen Scott, the famous sculptor and widow of the explorer Captain Scott. When he retired from politics in 1935 he became Baron Kennet.

John Crowley's post-war life was not so auspicious. After leaving the navy on 27 February 1919 he returned to Bath and then took a job with the London, Midland and Scottish Railway, in due course moving to the Swansea valleys where he spent the rest of his life. He married in 1927 and had two children. John's health was never good, perhaps the legacy of his being gassed, and he died in 1939 from tuberculosis and from the effects of an accident on the railway. In many ways, that one extraordinary night in Zeebrugge harbour was the highlight of John's long naval career, at sea and on land, and for him, as for many others in his situation after the war, things were never the same again.

A TALE OF TWO BROTHERS

JOEL HALLIWELL
1881–1958
THOMAS HALLIWELL
1886–1916

During the First World War 628 Victoria Crosses were awarded, almost half of the total given throughout the history of this supreme decoration for valour. There were a number of factors

that influenced this, not least the long years of close combat associated inevitably with trench warfare, which inspired numerous acts of astonishing courage and individual bravery.

Joel (on left of photograph) and Thomas Halliwell (on right of photograph) were two of the four children of a Manchester cotton-dyer. They were born in Middleton, a Lancashire textile town midway between Rochdale and Manchester city centre. Joel was born in September 1881. After school he worked in the local cotton mills. Soon after the outbreak of war, on 13 November 1914 he enlisted in the 11th Battalion of the Lancashire Fusiliers. He was then 33 years old.

After a complicated history stretching back to Devon in the 17th century, the Lancashire Fusiliers was reformed as a county regiment in 1881. In the First World War it was much expanded, with Territorial and New Army Service battalions being added. The 11th (Service) Battalion was

'According to my mum, my grandfather was a modest man, quietly spoken, a lovely father with an eye for detail. He was the only person she knew who would regularly whitewash the coal cellar.'

JOANNE BLISS, JOEL'S GRANDDAUGHTER

A cigarette case, presented to Joel Halliwell by his Major in 1918.

formed in October 1914. After training in Wiltshire, it was sent to France in September 1915, and then fought on the Somme from the second week of July 1916 to the end of the campaign.

Thomas, Joel's younger brother, who was born in 1886, was also a mill worker, and married with one son. Despite this, he signed up ten days after his brother, on 23 November 1914, joining the 6th Battalion of the Border Regiment. Formed in 1881 from earlier foot regiments, this served in South Africa, India, Burma and other parts of the Empire. Many new battalions were created during the First World War, including the 6th, a New Army Service battalion, which was sent first to the Dardanelles in July 1915. A year later the battalion arrived in France and took part in the later battles of the Somme campaign. On 2 October 1916 Thomas was seriously injured and died of his wounds later that day, probably in a casualty clearing station.

The brothers were close but all Joel ever knew was that his brother had died on the Somme. They may not even have met, even though both were fighting in the same campaign. Thomas is buried in Warloy-Baillon Communal Cemetery Extension, along with many colleagues from the later Somme battles. His wife later remarried and no one visited his grave until 2013, when Joel's daughter and granddaughter were taken to it during the filming of the *Antiques Roadshow*'s commemorative special at the Somme.

Meanwhile, Joel fought on through 1917 and the early months of 1918, surviving the ferocious onslaught of the German Spring Offensive in March and April 1918. When this finally ended in the Somme area, Joel's battalion was sent south, to the Aisne sector to recuperate. On 27 May 1918 General Ludendorff launched the third phase of the Spring Offensive, an attack on the Aisne designed to open up a route to the Marne and thus to Paris. The defenders were French troops, four British divisions recently moved south, including the 11th Battalion of the Lancashire Fusiliers, and recently arrived American forces. In a dramatic and unexpected attack, the German army swept through the defenders along a 25-mile front and had advanced nine miles by nightfall.

By 30 May, the Germans had captured 50,000 Allied soldiers and 800 guns, and Paris seemed within reach. However, over the next few days the German attack faltered, thanks to fierce Allied resistance, supply problems, lack of reserves and fatigue, and on 6 June 1918 Ludendorff had to call a halt, as he had been forced to do with the two earlier phases of the Offensive, and for similar reasons.

In the chaos of that first day, with the Allies fighting desperately to hold the German attacks, Joel was captured, but he escaped and made his way back to the retreating British line. On his way he heard cries for help, so he captured a runaway German horse and rode repeatedly into No Man's Land under heavy shell fire to rescue ten wounded British soldiers. He only stopped when the horse was shot from under him. He then walked for a mile through the battlefield to bring water to the rescued wounded. For this action Joel was awarded the Victoria Cross. In general there are two types of VC winners, those who carry out a single astonishing act of bravery, and those who consistently risk their lives over a period of time to save others. Joel was in the second category, and it is almost impossible today to imagine the courage he required to return ten times into the maelstrom of shell and machine-gun fire.

After the war Joel Halliwell had a hero's return to Middleton. There was a Civic parade, and he was given a gold watch, a silver cigarette case and an illuminated address. According to his mother, he looked very thin when he came home. A modest man, he always maintained that he had only done his duty, as would anyone in his position.

Joel married Sarah Greaves and they had three daughters. He returned to the mill, ran a pub and a fish and chip shop and then worked for Middleton Corporation. He kept his Victoria Cross in the sideboard drawer in the living room. He tried to serve again in the Second World War but was disqualified on medical grounds. When Joel Halliwell died in June 1958, he was given a funeral with full military honours.

A CONCEALED FIRST MARRIAGE DISCOVERED YEARS LATER

MARIA KING
1895–1981
JACOB JOHN FRANKS
1892–1918

Maria and William Frederick Lane were married in about 1923, a typical couple who had got together and made a life for themselves after the war had ended. William, always known as Fred, was a neighbour whose first wife

and baby had died of tuberculosis. He had enlisted in the Royal Navy in 1910 and served as a stoker all through the war, including service in the Dardanelles and at the Battle of Jutland. Maria and Fred had a happy marriage, with six children. Fred, always a good husband and loving father, was in the police for the rest of his working life and died in the 1960s. Maria finally followed him in 1981. It was only then, when the house was cleared by their children and grandchildren, that photographs of another soldier, Jacob John Franks (on left of photograph), came to light, along with his medals. Even more unexpected was the discovery of a marriage certificate for Jacob and their grandmother, who had been born Maria King.

'My grandmother never mentioned that she had been married before and we knew nothing about Jacob Franks until she died. We did wonder why she always got upset on Remembrance Day.'

GARY COOTES, GRANDSON

The papers and medals whose discovery, after Maria Lane's death in 1981, revealed the existence of her first husband, Jacob Franks.

Jacob John Franks, the son of a haberdasher in east London, was born in 1892. Jacob worked first as a farm labourer but also enlisted in 1910 in one of the Territorial Force regiments associated with the King's Royal Rifle Corps (KRRC). On the outbreak of war he joined the KRRC's 3rd Battalion, and landed in France in December 1914. Later, he was posted with the battalion to Salonika. At some point he was promoted to Sergeant and transferred to the Royal Fusiliers, joining 2/2nd (City of London Battalion) of the London Regiment. This was disbanded in 1916 and reformed, returning to France in January 1917. Jacob was then with the battalion for 1917 and much of 1918. During a period of leave he married Maria King at Bethnal Green Registry Office on 13 April 1918.

Jacob returned to the front and then, on 1 September 1918, he was killed during an attack on Bouchavesnes, a village on the Bapaume to Peronne road, an important objective during the Allied advance. The village was captured by the Australians three days later. Jacob's body was never found, and his name is listed on the Vis-en-Artois Memorial to the Missing.

Maria, a widow after four months of marriage to a man she had probably never seen after their wedding, must have been devastated but, for some reason, kept her misery to herself. It may have been a shared sense of grief that brought Maria and Fred together, Fred having lost his wife and child. Maria then buried the memories, and even the facts, of her first marriage. She never mentioned Jacob to any of her children or grandchildren, and so they were all shocked and surprised by the discovery of this long-held secret.

In 1977, Gary, Maria's grandson, was serving in the Royal Green Jackets, into which the old King's Royal Rifle Corps had been absorbed. He attended a family wedding in his uniform, which retained the black buttons and black detailing of the former regiment. Maria, seeing him, said, 'Oh, that's the old KRRC regiment isn't it?' At the time, Gary wondered how she knew, but it wasn't until she died some years later that all was revealed.

A SOLDIER WHO COLLECTED SOUVENIRS ON THE BATTLEFIELD

PERCY WEEKS
1891–1918

An unusual legacy from the First World War is a German belt decorated with regimental cap badges, collected by Percy Weeks, who was born in Handsworth, Birmingham, in 1891, the youngest of three children. His

father George ran a plumbing business and Percy and his older brother Sidney joined it when they left school. When their father died, the boys took over the business but Percy, feeling that his brother was not giving him a fair share, soon left and became a tram conductor. At some point, Percy volunteered for the local Territorial Service regiment and was trained as a medical orderly. When the war started, he tried to join the Royal Army Medical Corps but was sent instead to the 1/8th Battalion of the Royal Warwickshire Regiment. This, one of the regiment's Territorial Force battalions, had been formed at Aston Cross, near Birmingham, in August 1914. In March 1915 Percy landed in France with the battalion, as part of the South Midland Division, later the 48th Division.

The Royal Warwickshire Regiment has a distinguished history, reaching back to the 17th century, and including service during the Napoleonic

'As a small child I was always aware of Percy, my grandfather,
he was always remembered within the family. My grandmother had
the Royal scroll commemorating his death hanging by her bed.
We finally visited his grave when my father, his son, was 75.'

RALPH PAGE, GRANDSON

Wars, in South Africa and on the North West Frontier. Like many other regiments, it acquired its county affiliation in 1881. Two of the regiment's regular army battalions were sent to France in 1914, taking part in many of the early battles of the war. The Territorial Force and New Army battalions followed, mostly in 1915. The regiment's battle honours include most of the major engagements of the First World War.

The details of Percy's army career are not known, although he was for a while an officer's batman. On 1 July 1916, the opening day of the Battle of the Somme, he fought with his original battalion, the 1/8th, taking part in the attacks on the Quadrilateral, the heavily fortified German strongpoint near Serre, known also as the Heidenkopf. Percy was wounded twice during his career, and the more serious incident, when a bullet aimed at his heart was deflected by the metal rim of his wallet into his shoulder, probably occurred during this battle. He was sent back to Britain to recover but, judging by family stories from this time, he was also in a highly nervous state and probably suffering from shell shock. In spite of this he was sent back to the front, reached the rank of Sergeant and was preparing for a commission.

When he returned after his injury Percy was transferred to the regiment's 1st Battalion, and was certainly with them in July 1918. By this time, Percy seems to have become a souvenir hunter. He had acquired a belt from a dead German soldier, and onto this he attached a collection of regimental cap badges. The collecting of souvenirs seems to have been a regular feature of army life, with most soldiers content with the odd bits and pieces they found either on dead bodies or lying around in the chaos of the battlefield. Some, however, took the whole exercise much more seriously, looking for helmets, pistols, swords, uniform regalia, binoculars and other expensive pieces of equipment. Percy seems to have been in the former group, probably content to carry his cap badge belt in his pack, and add to it whenever he could. Items like cap badges were also exchanged by soldiers during casual encounters.

On 8 August 1918 the British Fourth Army launched a major offensive east of Amiens, part of the broad-based attack that was ultimately to bring about the defeat of Germany and the end of the war. This offensive was successful, but at a high cost, and heavy fighting continued through August in the advance towards Vis-en-Artois. On 29 August, the battalion's immediate objective was the village of Remy, and the next day the attack was launched at 10.00. German machine guns and artillery disrupted the attack which had already been hindered by the swampy ground in the area. Communications failed, cohesion was lost and the attack was stopped. The battalion's casualties were 6 officers and 166 men. Among the dead was Sergeant Percy Weeks who is buried in Eterpigny Military Cemetery, a delightful small battlefield cemetery just outside the village, and close to where he died.

Before the war, Percy had married Dorothy Williams in Handsworth and they had two children, a son born in October 1913, and a daughter born in May 1915. It seems that Percy had only two periods of leave during the war, and so neither of his children remembered him very well. His daughter, then aged three, had a clear recollection of seeing her mother on her knees, head against the bath, crying as she clutched the telegram announcing her husband's death.

After the war Dorothy Weeks met Samuel Ralph Henry Page, a soldier who had served with the Royal Field Artillery in Mesopotamia. His wife and daughter had died of tuberculosis in 1915. They married in 1925 and had one son, born in 1932. When Samuel went to register the birth, he named his son Michael Percy Page, the second name in memory of Dorothy's first husband. Michael's son Ralph is now the holder of Percy's memory, along with his German belt.

Percy Weeks's souvenir belt, acquired from a dead German soldier, on to which he attached his collection of regimental cap badges.

A SOLDIER WHO SENT HIS WIFE 188 POSTCARDS

THOMAS JAMES DRAPER
1893–1918

Thomas James Draper, who came from Sussex, was born in 1893. Little is known about his family or childhood, and only his mother is listed on his service record. When war broke out, Thomas enlisted in the Royal Field Artillery (RFA) and was ultimately attached to the 1st/36th Division

Ammunition Column. Originally formed in Ireland as part of the 36th Ulster Division, this column trained in Sussex and then joined the division in France in October 1915. They fought on the Somme in 1916 and at Messines, Ypres and Cambrai in 1917. In 1918 they fought on the Lys and in the final advance through Flanders. It is possible that Thomas served in another RFA battery or division before joining the 36th but his records are incomplete. Family stories suggest he was in France in 1914, and he may at some point have been a despatch rider. However, records that do survive place him in 1918 as a Gunner with the 1st/36th Division Ammunition Column.

Before the war Thomas had married his wife, Elizabeth, and they had one son, Ronald. Throughout his service on the Western Front, Thomas stayed in touch with his family by sending home postcards. Today, 188 survive which, over the four years he served, work out at nearly one a week.

'Sadly, we know little about him and had no photos of him as an adult at all, until we found some by chance last Christmas. The postcards show how much he loved his wife and family. We put a cross for him on the Memorial every Remembrance Day.'

TRUDY DRAPER, GRANDDAUGHTER BY MARRIAGE

Most have simple, loving messages to his wife and child and give no details about dates or where he was. It was the only way he could tell them he was still alive.

The postcard, which had been introduced in its modern form early in the 20th century, was at its peak of popularity by 1914, with millions being sent every year. The postcard-sending habit was carried on by soldiers throughout the war, as they were quick to write and easily sent via the efficient army postal services. They were also liked by the army because there was little room for messages and they were easy to censor. Indeed, the army quickly introduced pre-printed Field Service postcards on which soldiers merely had to tick the relevant boxes and write the address. However, when soldiers were out of the front line or in reserve they had access to a huge variety of pictorial and other decorative cards, many of which were produced in France to sell to the British.

Best known among these are the embroidered cards, of which there were hundreds of versions, featuring regimental badges, patriotic symbols and messages relevant to particular family members or events such as birthdays. The traditional industry of Belgium and the North of France was textile-making in all its forms and so, despite the problems caused by the war, this local industry quickly developed the machine-embroidered decorative postcard. Typically, these cards contain a pocket, holding a small card for a more personal message.

A typical embroidered postcard, made by the Belgian and French textile industry in huge quantities for British soldiers. This was one of 188 postcards sent by Thomas Draper to his wife.

One of the typical embroidered postcards sent home by Thomas
Draper to his wife, this one from France in 1917.

Many of the cards sent by Thomas to his wife were these embroidered cards. One sent on 19 June 1918 wished his wife happy birthday and said that he hoped to be with her on her next birthday. It was not to be, for on 29 September 1918 Thomas died in a dressing station in Ypres from wounds received following the explosion of a shell. In December his widow received a letter from the Red Cross explaining the circumstances of his death, and saying that he had been buried in the Old Prison Cemetery in Ypres. Elizabeth kept this letter until she died. She never visited her husband's grave, although the Red Cross sent her a picture of it, and, some time later, she remarried and had two more children. At the time of Thomas's death his son, whom he had not seen for four years, was five. It is possible Thomas only saw his son twice.

A SOLDIER WHO LOOKED AFTER TURKISH PRISONERS OF WAR

HYMAN LEVY
1899–1974

When they fled the pogroms in Poland towards the end of the 19th century, the Levy family settled by chance in Edinburgh. They had 15 children, of whom Hyman Levy was the second eldest, born in 1899. His father, a cobbler, had difficulty reading and writing English, and so he registered the births of his children with various versions of the family name, including Levy, Levi and Levey. Times were hard and Hyman remembered going to school in bare feet. However, he was studious and always immersed in books. When he left school he worked for the Edinburgh Post Office as a telegraph boy and his introduction to the war was making the rounds on his Post Office bicycle, delivering telegrams announcing the deaths of loved ones to families in the city.

In February 1918 Hyman, along with a number of other telegraph boys, was

'My grandparents fled to Britain from Poland and so my father grew up in somewhat straightened circumstances.
He was the studious one of the family and so made a good life for us. He was a generous and clever man.'

RHODA KIRK, DAUGHTER

called up, having signed his attestation papers in October 1917. Initially he was directed towards battalions associated with the Jewish Legion, but chose to stay with his friends from the Post Office and joined the 26th Battalion of the Royal Fusiliers.

In the early part of the war, the position of Jewish volunteers was equivocal. It is estimated that about 10,000 volunteered in Britain and fought in many regiments and in many campaigns, before the introduction of conscription in 1916. However, anti-Semitism was also widespread at all levels of the army. At the lower levels, little distinction was often drawn between German nationals and Jews from Russia or Poland who had emigrated to Britain, while at the higher echelons recruiting officers were being quoted as late as November 1915 as saying that 'Lord Kitchener does not want any more Jews in the British army'. At the same time, there was pressure to form Jewish battalions, and even Jewish regiments. In 1915, a Zion Mule Corps was formed which saw service in Gallipoli. This was part of a much wider, but ultimately unsuccessful, plan to recruit Jews from Palestine and other parts of the Middle East to fight the Turks and the Ottoman Empire. Finally, in 1917 the Jewish Legion was formed, as the 38th and 39th battalions of the Royal Fusiliers. Three more battalions followed, and in the end the Jewish Legion comprised 5000 soldiers drawn primarily from Britain, the United States, Canada and Palestine. By June 1918 it was fighting in Palestine, in the area around Jerusalem. Jews killed in action while serving in the British army were buried with the conventional Imperial War Graves Commission stone, additionally marked with a Star of David. Interestingly, in the light of later events, Jews killed while serving in the German army were also given distinctive grave markers.

Little is known about Hyman's military career. He joined up with his friends and, in the event, they all survived, unlike Hyman's eldest brother

John who was killed in October 1917. At some point Hyman, by now in the 38th Battalion, Royal Fusiliers, part of the newly formed Jewish Legion, and serving in Palestine, was promoted to Sergeant and put in charge of Turkish prisoners of war, either at a base depot or in a small camp. There are many reports of Turkish prisoners being treated harshly but Hyman was a generous and humane man who supplied those in his care with materials from which they could make decorative objects to sell and make small sums of money with which they could buy food and other necessities to improve their lives. This tradition, probably started by French prisoners held in Britain during the Napoleonic Wars, was practised quite widely during the First World War and particularly among Turkish prisoners.

The best known of these are the beadwork snakes, made by Turkish prisoners in all sizes and with varied inscriptions, which, judging by the number that survive, must have been produced in huge quantities. For Hyman, his prisoners made a collection of woven hessian bags, designed as presents for his sisters and various friends back in Edinburgh. One of these survives in the family.

After demobilization Hyman returned to the Post Office and then gradually worked his way up the ranks of the civil service. He married and moved to London, working for a while at the main sorting office at Mount Pleasant. During the Second World War he worked for the Air Ministry. At some point Hyman changed his name by deed poll to Harry Leigh. His daughter Rhoda, then at primary school, remembers the confusion this caused with her school register. Hyman Levy died in 1974 from emphysema, having been a heavy smoker for much of his life.

Opposite and above: One of the woven hessian bags made for Hyman Levy by Turkish prisoners of war while they were in his care.

A ROYAL FLYING CORPS PILOT ON DUTY DURING THE FIRST TRANSATLANTIC FLIGHT

JAMES WILLIAM WHITE
1900–1977

James William White was born in February 1900 in north London, where his father William owned a small general store. After leaving school James worked as a clerk for the Post Office at Mount Pleasant, one of London's main sorting offices. In 1917, having lied about his age, he enlisted in the Royal Flying Corps and trained as a pilot. In 1918 he joined 108 Squadron.

This had been formed in Wiltshire in November 1917 as a bomber squadron, and it was sent to France in July 1918, based initially at Capelle, near Dunkirk. Here James flew the two-seater Airco DH9a on day bombing and reconnaissance missions over northwest Belgium.

The DH9 was designed by Sir Geoffrey de Havilland as a replacement for the successful and popular DH4. In squadron use from November 1917, the DH9 proved to be under-powered and unreliable, and its limited manoeuvrability meant that many were shot down. Nevertheless, it was widely used, and by July 1918 was in service with nine squadrons on the Western Front. By this time the Royal Flying Corps and the Royal Naval Air Service had been absorbed into the new Royal Air Force, which was launched on 1 April 1918, although army ranks remained in use in the new service until August 1919.

'My father was famous for his tenacity. He never knew when to give up. He could be strict and remote but he was blessed with a wonderful wife! He was a great traditionalist and was always enthusiastic about the RAF and all things military.'

ELSPETH BREWER, DAUGHTER

In September 1918 James's DH9 was shot down in combat, with one bullet passing through both him and his navigator. He managed to land the aeroplane, in spite of his injuries, and both crew members survived. He was taken to a base hospital near Dunkirk, where he recovered and was then sent back to England to convalesce. Although exempted on medical grounds from front-line service, James remained in the RAF, and in June 1919 he was serving in Western Ireland, possibly at the Oranmore RAF base. This had been established in May 1918 by the Royal Flying Corps and at various times 2 Squadron, 100 Squadron and 15 Squadron were assigned to it.

Early in the morning of 15 June 1919 John Alcock and Arthur Whitten Brown crash-landed their specially converted Vickers Vimy bomber into a bog at Clifton in Connemara, having completed the world's first transatlantic flight. This was the conclusion of a spectacular aviation achievement. They had left St John's, Newfoundland at 13.45 on 14 June and the flight took 16 hours to reach Galway, their intended landfall. That morning 2nd Lieutenant James White was the Duty Officer at the nearby airfield, and he must have been involved in relaying messages to London about the success of the flight, and maybe even meeting Alcock and Brown.

James left the RAF in October 1919 and then trained to be a dental surgeon in London. In 1923 he married Ethel Elisha and they had two sons and one daughter. James's injury had some lasting effects but, as a keen sportsman, he played football and golf and his many interests and enthusiasms were tolerated, and encouraged, by his wife. A man of conservative attitudes and regular habits, he died in 1977. When he left the RAF, James kept his old flying jacket, and this has been carefully looked after, first by his children, and now by his grandsons.

Top: A Royal Flying Corps sweetheart brooch given by James White to his wife. Left: James White's Royal Flying Corps leather flying jacket.

Church Army Recreation Hut
OR TENT.

ON ACTIVE SERVICE
WITH · THE · BRITISH · EXPEDITIONARY · FORCE

My Dear Brother   18/5/18

Just a few lines hoping to find
you in the best of health as it leaves me at
present well its a long time ago I wrote to
you but now I got time I thought I would
I am in another Regiment now and my
address is Pvt. A. Coombs 37505-128 L 9
J S B D APO S 15 12 W S; Bⁿ.
so now you can write to me, well I dont
mind for we got to win the war. and
I suppose I will make as good ▓▓▓▓ for
the ▓▓▓▓▓▓▓▓▓▓▓▓▓▓▓▓▓▓ as any. Its
dam hard luck when a man comes a long
way and ▓▓▓▓▓▓▓▓▓▓▓▓▓▓▓▓▓▓▓
when her about ▓▓▓▓▓▓▓▓ dont you think
so Well I hope Beat and little Jim are well
and that you are getting on al yourself.
well Jack I would like to get a leave
before I am knocked out but. if I dont
ever come home dont forget Mother
and Father. We are getting some fine
weather at present I hope its the same

Letter from one of Kit Coombs's brothers to another, on standard issue
Church Army stationery, with deletions by the censor.

A MUNITIONS GIRL
WHO COURTED A SOLDIER

KETURAH MARY COOMBS
1892–1980

Throughout the First World War women took over many of the jobs traditionally associated with men, notably in the transport and manufacturing industries. Typical was Keturah Mary Coombs, always known as Kit, a Dorset girl who worked in a munitions factory. Born in October 1892, Kit was a feisty church-going girl who never swore or blasphemed throughout her life. She worked at first as a domestic servant on Portland, and then volunteered to go and work in a munitions factory in Coventry to help the war effort.

The rapid escalation of the First World War brought an ever-increasing demand for ammunition of all kinds and so the Ministry of Munitions established a network of 12 National Filling Factories, where the empty brass shell cases were filled with explosives, made at the National Explosives Factories and transported to the various Filling Factories by train, and completed with fuses. This dangerous work was carried out largely by women. The factories were built with sections to separate all the ingredients and components but accidents still occurred. The women workers also suffered from the

'My great-grandmother was tiny, but very strong-willed. I remember her feeding me and my sister boiled sweets from a never-ending bag in her pocket and lighting matches on the heel of her shoe to amuse us.'

NICKY WHITTENHAM, GREAT-GRANDDAUGHTER

inhalation and handling of chemicals which caused many unpleasant side effects, including discolouration of the skin, inflammation of the eyes and the risk of illness. The National Filling Factory at Coventry was built over a 14-acre site at Whitmore Park.

Kit, a country girl at heart, did not enjoy working in a factory. Apparently, the main problem was not the work, but the coarse and foul-mouthed nature of her fellow workers. However, she stuck it out for several months, before returning to Dorset. It was during this time that she met Ernest Edward Keefe, a soldier recovering from wounds at a military hospital that had been set up in the Prince Regent Hotel on Weymouth's esplanade. Opposite the hotel is one of Weymouth's famous decorative Victorian esplanade shelters and, according to the family, it was here that

they did their courting and fell in love, sitting looking out to sea over the sandy beach. The shelter still stands and Kit's daughter Jessie remembers sitting there with her mother after her father's death in 1935.

Ernest was born in Brentford, Middlesex in 1886 and had a hard childhood with a bullying drunkard of a father who died young. At the age of 16, Ernest had a spell in Reading Gaol. He enlisted at the start of the war, possibly in the Royal Fusiliers. His military records do not survive, but a photograph shows that he was a Lance Corporal. Ernest was wounded at the Battle of the Somme in 1916, and there is a family story that he rescued a wounded German soldier who gave him his jack-knife in gratitude.

Ernest recovered and went back to the front and was wounded again in 1918 and left for dead on the battlefield. However, he was rescued eventually and sent back to Britain to recover, presumably to Weymouth. This injury left him partially disabled and in frequent pain, due to the shrapnel that had been left in his body, and he also suffered from the lasting effects of shell shock, all of which contributed to his early death at the age of 49.

Opposite: Ernest Edward Keefe, Kit Coombs's husband, whom she met during his convalescence in Weymouth. Above: Kit Coombs (centre, wearing a white hat) with a group of munitions girls.

Ernest and Kit married in 1925 and had a daughter and a son. After Ernest's death, Kit brought up her children alone and, during the Second World War, she worked as a nurse at Weymouth's Westhaven Hospital. Jessie, her daughter, married in due course but her son Ted continued to live at home. He used to talk about going on coach trips to stately homes and cathedrals with his mother, and he also remembered her chasing him round the house with a poker when he came home after a few drinks. Kit died in Weymouth in July 1980, and with her the memory of a time when women, working in factories and in other previously male-dominated areas to aid the war effort, enjoyed a new sense of independence and equality.

Kit's two brothers also fought in the war but all that remains of their story is a letter sent from one brother to another in May 1918, which includes the comment, 'I hope Kit is still home and she stays there.'

A SOLDIER WHO OUTLIVED
HIS DEATH CERTIFICATE

WILLIAM HENRY BELL
1897–1975

William Henry Bell, always known as Billy, was born in October 1897 in Everton, Liverpool. He was one of eight children and his father Jack was a Master Boatman and Dock Pilot on the Mersey. By the age of 11 he was working part-time as a grocer's boy and later he joined his father on the river. On 29 May 1914, his younger brother Robbie, a 14-year-old deckhand,

was one of the 1012 people lost when the liner the *Empress of Ireland* sank after a collision in the St Lawrence River in Canada.

When war broke out Lord Derby called on the men of Liverpool to enlist in new battalions being formed by the King's (Liverpool) Regiment to fight in France. Thousands rushed to join up, including Billy. When he applied, saying he was 17, he was told to come back in a year's time. Instead, he walked round the block and then applied again, saying he was 18. In fact, he was 16 when he enrolled on 29 August 1914 in the 18th Battalion, one of four known as the City of Liverpool battalions or, more popularly, as the Liverpool Pals. Many who signed up were from the shipping, insurance

'As a child I can remember my granddad taking me to Liverpool Town Hall and showing me his name on the Roll of Honour – with typical Scouse humour he told me he had been "seriously killed".'

CHRIS BROTHERSTON, GRANDSON

and brokerage industries and so were connected professionally or by friendship, the principle behind the Pals battalions. In November and December 1914 Lord Derby presented the men of these battalions with silver cap badges.

After extensive training the 18th Battalion sailed for France in November 1915, following in the footsteps of the King's Liverpool's regular battalions that had been fighting in France since August 1914. Three weeks earlier, on 18 October, Billy had married Catherine Wilson. While he had added years to his age in order to enlist, she had subtracted a year from hers so as not to appear older than her husband, a secret she kept until she died. Through the early months of 1916 the 18th Battalion was kept largely in reserve but on 1 July 1916 it was flung into action on the Somme, fighting on the southern end of the line in the attack on Montauban. In this sector, the attack was successful and the Liverpool Pals attained their objectives with relatively few casualties. They fought on through the later phases of the Somme offensive and then, in April 1917, they took part in the Battle of Arras. Next, at the end of July 1917, came the start of the Third Battle of Ypres, with many of the King's Liverpool's battalions involved. The nature of this battle was described later by an officer from the Liverpool regiment: 'Those who took part in it will never erase from their minds its many ghastly features, among which the mud and the multitude of dead will stand out pre-eminent.'

In 1918 the Pals battalions fought at St Quentin, and were then swept backwards by the force of the German Spring Offensive, along with much of the British army. A fiercely fought and often desperate retreat finally stopped the German advance, with the 18th Battalion playing an important part in the final days of the battle.

At some point in 1918, Billy, by then a Colour-Sergeant, was buried by an exploding shell. Those close to him assumed he had been killed and reported his death back to their Headquarters, and Catherine was accordingly informed that her husband had been killed in action. The news spread round the family, and only Catherine stood by her belief that Billy wasn't dead. In due course, she was proved right. Billy had been dug out and rescued by some soldiers from the King's Own Yorkshire Light Infantry, but the news did not get back in time to stop the telegram to

William Bell's erroneous death certificate, which he refused to return
to the authorities when he was demobilized in 1919.

Catherine announcing his death. Restored to life, Billy fought on until
the signing of the Armistice, by which time he was serving with the 4th
Battalion of the King's (Liverpool) Regiment, and was finally demobilized
in 1919, after the award of his Military Medal on 13 June 1919, for 'Bravery
in the Field'.

Billy came back to Liverpool, where he found the certificate headed To
Our Glorious Dead. Despite pressure from the army authorities, he refused
to hand it over, saying he would dine out on the story for the rest of his
life, which he did. After the war Billy returned to the Mersey, working
in the docks, serving as a pilot and occasionally working on colliers on
coastal routes and on ships on the South America run. He and Catherine
had 11 children.

Until his death in 1975 Billy kept the personal effects of a German soldier
called Herman Pringel, but no one knew where or how he had acquired
these. He bore no ill feelings against German soldiers, saying often that
they had all been in the same boat. In his old age, Billy Bell stayed loyal
to a pint of Guinness, Capstan full-strength cigarettes and the *Liverpool
Echo* crossword.

A SOLDIER WHO RESCUED A WOUNDED GERMAN

WILLIAM TURNEY
1882–1935

Born in April 1882 in Morley, Leeds, William Turney, always known as Willie, was the illegitimate son of Harriet Turney, a powerloom weaver, and he was brought up within the Turney family. His mother, who was treated as an outcast, suffered from periods of mental illness and died young. Willie worked in the textile trade and in June 1905 he married Emily Newall, a girl from the same street in Morley. Emily gave birth to still-born twin babies during the war, and they had no other children.

At some point Willie enlisted, either as a volunteer or a conscript, in the Army Service Corps (ASC). Little is known about his military service as his records were lost, along with many others from the First World War, when the warehouse in which they were stored was destroyed during the London Blitz in the Second World War. Although regularly abused by front-line soldiers, who referred to the ASC as Ally Sloper's Cavalry after

'My great-uncle Willie was very good with his hands, very inventive but he was not a proud person and I don't think he talked much about the war. If anything, the story of the German and the ring had to be prised from him.'

NICK ROBERTS, GREAT-NEPHEW

a cartoon famous for being useless and lazy, the Army Service Corps was a vital part of the army in general and the British Expeditionary Force in particular. Indeed, the war could not have been fought without it.

Set up in 1888 as an independent organization responsible for all the army's supply and transport arrangements, the Army Service Corps served on every front. It was a massive, yet efficient organization, staffed at the end of the war by over 325,000 officers and men. It managed the supply chain for food, equipment and ammunition between Britain, the numerous base depots and the various front lines, using railways, waterways, horse and motor transport. By 1918 the Allied armies included 3,000,000 men and 500,000 horses. They required each month 90,000,000 pounds of bread, 32,000,000 pounds of forage and 13,000,000 gallons of petrol.

One day in 1918, Willie was driving an ASC lorry laden with a bread delivery for soldiers on the front line. In the confusion of the war-torn landscape he missed the road and strayed into No Man's Land. After several years of war in a conflict in which opposing armies often fought to and fro across the same ground, there was little to see except devastation. Villages, farms, woods, roads, indeed all the familiar features, had been obliterated and so getting lost was all too easy. Maps changed on a daily basis, along with the trench network. Men could, and did, vanish and wounded soldiers could lie out in No Man's Land for days, awaiting rescue or death.

While trying to find his way Willie came across a long-lost and badly wounded German soldier. Taking a loaf of bread from his lorry, Willie gave it to the soldier who thanked him, saying 'Danke, dass du mir das Leben gerettet hast' (Thank you, you have saved my life). The German soldier gave Willie his ring, which Willie then continued to wear for the rest of the war as a lucky talisman. As for what happened

Ring given to William Turney by a wounded German soldier.

to the German soldier, this is not recorded, and even his name remains unknown.

After the war Willie tried his hand at various business ventures and schemes, without much success, and then he moved to Denby Dale as Warden of a Quaker Residential Holiday Home. Willie was certainly a Quaker but it is not known when he chose this way of life. Had he been a Quaker before the war, he would most likely have been either a Conscientious Objector or served with the Friends Ambulance Unit. However, his act of generosity towards the German soldier indicates a Quaker attitude. From Denby Dale Willie moved to Manchester, as Warden of a Friends Institute in the city. While here, Willie developed diabetes and so he retired and he and Emily moved to Timperley, near Altrincham, where he died in 1935.

Within the family, Willie is best remembered for his enthusiasm for inventing things, even if none were successful. However, his German ring, and the story attached to it, have always been highly regarded by the family, as a rare act of kindness and fellowship.

A DRIVER WHO LOVED HIS HORSES

HARRY WAINWRIGHT
1897–1975

Over the last few years the role played by horses in the First World War has been properly appreciated, but it is still easy to forget that in the early 20th century the world was largely horse-powered, in warfare as in all other areas of human activity. Equally important, therefore, was the role played

by those who looked after horses.

Born in 1897, Harry Wainwright (on right of photograph) had always worked with horses, since leaving school and joining his father at the local coal mine in Kippax, south of Leeds. where he probably looked after the pit ponies. When he enlisted in Leeds on 10 October 1914, this experience drew him to the artillery. He joined the 1st West Riding Brigade, later the 245th Brigade, of the Royal Field Artillery (RFA), which had been established as part of the Territorial Force before the war, attached to the 49th Division. Harry became a driver in A Battery and, after a period of training, he sailed to France in April 1915. His first action was at the Battle of Aubers Ridge in May and from then on he was never far from the fighting.

Harry fought through the Somme campaign, starting in Authuile Wood near Thiepval on the opening day, 1 July 1916. In 1917 he was at Messines

'My grandfather was a quiet, gentle man who smoked his pipe, drank pints of tea and enjoyed reading westerns from the library. He never talked to me about the war, though he did tell my dad the major battles he had been at.'

GARY WAINWRIGHT, GRANDSON

and Ypres and in 1918 in the Battle of the Lys and then with the Allied advance to the Armistice. A Battery of the 245th Brigade fired its final barrage at 14.00 hours on 10 November 1918. As a driver, he experienced the worst, and the best, of the war. Life in an RFA Battery was one of constant mobility, with the guns regularly moved and re-sited. Sometimes this was pre-planned, other times it was done in the chaos of battle under fire or gas attack. He saw his colleagues, and his horses, killed and maimed all around him as they struggled, time after time, to get the guns out of a dangerous position. In 1918, he lived through the horrors of a desperate fighting retreat, and the dangerous excitement of a rapid advance.

Harry loved his horses and did his best to make sure they were well cared for. Indeed, he said that the horses looked after him as much as he looked after them. On freezing cold nights he slept with them, kept alive by their body heat. He never wanted to hurt his horses and so he replaced the sharp pointed stars in his spurs with French centime coins. These spurs, with their coins in place, are now owned by Harry's grandson, Gary.

After the war, Harry stayed in France with the army until February 1919. He returned to England but was not demobilized until March 1920, a total of five and a half years in military service. Back in Yorkshire, one day he attended a local auction with a friend, Gertrude Monks. A bed came under the hammer and he asked Gertrude if they should buy the bed and get wed. She agreed, they were married and had two sons. Harry spent the whole of his working life underground at the Allerton Bywater coal mine.

A quiet, thoughtful man, Harry Wainwright was typical of a generation who fought through the war and survived. Somehow, he put away the years of dreadful horror that were perhaps softened by the memories of the comradeship of military life. In his case, the constant presence of his beloved horses probably made it more bearable. Like all those who survived, he never talked about the war. Before he died in 1975 Harry said that the only words he wanted on his tombstone were In Remembrance, as that is all his pals ever got.

Harry Wainwright's spurs, with the points replaced by French coins.

R. 28.
Attested Man.

Local Tribunal for ___ THE URBAN DISTRICT OF PORTLAND,

Address ___ COUNCIL OFFICES,

___ PORTLAND.

Date ___ *Mar 4th 1916*

NOTICE OF DECISION.

Particulars of claim:— *Exemption from Combatant service, or any service assisting combatants or any service which necessitates taking the military oath.*

SIR,

The Tribunal have considered this case, and have decided that ~~there are not sufficient grounds for allowing the claim.~~ *exemption be granted from com' tant service only.*

Yours faithfully,

R. A Coleman

For the Tribunal.

[This document should be folded, fastened, and posted without an envelope.]

[505] 41b89/80 100m 12/15τ G&S

Above: William Stone's Certificate of Exemption granted by the local Conscientious Objectors' Tribunal. Opposite: William Lowman Stone with a choir group formed by NCC colleagues.

A CONSCIENTIOUS OBJECTOR WHO SERVED IN THE NON-COMBATANT CORPS

WILLIAM LOWMAN STONE
1892–1975

William Lowman Stone was born in 1892, into one of a small group of families closely associated with the isolated community of Portland, Dorset, since at least the 18th century. The branch into which William was born were strict Methodists with a strong Christian faith, and he

grew up never touching alcohol or tobacco. Educated locally, William went to work in one of the many quarries, the major source of employment on Portland. When war broke out, Stone continued to work as a quarryman, relying on his faith, and his ability to resist social pressures, to support his position as a declared Conscientious Objector. His decision not to fight does not seem to have been an issue within the family, though in Mrs Graham's experience it has never been talked about. William died in 1975 and since then the suitcase containing all his diaries, letters and documents has been looked after by Mrs Graham.

In March 1916 the passing of the Military Service Act paved the way for the introduction of conscription. Conscientious Objectors who had

'Though strict with himself, he was always fun to be with. He loved being with the family and was always good to me. He was always there for anybody, had time for everyone. He was a gentle giant.'

GILL GRAHAM, NIECE BY MARRIAGE

hitherto been able to avoid military service, though not without difficulties, were now faced with a hard choice. Many, including William, chose to face a tribunal before conscription became universal. On 4 March 1916, William was granted exemption by the local tribunal 'from combatant service only', and in due course was enrolled as a Private in the 1st Southern Company of the Non-Combatant Corps.

The Non-Combatant Corps, generally known as the NCC, was established in March 1916 to help overcome the problems posed by conscription to Conscientious Objectors. It was part of the army and its officers were regular soldiers. Despite this, some newspapers of the day referred to the NCC as the No Courage Corps, a typical reflection of attitudes to Conscientious Objectors that were then quite common. The Conscientious Objectors who joined the NCC willingly wore army uniforms, had the rank of Private and were subject to army regulations and discipline. They carried NCC cap badges and shoulder flashes. They were not expected to take part in battles, or to carry or handle arms and munitions. By the middle of 1916 there were eight NCC companies, providing labour for docks, depots and camps, for construction and maintenance operations and for cleaning and sanitation. Over 3000 Conscientious Objectors accepted service in the NCC and in the Royal Army Medical Corps and were generally well treated. Some with stronger views were forcibly enlisted into the NCC. They were generally treated more harshly, and those who refused to wear uniform were charged and court martialled, and often imprisoned or sentenced to hard labour.

In 1917 William was sent to France with the 1st Southern Company, to work primarily as dock labourers in the ports of western France, notably Bordeaux. From that moment, he kept a daily diary. The first entry, 17 October 1917, describes leaving Portland while the last, in December 1918, is a detailed record, including train times, of his journey home. Throughout the period he also wrote regularly to his mother and other members of the family, and most of these letters survive. Together, they offer a rich insight into daily life in the Non-Combatant Corps, thanks to William's eye for detail. There is a mass of information about ships, their cargoes and the dock-side procedures and about life in the camps, along with comments on many matters including railway construction, the appearance of 'coloured' troops, the habits of members of the Chinese Labour Corps, the food enjoyed by Canadian soldiers and the daily French lessons. Every day, including Armistice Day, ended for him with a bible reading, duly noted in the diary.

> Monday November 11 [1918]
>
> We went to work very expectant of good news. At dinner time Ted Hemmings announced to us that the armistice had been signed. A rousing cheer went up. After dinner the boats in the river were decorated and they all blew their sirens for about two hours. Everybody was excited and in the town it was difficult to get through the streets for the crowd. We had no French class as some of the chaps had gone to town. I had a letter from mother and wrote one to her in return. We are all wondering now when we shall be sent back to England. Daily reading Psalm 46.

After his return home in December 1918 William Stone became an agent for the Prudential Insurance Company in Portland. Perhaps because of the echoes of his life as a Conscientious Objector, he seems to have had a solitary life until his marriage in 1932. He had no children, his brother died and his sister never married but he always enjoyed the company of children and was popular within the family.

The watch given to David Jenkins by a grateful Turkish officer whom he had looked after. Attached to the chain are British sporting or commemorative medallions, presumably added at a later date.

A WELSH MINER WHO SERVED THROUGH THE WAR WITH THE RAMC

DAVID THOMAS JENKINS
1892–1958

As soon as he was old enough, Dai Jenkins, born David Thomas Jenkins in Kenfig Hill, South Wales, in March 1892, followed in his father's footsteps and became a coal miner. The eldest of six children, Dai also took after

his father as a St John Ambulance volunteer at the pit. This organization, taking its name from, but having no direct connection with, the Order of St John, was set up in 1877 as the St John Ambulance Association, to teach first aid in railway centres and mining districts. At that point, industrial accidents were common, and medical care was rudimentary or non-existent. Ten years later the St John Ambulance Brigade was established to provide first aid at public events, and has continued to do so ever since. The organization spread rapidly throughout Britain and other parts of the world. Despite its Christian origins, the St John Ambulance was always non-denominational and open to all.

By 1912 Dai had married Rachel and they went on to have six children. When war broke out Dai, keen to use and further develop the medical skills he'd learned with the St John Ambulance, joined the Royal Army

> 'My grandfather was a very generous man, always helping
> other people. He gave his life to the St John Ambulance,
> I think he really wanted to be a doctor.'
>
> MARTIN JENKINS, GRANDSON

Medical Corps (RAMC). This had been founded in 1898, bringing together under one umbrella all the army's medical services which hitherto had been operated on a rather ad hoc and largely regimental basis. Initially, Dai served in army hospitals in Tidworth and Aldershot and, when he was fully trained, he was sent in 1915 to serve on a hospital ship in the Mediterranean, probably to treat the wounded from the Dardanelles. From here he was sent to Mesopotamia, to join the RAMC units attached to the Indian Expeditionary Force D.

This force, formed largely from Indian Army divisions, though with some British units and strengthened in 1916 by the British 13th (Western) Division, had been sent to Mesopotamia in October 1914, primarily to secure the oilfields. This aim, fairly quickly achieved, was then expanded into a major war against Turkey. It was a difficult landscape in which to fight, being remote, inaccessible and with dramatic climatic variations. Transport was dependent upon the rivers, creating great supply and support problems. Moving the wounded back from the front line was also difficult and time-consuming and so medical conditions on the battlefield were primitive and inadequate. As a result, injuries and disease were the biggest killers.

At first the British achieved military success but the Turkish resistance quickly increased and advances were soon halted or reversed, usually at high cost in casualties. From December 1915 the British army was besieged at Kut al Amara and, when this army finally surrendered on 29 April 1916, Dai was among those captured. Luckily he was released, along with a party of 250 wounded, and sent down the Tigris to Basra. Thus, he escaped the terrible fate that awaited most of those who had surrendered after the siege of the Kut garrison.

By 1917 Dai was a Sergeant and he continued to serve in Mesopotamia for the rest of the war. The British had learned the lessons of 1915 and 1916 and by using better tactics, a better trained army and improved supply systems, they won a sequence of victories against the Turks in 1917, including the capture of Baghdad in March. This brought to an end German ambitions in the region, and led to the signing of an armistice with Turkey on 1 October 1918. It had been an expensive campaign, with about 30,000 dead, over 12,000 of whom were the result of disease, and 52,000 wounded.

At some point, probably in 1918, Dai treated a captured Turkish officer who had been wounded. In gratitude this officer gave Dai his watch. When he was finally demobilized in 1919, he took it home with him. When he got back to South Wales, Rachel, his wife, greeted him by saying he had been the first to go and the last to come back.

Dai returned to the pit, combining his work as a miner with his continuing St John Ambulance work. Thanks to his medical training and extensive wartime experience, his skills were often in demand, both at the pits, and with the local doctors. Many believed that this was his true calling and he should have been a doctor. During the Second World War he served with the Home Guard and as a Police Special Constable.

After the war Dai suffered increasingly from illness. Family photographs reveal that the healthy young man who had boxed for the army had aged 20 years during the war. He had bouts of malaria, a legacy of his service overseas, but more significant was the silicosis, the result of years of work as a coal miner underground, and it was this that killed him in January 1958, at the age of 65.

Dai carried the Turkish watch for the rest of his life and left it to his son Bill. When Bill died at the early age of 42, the watch passed to his son, Dai's grandson, Martin. In 2012 Martin gave it to his son Owen, an army search dog handler, as he was about to embark on a tour of Afghanistan. This battered watch, once the property of a now unknown Turkish officer, has seen – over four generations – the dust of Mesopotamia, the coal dust of South Wales and the desert sands of Helmand Province.

A SOLDIER WHO HELPED
A WOUNDED GERMAN

FREDERICK WILLIAM GLEED
1897–1954

Families today inevitably remember their relatives who were killed or wounded and there is, as a result, sometimes a tendency to overlook those who served right through the war and survived. Yet, even if never wounded, they still experienced dreadful things on a daily basis and their actual survival was itself sometimes the cause of mental anguish. Frederick William Gleed, always known as Fred, was born during the summer of 1897

near Wargrave-on-Thames, Berkshire. His father was Head Gardener at Yeldall Manor and so Fred grew up as a country boy.

After leaving school Fred worked as a junior gardener. One day in the autumn of 1914, when his complaints about a dangerous machine he was operating were ignored, he left and walked to Maidenhead to enlist in the 2/4th Battalion of the Royal Berkshire Regiment. This Territorial Force battalion had been formed in 1914 and was used at first for Home Defence duties. It was sent to France in May 1916, and Fred soon found himself in

'My grandfather served right through the war but when he
ame home he felt disillusioned for a while so he never wore
a poppy or took part in Remembrance events. He was a kind man
who loved animals and working on the land.'

FRED GLEED, GRANDSON

336

the trenches. In November he took part in the closing stages of the Battle of the Somme. For much of the war Fred served as a Runner, carrying messages to and from the front line. This was a very dangerous occupation, with a high mortality rate, but somehow Fred survived through 1917 and 1918 and, after the Armistice in November 1918, he was sent to Cologne with the army of occupation, where he remained until he was demobilized in January 1920.

His brother joined the Royal Marines when he was 16, having lied about his age, and was sent overseas. When his mother found out, she wrote to the War Office and, to everyone's surprise, he was removed from his ship and sent home. Later, he rejoined the navy and survived the war.

In the course of his duties, Fred sometimes came across wounded men, lying out in No Man's Land. On one occasion, he found a fellow soldier from the Royal Berkshire Regiment, seriously injured with a stomach wound. He directed stretcher-bearers to the man, but assumed he had died. Much later, in 1923, he met this man by chance in Maidenhead High Street, who was alive and well and very grateful to Fred. Another time he came across a badly injured German soldier, whom he carried back to the British lines. In gratitude, this man, Fritz Bierstedt, gave him his Iron Cross and a postcard from a friend that gave all his regimental details in the address. This card was looked after for years by Fred's mother, along with his tin helmet, and much later his grandson was able to trace Fritz Bierstedt via the Volksbund Deutsche Kriegsgraberversorge (the German War Graves Commission), and found out that he had died on 22 June 1918 and been buried in Méricourt Military Cemetery, among 83 German graves there.

The details of Fred's service are not known, apart from stories treasured by the family. Apparently, the only time

The Iron Cross given in gratitude to Frederick Gleed by the German soldier, Fritz Bierstedt, whom he had rescued.

he had to report to a doctor was after he had sat on his fork and been pierced by the prongs.

After the war, like many survivors, Fred struggled to find work and became quite disillusioned. Eventually he returned to gardening and farm work. He married Bertha in 1923. She had previously been engaged to a soldier killed at Messines in June 1917. She never allowed her children, or her grandchildren, to play at soldiers in her presence. Fred was a gentle man, one of the last to work with horses on the farm. He enjoyed a pint and was an outstanding darts player. During the Second World War he was a Special Constable. He never arrested anyone and the only time he lost his temper was when he found an Italian prisoner of war with a local girl. Fred died from bowel cancer in 1954.

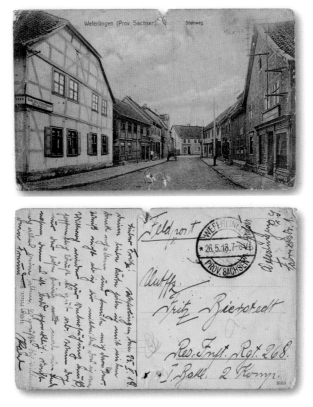

The postcard (front and back) that enabled Frederick Gleed to identify the wounded German he had rescued.

AN ARCHITECT KILLED AT THE END OF THE WAR

ALFRED TINNISWOOD
1879–1918

While some First World War stories are familiar to the family, others can remain hidden for generations until a chance discovery reveals them. The story of Alfred Tinniswood, who was born in December 1879, is one of the latter. It was only when his grandson Nigel was clearing the house after the death of his mother, Alfred's daughter, that he found a little suitcase

containing his grandfather's diaries of his army life, from training to the start of fighting, along with a sketchbook and other documents.

Little is known about Alfred's early life, other than that he was an artist and architect. In 1911, when he was attached to the London County Council's Architect's Department, he was made a Licentiate of the Royal Institute of British Architects. On 29 November 1915 Alfred enlisted in the 28th (County of London) Battalion of the London Regiment, more familiarly known as the Artists' Rifles. This volunteer corps had been formed in 1859 by Edward Sterling, an art student, and was at the

> 'My grandmother came from a typical Victorian background
> where nothing was ever discussed. So, she never mentioned
> my grandfather and we knew nothing about him or his war.
> My mother was one when he was killed and it was
> only after her death that his story came to light.'
>
> NIGEL ROPER, GRANDSON

start designed to attract painters, musicians, architects and others from the creative world who wanted to join the volunteer movement. Its first headquarters was at Burlington House, the home of the Royal Academy. The Artists' Rifles, which soon attracted volunteers from outside the art world, fought in South Africa, as part of the City Imperial Volunteers. When the London Regiment was formed in 1908 it incorporated many volunteer units, including the Artists' Rifles, which became its 28th Battalion.

Alfred became an instructor in field engineering and in November 1916 he was commissioned as a 2nd Lieutenant in the Royal Engineers, at some point joining the 412th Field Company which was attached to the 52nd Division. In 1916 this company was in Egypt and in 1917 it fought in Palestine. In May 1918 the company arrived in France, serving initially near Vimy and later near Arras. Alfred's records do not survive and so he may have been in France with another Royal Engineers Field Company before joining the 412th. He was first in action at the Battle of Cambrai, and then, in the latter part of 1918, he was with the company at the Battle of the Scarpe, and in the advance towards the Canal du Nord. On 1 October 1918, while working to repair a canal bridge at Moeuvres, near Marcoing, Alfred was killed by a shell.

Alfred left behind his wife and his one-year-old daughter and from that point he, in effect, disappeared. Alfred's wife never mentioned him and his daughter had no memory of him. It was only when his grandson

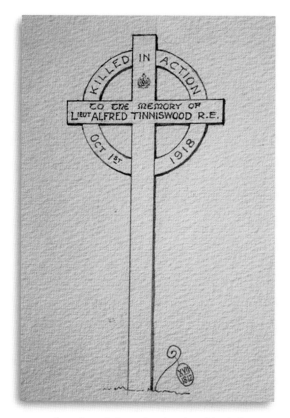

Opposite and above: Drawings by a friend of
Alfred Tinniswood, showing his wooden grave-marker
and the cemetery where he was buried.

discovered the suitcase that Alfred's story was revealed. Apart from the
diaries and sketchbook, the suitcase contained letters to his wife from
friends and comrades, and sketches by his friends showing the bridge
where he was killed, the cemetery where he had been buried and his
wooden grave marker. Thanks to the discovery of the suitcase, Alfred
Tinniswood came back into the heart of his family, after nearly a century
of silence and oblivion.

Nigel, his grandson, has since been to visit his grave in Moeuvres
Military Cemetery, and found that, other than the standard War Graves
Commission headstones which have replaced the original wooden crosses,
it looked just like the sketches of 1918.

A TALE OF TWO GRANDFATHERS

WILLIAM JOHN TAYLOR
1894–1946
REGINALD CUFFE
1896–1933

Families throughout Britain are linked firmly to the First World War by the stories of their grandfathers and great-uncles who fought in the conflict.

Today, some are barely remembered, while others have been meticulously researched by their descendents. The two soldiers from this family had very different military careers and experiences but family research has brought them together.

William John Taylor (far left of photograph, seated), known for reasons now forgotten as Brul, was born in Cardiff in 1894. His father, John Taylor, was a haulier who, at the time of his marriage in 1891, could neither read nor write; he had seven children. Little is known about William's early life or education but by 1912 he had become involved with the Territorial Force. When war broke out, Brul was called up for service in September or October 1914 as part of a draft of 200 men joining the Army Service Corps (ASC). This was the start of a long career with the ASC, the vital supply and transport arm for the army.

There are few records of Brul's career but he seems to have remained in Britain until 1916. In July that year, by then a Lance Corporal, he was

'My two grandfathers are my family heroes and I am thrilled that their story can be told. My great-uncles were also in the war, one of whom went down with HMS Defence at the Battle of Jutland. We must remember them all.'

JEFF CUFF, GRANDSON

sent to France, where he served for the rest of the war. He was attached to the 3rd Division and so took part in many of the major battles and campaigns of the last two years of the war. Involved as he was with the daily problems of maintaining the supply of food, ammunition and equipment to the front line, usually on horse-drawn wagons, he was exposed to all the dangers of front-line life and his war experiences were as extreme as any fighting soldier. He witnessed dreadful things on a daily basis and in one battle was gassed. In another he was wounded by shrapnel,  ending up with a metal plate in his head. Somehow he survived and was with the ASC until the Armistice. After the war he remained for a while in the army, becoming a Lance Sergeant in February 1919 and later a Sergeant-Major.

Brul left the army in June 1920, returned to Cardiff and used his army experience as a haulier to get a job with the Park Coal Company, where he remained for the rest of his life. At some point Brul married his childhood sweetheart, Winifrid Simpson, and they had eight children. However, he was a broken man and his life was blighted by his experience of the war. The lasting effects of the gassing shortened his life. Doctors told him he would die at about 50, and he did, in 1946, aged 52. Like many former soldiers, he spent long hours in the local pub, drinking to forget his memories. He clearly suffered from what would now be recognized as post-traumatic stress syndrome. He was hard on his sons, though his daughters adored him. He missed his comrades, both dead and alive, with whom he had shared the most extreme experiences, and he felt, like much of his generation, that these were his real family.

Meanwhile, in Dorset in April 1896, Reginald Cuffe (above) was born, as one of four children. Little is known about his early life but he became a certified nurseryman and florist. In about 1912 he and his brother Frank became involved in the Territorial Force and when the war came they both enlisted in the 1/4th Battalion of the Dorsetshire Regiment. Reginald was a first-class shot and a drummer in the regimental band. This famous county regiment, whose cap badge reflected its long association with

India, was established in its modern form in 1881. It fought on the North West Frontier and in South Africa and was expanded on the outbreak of the First World War to nine battalions, six of which fought overseas, notably at Gallipoli and in Mesopotamia, Palestine and India.

The 1/4th Battalion was formed in Dorchester in August 1914. Its first duties were guarding the naval facilities at Devonport dockyard but it was soon sent overseas, leaving for India on 9 October 1914. It landed in Bombay on 10 November and there then followed some months of primarily Imperial duties in various parts of India. Meanwhile, the war in Mesopotamia was becoming steadily more troublesome. The Dorsets' 2nd Battalion was sent there, only to become embroiled in the siege of Kut and in due course was forced to surrender to the Turks along with the rest of General Townshend's army on 29 April 1916. Only 70 of the 350 men of the 2nd Battalion that surrendered were to survive captivity.

During and after the Kut disaster, a much larger and better organized British army under the command of General Brooking was assembled and sent to Mesopotamia, and that included Reginald and Frank in the 1/4th Battalion. On 18 February 1916 their battalion left India and landed at Basra, where they were immediately involved in strengthening the city's defences, railways and docks. On 29 April 1916 the battalion started on a long

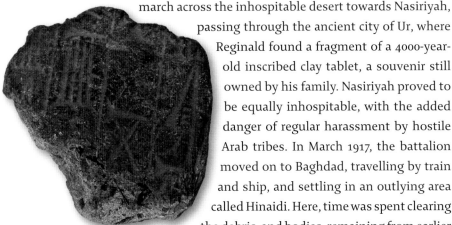

march across the inhospitable desert towards Nasiriyah, passing through the ancient city of Ur, where Reginald found a fragment of a 4000-year-old inscribed clay tablet, a souvenir still owned by his family. Nasiriyah proved to be equally inhospitable, with the added danger of regular harassment by hostile Arab tribes. In March 1917, the battalion moved on to Baghdad, travelling by train and ship, and settling in an outlying area called Hinaidi. Here, time was spent clearing the debris, and bodies, remaining from earlier

The 4000-year-old clay tablet found by Reginald Cuffe in April 1916 in the ancient city of Ur in Mesopotamia.

battles. There were frequent attacks on local Turkish and Arab units.

In September 1917 the battalion moved to Fallujah and thence to Madhij, to become part of an attacking force designed to drive the Turkish army from the Ramadi Ridge. In a desperate battle, with the Dorsets fighting alongside Gurkhas, the Turks were finally defeated, and their whole army in the area surrendered. The Dorsets, who had suffered 176 casualties, then moved back to Madhij for the winter. In February 1918 the campaign was resumed, with the capture of Hit in March, followed by further successes culminating in the Turkish defeat at Khan Baghdadi. The battalion remained in the area until the Armistice in November 1918, and then became part of the army of occupation for a year. In November 1919 they returned to India and from there they were shipped back to Britain, arriving in Plymouth on 3 January 1920. The following day the 1/4th Battalion finally arrived back in Dorchester, where a full civic reception awaited them.

For Reginald and Frank the war experience in Mesopotamia was very different to the more familiar setting of the Western Front. Heat and cold, disease, the inhospitable desert, supply problems and an unpredictable and often elusive enemy were challenging conditions that made fighting as difficult as anything that they had experienced in France or Belgium. Yet, the Mesopotamia campaign is still little known and its importance rarely appreciated.

Back at home, Reginald married Eva Critchell in Weymouth and they had two children, one of whom died young. He worked with friends for the Great Western Railway (GWR) in Cardiff, and being a football-lover, won the Ingram Cup for the GWR in 1932. After his marriage ended, Reginald returned to Weymouth, working again as a nurseryman and landscape gardener, and remaining a cheerful and outgoing man despite his family problems. He was always loved by his surviving son, who in due course became a great family man with six children. Reginald also enjoyed racing and in 1933 he and some friends had a massive jackpot win on the Derby. His share was £1000 and he spent £85 on a motorcycle. A week later, riding it in bad weather, Reginald had an accident and was killed, a strange link with T. E. Lawrence, who had fought in Mesopotamia and who was to die in a motorcycle accident in Dorset two years later.

POST WAR

THE SIGNING OF THE ARMISTICE ON 11 NOVEMBER 1918 brought the fighting in Europe to an end but the war was not formally over until June 1919, when Germany finally signed the Treaty of Versailles. This is why many war memorials, and many commemorative mugs and plates, give the dates of the war as 1914–1919. They also use such terms as the Great War and the World War, both of which were in use by 1914. The Treaty of Versailles redrew the map of Europe, laid the foundations of the League of Nations and imposed such punitive reparations on Germany that, combined with the acceptance of responsibility for starting the war, the build-up to the Second World War became inevitable.

In some places, fighting continued after November 1918. British troops fought on the North West Frontier until the early 1920s to bring under control tribal uprisings in Waziristan and Afghanistan. There was also periodic unrest in the Middle East, which had been divided between France and Britain under the terms of the Sykes–Picot Agreement of 1916. Arab tribal leaders who had supported the Allies found that wartime promises were not being honoured, and the disputes that followed laid the foundations for present-day conflicts in the region.

Fighting also continued in North Russia until 1919, following the Allies' ill-considered intervention in support of the White Russians in 1918, ultimately designed to bring the former Russian government back into power, and thus reopen the Eastern Front campaign against Germany. British, French and American troops, backed by a substantial naval force and limited aircraft, had some successes in the bitterly cold winter, but were eventually forced to abandon a hopeless exercise. Afterwards, the British government attempted to draw a veil over the whole enterprise, making the North Russia Intervention the least known campaign of the war.

No one knows exactly how many died in the First World War, but the total probably runs into tens of millions. Apart from those killed in the global fighting, hundreds of thousands died from disease, notably in the Spanish influenza epidemic that swept across the battlefields from 1918. Alongside the deaths, there were many more soldiers who never recovered from the physical and psychological effects of being injured, or simply taking part. A generation of devastated families was the lasting legacy of the 'war to end war'. Twenty years later, those same families saw it start all over again.

In this chapter, stories depict some of those post-war campaigns. Others highlight the lasting effects of the war, on families in Britain, Australia and Germany, and reveal how objects can sometimes bring long-forgotten stories to light. The final account, told by a Senior Chaplain, offers a rare insight into the story of the Unknown Warrior, which since 1920 has been the national symbol of mourning for the British dead of the First World War.

TEN BROTHERS GO TO WAR

THE CALPIN BROTHERS

During the First World War many family members served together or at the same time. There are plenty of cases of two of more members of one family being killed, with over 300 pairs of brothers killed on the same day. At least three families, the Souls, the Beecheys and the Cranstons, each lost five sons.

By contrast, the Calpin family sent ten brothers to the war and all came back, although one died during wartime. The family had originally emigrated from Ireland during the Great Famine in the 1840s, and settled in York. Mr and Mrs Calpin, who married in the 1870s, had ten boys and one girl. Several of the boys worked for Rowntree's, the local chocolate manufacturer, and some had enlisted in the army or the Territorial Force before the war. All signed on soon after the outbreak of war.

John, born in 1875, was 39 when he went to fight in France. Gassed in 1915 or early 1916, he was sent home, but died in 1916. Patrick, born in 1878, was attached to the Remount Service. James, born in 1881, William, born in 1882, Martin, born in 1885, and Thomas, born in 1887, served in various battalions of the West Yorkshire Regiment. Arthur, born in 1890, served with the East Yorkshire Regiment. Henry, born in 1892, served with the Royal Field Artillery. Ernest, born in 1893, and David, the youngest, joined the Royal Navy.

Ernest was on the battleship HMS *Dreadnought* in March 1915 when she rammed and sank the submarine U-29, the only German submarine sunk by a battleship in the First World War. Ernest served again in the Second World War, and suffered a serious head wound. He died in 1957.

At the end of the war, Mr and Mrs Calpin received a letter of thanks from the Lord Mayor of York, praising them and their sons for doing their duty.

'My grandfather died when I was seven, so I never asked him about the war. He was good fun but a bit of a ruffian.'

MICK CALPIN, GRANDSON

A DORSET MAN WHO DIED FOR AUSTRALIA

EDWIN HENRY DIBBEN
1881–1914

Over the last few years the name Fromelles has become more widely known but for nearly a century the name of this famous battle had been largely forgotten, along with the thousands of Australians who fought and died there. Edwin Henry Dibben, always known as Harry, was one of those soldiers, although he had been born in Buckland Newton in Dorset in 1883.

His father was a farmer and had seven children but Harry, unlike his brother, left the farm and trained in Dorchester as a coachbuilder. In 1906 Harry emigrated from Britain, first to South Africa and then to New Zealand and finally to Australia, where he arrived in 1912, and worked as a motor mechanic in Sydney. On 23 August 1915, when he was nearly 33, he volunteered for the Australian Imperial Force. Surviving documents from this time describe him as blue-eyed, with brown hair and a fresh complexion. After training, he sailed from Sydney on 20 December 1915 bound for Egypt with a batch of new recruits who were to join the Australian survivors of the Dardanelles campaign. Initially he was with the 13th Rifle Brigade but was transferred early in 1916 to the 54th Battalion of the 14th Brigade. A period of intense training followed, including route

'I became aware of my great-uncle Harry in the 1980s when I was given a family tree. I knew he had died in the war, but couldn't understand why so little was known about him, and why he wasn't listed on the war memorial at Buckland Newton. I decided to find out.'

RICHARD DIBBEN, GREAT-NEPHEW

marches in the full heat of the desert summer. While in Egypt Harry sent his brother Will a postcard, and it was the discovery of this years later that inspired his great-nephew Richard to research his life.

In June 1916 the 14th Brigade left Egypt, sailed to Marseilles and was then transported by train to the north of France. Feted all the way by French people, the soldiers were based first at Thiennes, and then moved via Estaires to Fleurbaix. The more experienced troops they were replacing had gone south to the Somme. Although the living conditions were primitive, they enjoyed the summer weather, sharing their lives with French families and in some cases working on local farms. However, all this was soon to change.

From late 1914 and through much of 1915, the main British battleground on the Western Front had been the Ypres area. Ypres itself had been held, at huge cost, and a series of related, and largely unsuccessful, battles had been fought as the British tried to push eastwards to secure the area. The German response had been to strengthen their lines by building a linear fortress with concrete machine-gun emplacements and deep dugouts, against which British artillery was relatively ineffective. A key spot in the area south of Ypres was the higher ground represented by Aubers Ridge, which the British tried, and failed, to capture several times. Another important point was the village of Fromelles, and the nearby raised ground known as the Sugarloaf, which was 17 miles southwest of Ypres and, more importantly, only 10 miles west of Lille, a vital German command and supply centre, the loss of which would probably have ended the war. Despite its strategic importance, the British had developed the habit of using this area as a training ground for inexperienced troops, and so the losses had always been considerable. The Allied Commander in the area was Sir Richard Haking, whose policy seemed to be to force the line forward regardless of cost. It has to be remembered that, in 1915, there was no other strategy for an army committed to attack, as the British were. However, after the failure of the Battle of Aubers Ridge in May 1915, this had become a quieter sector. The lack of activity gave the Germans ample opportunity to further strengthen their lines.

By the summer of 1916, Haking was ready to resume his attacks, the main focus of which was now to prevent German reinforcements being sent south to the Somme, where the major Allied campaign was to start on 1 July. In early July an attack was planned for Fromelles but initially it was delayed, partly due to the weather and partly due to a dawning realization that any attack over the open ground in front of the Sugarloaf could be a disaster. However, Haking was confident of success, and determined that the attack should take place. It was to be carried out by the British 61st Division, comprised largely of reasonably experienced Territorial battalions, and the 5th Australian Division which, by comparison, was largely inexperienced. The attack was launched on 19 July 1916 and ended the next day. It was, as predicted, a disaster and, although gains were made, the battle ended with nothing significant achieved. The losses were huge. British and German casualties were around 1500 but 5533 Australians were killed or wounded and a further 400 were taken prisoner. Fromelles was the first Australian battle on the Western Front, and it was widely felt, at the time and subsequently, that thousands had been sacrificed pointlessly. For many in Australia, it was the Dardanelles all over again. Australia never forgot Fromelles but the British did their best to draw a veil over the disaster, and it quickly became a battle that never figured in the litany of famous Western Front battle sites.

Harry Dibben, in A Company in the Australian Imperial Force's 54th Brigade, fought well and a section of German trench was captured. In the course of this, however, Harry was shot and critically injured. As so often happened, the gains could not be consolidated, and the Australians had to withdraw, leaving Harry and

The postcard (front and back) sent from Egypt that inspired Harry Dibben's great-nephew, Richard Dibben, to research his great-uncle's life.

many others behind. After the battle, the Germans collected all the dead, loaded the bodies onto railway wagons and took them back for burial in a series of mass graves at Pheasant Wood. This was well documented by the Germans, and bodies were identified wherever possible. Harry's family was told that he was missing. In 1917 his sister Mabel made an enquiry via the Red Cross and received a reply saying that, from German records, he had been identified among the dead. At this point, Harry and all his colleagues disappeared. Despite contemporary German and Australian records, and despite aerial photographs that clearly showed them, the mass graves at Pheasant Wood were forgotten and when the Imperial War Graves Commission searched the area for bodies in the 1920s, the mass graves were somehow missed.

It was not until the 1990s that the Fromelles story was rediscovered. Lambis Englezos, a Melbourne teacher, became interested in the story of Fromelles and its Australian history. Soon, he noticed the significant discrepancy between the known number of dead from the battle and those accounted for in actual burial sites and on memorials to the missing. From German and Red Cross archives he was able to establish that mass burials had taken place, and his evidence was supported by the aerial photographs taken at the time that showed the graves. For a while no one listened but in the end the evidence was so convincing that an electronic survey of the site was carried out. In 2008 this confirmed the presence at Pheasant Wood of eight mass graves, undisturbed since 1918. In May 2009 a full exhumation began, backed by a DNA analysis to try to identify the soldiers, most of whom were Australian. In January 2010 the burial with full military honours of the 249 bodies started in the newly built Fromelles Military Cemetery.

Richard Dibben, Harry's great-nephew, had supplied a DNA sample in November 2009, and in March 2010 he received a phone call from the Australian army in Canberra to say that his sample had matched one of the exhumed bodies. At that point, Harry Dibben, in effect, came back from the dead. In July 2010 Richard, with other members of the Dibben family, attended the dedication of the new cemetery, a truly memorable moment that finally brought closure to Harry and his life. The name of Edwin Henry Dibben was also added to the war memorial in Buckland Newton, Dorset, where the whole story had started.

Henry Jenkins's ditty box, a chance discovery by his grandson Alan,
which revealed the story of his life.

A SAILOR BROUGHT TO LIFE
BY A CHANCE DISCOVERY

HENRY JENKINS
1882–1925

Henry Jenkins came from a long-established Pembrokeshire family, one that his grandson Alan now feels connected to, after recently discovering a long-forgotten box containing his grandfather's papers. Henry was born in Lawrenny in March 1882, one of a pair of twins in a family of seven children,

and his father was a ferryman and boatman working around Milford Haven. After school, Henry worked as a farm servant and then, in 1900, he enlisted in the Royal Navy, signing on in Portsmouth for 12 years. After training he served on the battleships HMS *Impregnable* and HMS *Lion*, and on the cruiser HMS *Black Prince*. Further periods of training followed, some on HMS *Victory*, interspersed with service at sea. As a Leading Signalman on the *Cressy*-class cruiser HMS *Euryalus*, he assisted the victims of an earthquake in Italy. By 1911 he was a Ship's Corporal on the cruiser HMS *Blake* and in 1913 he was posted to HMS *Dido*, a former cruiser then starting a new life as a depot ship. In 1912 he married Alice Tuck, and they had three children, with the family based in Portsmouth.

> '*I was told that my grandfather was a lovely man, warm and affectionate but a bit of a martinet. More important, I realize now that my life was shaped by his life and his experiences, though I didn't know this when I grew up.*'

REVEREND ALAN JENKINS, GRANDSON

One of the photographs discovered in Henry Jenkins's ditty box.
He is probably the man on the right.

Henry was on HMS *Dido* when the war broke out, and he remained on her until 1917. His war experience was, therefore, relatively quiet and an important reminder that many soldiers and sailors rarely, if ever, see action. This changed in 1917 when Henry joined HMS *Nairana*, a newly converted aircraft and seaplane carrier that had started life as a merchant vessel being built on the Clyde for an Australian company. Her first attachment was at Scapa Flow, where she was used largely for training purposes, and so Henry's quiet war continued. However, in the summer of 1918 she was sent to Russia as the primary aircraft carrier in the naval flotilla sent to support the North Russian Intervention. Here, on 1 August 1918, Henry had his first taste of action when HMS *Nairana* made history by taking part in the world's first combined operation involving sea, air and land forces in a successful attack on a fort held by the Bolsheviks on the mouth of the Dvina River. This new type of strategy, which had been developed during the last months of the war, reflected the availability of better communications, a better understanding of the use of air power and, most importantly, a move away from traditional inter-service rivalries.

Later, Henry received a share of prize money for the capture of Bolshevik vessels in August 1918. When Henry left HMS *Nairana*, the ship's company presented him with a watch. He remained in the navy after the war, and his last posting, as Master-at-Arms, was on the battleship HMS *Iron Duke* in 1923.

After leaving the navy, Henry and his family moved back to Pembrokeshire, living near Tenby, and he worked as a salesman. In 1925, while returning from a visit to a client, he was killed when his motorcycle was in collision with a baker's van. His wife Alice remarried and seemed at that point to detach herself from her former life and Henry almost disappears from history. The children she had had with Henry were sent away, and the connection with Pembrokeshire was severed. According to Alan, Henry's grandson, his father, Henry's son, was sent away to school at the age of seven and in due course followed Henry's footsteps and joined the navy. He rarely mentioned his parents and so Alan grew up knowing nothing about his grandparents.

Alice Jenkins died in 1940 and her second husband then gave all her belongings back to her first husband's brother. This included Henry's 'ditty box', a plain wooden box in which seamen traditionally kept all their personal papers. Alice's brother hid the box behind the cistern in an outside lavatory at the family home in Pembrokeshire and then forgot all about it. Many years later a cousin bought the house at auction and, in the course of demolishing the outside lavatory, found the box. Meanwhile, Alan, Henry's grandson, had started to trace his early Pembrokeshire roots and went to look at the former family home. It was only by chance that he met the new owner, but in conversation they established their distant family connection, at which point Alan was given his grandfather's box. He took it home, opened it and his grandfather's story was revealed, in letters, photographs, his service record and all sorts of bits and pieces that brought him to life. For the first time, in what was a very emotive experience, Alan felt he had met his grandfather. Alan, who is a Methodist Minister, also began to understand why he had always felt Pembrokeshire to be his home, even though he had had no connections with the area until he was sent by the Methodists to a Pembrokeshire parish.

A CYCLIST WHO FOUGHT ON THE NORTH WEST FRONTIER

CHARLES JOHN DAVIS
1896–1981

There are many aspects of the First World War that are frequently overlooked today, for example the role played by the Cyclist battalions and the campaigns in the North West Frontier. Charles John Davis brings

together these two stories. He was born in Bow, east London in 1896 to a warehouseman father. Charles did better for himself and by 1911 was working as a stockbroker's clerk in the City of London. A keen cyclist and sportsman, he always rode to work, and this habit took him into the war. One day in August 1914 he and a couple of friends were on their way to work when they were stopped in the road by a recruiting picket of soldiers and encouraged to join up.

The result was that on 31 August Charles enlisted in the 25th (County of London) Cyclist Battalion of the London Regiment.

The army's interest in cycling started in 1887, with the formation of the 26th Middlesex (Cyclist) Volunteer Corps, a unit involved in the development of military cycling tactics. In 1907 this became the 25th

'As a child I knew him very well, he was a lovely grandpa, very kind. And when we saw him he always gave us half a crown, so we loved him to bits. I know he'd be amazed if he knew we were talking about him now, and delighted that his old friends in his "forgotten" war are being remembered.'

NIGEL LOGAN, GRANDSON

Top: A postcard showing a group from the 25th
(County of London) Cyclist Battalion, still in civilian clothes.
Bottom: Military badge embroideries worked by Charles Davis
while recovering from illness in India.

Cyclist Battalion of the London Regiment. By 1914 there were 14,000 cyclists attached to various regiments, a figure that grew steadily through the war. Cyclist units were also a feature of French, German and Italian armies. The idea was that cyclists would be used as scouts and for reconnaissance, as a kind of bicycle cavalry, and their speed and flexibility would give them an advantage in house-to-house and street fighting. The reality of the conditions on the Western Front soon destroyed these notions, and so Cyclist battalions were largely kept in Britain and used for guarding camps and patrolling the coasts as part of the defence against the risks of invasion by Germany, a very real fear in the early part of the war. Charles and his colleagues spent most of 1915 patrolling the coasts of Sussex, Kent and East Anglia. In December 1915 the 25th Battalion, along with the regiment's other Cyclist battalions, were reorganized as infantry, and in February 1916 Charles found himself in India with the battalion, having left their precious bicycles behind in Britain.

The former cyclists joined other units being sent to reinforce the British army presence in India, and to strengthen the defences in the North West Frontier. In March 1916 the Seistan Force had been established, under the command of General Dyer, to protect India and the Middle East from enemy attacks via Afghanistan and the North West Frontier. This region had been a trouble-spot since the early 19th century, and a number of Victorian wars had been provoked by the perceived threats to India from this region, initially from Russia and later from Germany. In the First World War, the threat of a German campaign in the region was taken very seriously, because of the potential risk to India and to the oil supplies in the Middle East.

In the summer of 1917, Charles was involved in fighting the incursion by the Mahsud tribe, the first round in what was to become the Waziristan campaign. The fighting was very difficult, in intense heat, and with shortages of supplies, including water, and medical facilities, but order was restored. In May 1919, six months after the defeat of Germany, the Afghan army crossed the frontier and invaded a part of India. The British responded by assembling a large army which, supported by the Royal Air Force, drove the Afghans back. This campaign, generally known as the Third Anglo-Afghan War, ended with an armistice in August 1919. Among those who took part were the 25th Battalion of the London Regiment. Encouraged by unrest in Afghanistan, the Waziris started a new and much more substantial series of incursions in the later part of 1919. In November British attacks quickly pacified the Waziris but the Mahsuds, who had joined in, proved to be a tougher foe and the campaign dragged on for a year. Again, the Royal Air Force played an important role in the defeat of the Mahsuds, and this prompted a new approach to frontier control in this unstable region that relied heavily on air power, to which there could be no adequate tribal response.

By this time many British troops were war-weary and felt that they had done more than their duty, and so the campaign relied heavily on Indian and Gurkha troops. Charles, who had taken part in the Afghan War, and the Amritsar Riots in India in 1919, was taken out of the front line by a different problem. At some point, he developed dysentery, one of the many diseases that caused havoc among the British serving in the region, and became seriously ill. He was taken back to India and sent ultimately to a hill station in the Himalayas to recover. It was here that, encouraged by the Indian nurses and memsahibs, he took up embroidery as a kind of occupational therapy, and produced a series of detailed embroideries on old scraps of fabric depicting regimental badges. The 25th Cyclist Battalion is represented, along with a mixed selection of others. The random nature of these suggests that they may have been the regimental badges of fellow invalids in the hospital. When he came back to Britain, changed from the fit young man who signed on in 1914 to a white-haired scarecrow, he brought these with him, and they have been with the family ever since.

After the war Charles returned to his old job as a stockbroker's clerk and worked in the same business for the next 50 years. In 1923 Charles married a French woman, Marie Mathilde Guyan-Messager, who had come to Britain to work for her uncle, a briar pipe maker, and they had two daughters. When she died in 1949, he married her best friend and had a second long and happy marriage. Despite the long-term effects of his wartime illness, which left him with only one kidney, he retained his love of sport, and took up skiing in his fifties. Charles Davis died in 1981.

THE SOLDIER GIVEN A WALKING STICK BY QUEEN ALEXANDRA

BENJAMIN FREDERICK WHITELEY
1881–1959

Benjamin Frederick Whiteley was born in March 1881 into a Methodist family in Leeds, where his father had a bicycle shop. His mother died

young, and all Benjamin's brothers went into the bicycle business. At about the time his father remarried, Benjamin joined the Leeds Rifles. Formed as a Volunteer Rifle Corps in 1859, it was attached in 1881 to the (Prince of Wales's Own) West Yorkshire Regiment, becoming its 3rd Battalion. At some point Benjamin left the Leeds Rifles and enlisted in the regular army, joining the 2nd Battalion of the King's Royal Rifle Corps. This regiment had a very distinguished history, having originally been raised in North America in 1758. It fought in the Peninsular War, and in many Victorian campaigns including China, Afghanistan and Burma. It fought in South Africa, and it was here that Benjamin had his first experience of military

'I don't really remember my fierce but friendly grandfather,
though there is a photograph of him holding me as a baby.
My father told me he spent his time smoking, going on long walks
and doing the Daily Mail crossword. When offered the chance
to visit the First World War battlefields, he replied: "Why would
I want to go back there, where I left all my friends?"'

HELEN WHITELEY, GRANDDAUGHTER

action, serving as mounted infantry. By 1914 he was a Sergeant, and a well-established regular army career soldier. In 1910 he married, and his two children were born in 1911 and 1917.

By 13 August 1914 Benjamin was in France with the 2nd Battalion, at the start of a long association with the Western Front. He fought at Mons, on the Marne and the Aisne and at the First Battle of Ypres. By September 1914 he had become a Company Sergeant-Major and in December he was commissioned in the field as a 2nd Lieutenant. He was awarded the Distinguished Conduct Medal at the First Battle of Ypres, for 'Gallant conduct for leading all available men in a charge at Veldhoek', but was just as proud of his 1914 Star.

In January 1915 Benjamin was severely wounded during a bombing raid on German trenches when a British shell fell short and buried him in his trench. Several were killed, and his wife was told that he was dead. Luckily, she soon discovered that he had been rescued, though with serious head and leg wounds, and in due course he was brought back to Britain, to the Empire Hospital for Officers in Vincent Square, London, which specialized in head and spinal injuries. It was while he was recovering that Benjamin

The walking stick presented to Benjamin Whiteley by Queen Alexandra in March 1915, with a detail of the inscription.

was visited by King George V and Queen Alexandra in March 1915. This visit, and the conversation they had, probably came about because the King was Colonel-in-Chief of Benjamin's regiment. At the end of the visit, Queen Alexandra gave him a walking stick bearing her royal cipher on a silver band.

After a long period of recovery and convalescence, Benjamin went back to the army. At first he was only passed for light duties at the battalion's home depot but eventually he was passed fit for overseas service and transferred to the Machine Gun Corps, perhaps because the former Commanding Officer of his Battalion during the early months of the war, Brigadier General Eric Pearce-Serocold, was later involved with the Machine Gun Corps. Benjamin returned to France in September 1918 and fought through the last months of the war as a Captain with the Machine Gun Corps. However, Benjamin's war was not yet over and in August 1919 his battalion was sent to Russia for two months to support the withdrawal of Allied forces that had taken part in the Northern Russian Expedition, or North Russian Intervention.

The background to this little-known campaign was the Russian Revolution of 1917 and the abdication of the Tzar, which had led to the collapse of Russia as a fighting force and the Treaty of Brest-Litovsk of 3 March 1918 which ended Russian involvement in the First World War. This treaty not only released large numbers of German troops for service on the Western Front, but also caused great fear among the Allies faced by the rising tide of Bolshevism. A White Russian army of anti-Bolsheviks under the command of Admiral Kolchak was fighting the Red army in the north of Russia and so during the spring of 1918 the Allies decided to intervene to give support to the White Russians in the hope of re-establishing an Eastern Front. There was also a plan to protect Archangel and the port of Murmansk from the Bolsheviks. At this point the British and the French, hard-pressed by the Germans on the Western Front, had no troops to spare. However, President Wilson promised American support and by May 1918 an International Contingent had been assembled from American, Canadian, Australian and French colonial troops, along with Serbian and Polish elements. The British contribution was a quickly created 6th Battalion of the Royal Marine Light Infantry, largely made up of young conscripts and soldiers from base depots, none of whom had any fighting experience.

There was substantial Royal Naval support for the venture with a flotilla of 20 ships, including two seaplane carriers, and a small Royal Air Force contribution in the form of bombers, seaplanes and a Sopwith Camel fighter. Six tanks also took part.

The campaign was complex and largely unsuccessful, although Archangel was captured on 4 August 1918. Further advances were made, thanks in part to the support from the RAF aircraft, in this region and along the River Dvina. There were also successes by the Royal Navy, including attacks by high-speed Coastal Motor Torpedo Boats on Russian warships in Kronstadt naval base. In September, after two unsuccessful attacks on the village of Koikori by the British, there was a mutiny by one company of the Royal Marines. At the subsequent court martial, 13 Marines were sentenced to death, although these sentences were later revoked. By this time, a withdrawal was underway, although fighting continued until November. Given the limited success on the ground, there was increasing pressure in Britain to bring to an end the venture, which Churchill had presented as a means 'to strangle at birth the Bolshevik State'. In January 1919 the *Daily Express* famously declared, 'The frozen plains of Eastern Europe are not worth the bones of a single Grenadier.' The British, along with much of Europe, were sick of war. A full withdrawal from Russia started in the early months of 1919 and that was when Benjamin was sent there, with his battalion of Machine Gunners. By now, there were plenty of troops available to safeguard the withdrawal and by April 1919 it was all over. The North Russian campaign is one of the reasons why some memorials and commemorations give the dates of the First World War as 1914 to 1919. Fighting also continued in other areas, notably Mesopotamia.

Captain Benjamin Whiteley remained in the army until 1921, and was briefly recalled during the General Strike in 1926. In 1940 he was commissioned into the Royal Air Force Volunteer Reserve, becoming one of the founding officers of the RAF Regiment. Today, his memory is in the care of his granddaughter, Helen, who has also served in the RAF, along with his royal walking stick, his medals and several tunic jackets, all of which reveal that he was by modern standards a small man. His son, Helen's father, also went to Murmansk, serving as a naval officer escorting Russian convoys in the Second World War.

A SAILOR WHO FOUGHT IN RUSSIA

WILLIAM LESLIE TOKELEY
1881–1962

The Western Front inevitably dominates the history of the First World War, and so some other campaigns are little known today. William Leslie Tokeley, always known as Will, was involved in one of the least known, the Allied Expeditionary Force sent to North Russia. In 1899, at the age of 18, Will enlisted in the Royal Navy, signing on in Portsmouth for 12 years. He trained as a Signaller, was attached to the training ship HMS *Alexandria* and then served on several famous battleships, including HMS *Duncan*, HMS *Lion*, HMS *Resolution* and HMS *Impregnable*.

William Tokeley wearing Arctic clothing, designed by Sir Ernest Shackleton.

In about 1907 William was retired from the navy on grounds of ill health, married his wife Ellen, and joined the Merchant Service. For the next two years he served on a variety of ships, including the Anchor Line's SS *Caledonia* and the SS *Galeka*, a Union Castle Line vessel and then, in 1909, he came ashore and joined the Prudential Assurance Company.

At the outbreak of war, Will rejoined the Royal Navy and served through the war. The signing of the Armistice in November 1918 and the defeat of

> '*The war in the Arctic deeply affected my grandfather and he rarely spoke about the things he had seen. He felt everyone involved had been badly treated, lost faith in the government and hated Churchill, whom he held responsible.*'
>
> CHRISTOPHER TOKELEY, GRANDSON

Germany and the Austro-Hungarian alliance brought the First World War to an end on the Western Front, in Italy and in the Middle East. However, in a few areas fighting continued, notably in the North West Frontier region and in Russia. The latter, known as the North Russia Intervention or the Northern Russian Expedition, is one of the least familiar chapters in the history of the First World War, mainly because the governments of the Allies involved, notably Britain, France and the United States, did their best to draw a veil over one of their least successful ventures. There was no official history, and books written by those who took part, or who knew about the campaign, only appeared decades later. The most notable, *Archangel 1918–1919*, by General Edmund Ironside, the Commander of the Expedition, did not appear until 1953.

In 1918 Will was serving on HMS *M23*, one of the fleet of M15-class monitors introduced from 1915. These small, low-draught vessels were designed for shore bombardment and were usually equipped with one large-calibre gun, supported by secondary armament. When commissioned in July 1915, *M23* had a single 9.2-inch gun, later replaced by a smaller 7.5-inch gun. She served first in the Mediterranean, and was then attached to the Dover Patrol. On 6 April 1919, *M23* was sent to Russia as part of the large naval flotilla of over 20 ships supporting the Expedition, and arrived at Solombala, near Archangel, on 14 April. By this time, the Expedition was approaching its end, the initial gains made by the land forces having been steadily lost. Over the next few weeks *M23* was involved in frequent actions, mostly on the Dvina River and with the aim of keeping Bolshevik gunboats at bay. By September 1919, *M23* was helping with the evacuation of troops and she finally left Murmansk for Norway on 10 October. On 11 November 1919 *M23* was back in Chatham.

However, Will was not with her. *M23*'s log reveals that on 1 May 1919 one signal rating was discharged to hospital. This must have been him, as he arrived back in Portsmouth on 15 July 1919, on board the cruiser HMS *Fox*.

Nonetheless, the Arctic experience had a lasting impact on William Tokeley. He witnessed the intense cold that killed members of the Expedition, the inadequate equipment and preparations, and the muddle and uncertainty that accompanied an expedition whose politics, principles and planning were never clear-cut. With hindsight, the idea of halting the Bolshevik domination of Russia by a half-hearted intervention was doomed to fail. Even Sir Winston Churchill, one of the scheme's greatest supporters, acknowledged that at least 100,000 soldiers would have been necessary for the Expedition to have any chance of success. As ever, there were other agendas, namely the saving of large stockpiles of war materials in Archangel, the rescue of the soldiers of the Czechoslovak Legion trapped in Russia and their use with the White Russian forces to reopen the Eastern Front. In 1918, with the defeat of Germany still uncertain, this must all have seemed a good idea. By 1919, the Expedition had, in effect, failed and its prolongation was pointless.

After leaving the navy, Will returned to the Prudential and worked as an Area Manager until his retirement. However, he never overcame the bitter legacy of his Russian experience and became a life-long Socialist with a deep distrust of governments. He died in May 1962.

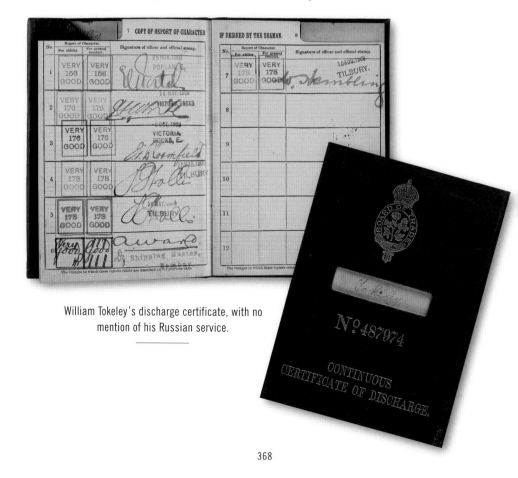

William Tokeley's discharge certificate, with no mention of his Russian service.

A STAFF OFFICER AND CLASSICAL SCHOLAR WHO WAS A PHOTOGRAPHER

THOMAS PEROWNE COE
1887–1974

Thomas Perowne Coe, who was always known by his second name, was a typical product of Edwardian Britain. He came from a notable Norwich family connected to the development of photography from the mid-1840s and

famous today as Britain's longest-established family photography business. While at Oxford, Perowne rowed for his college and joined the university's Officers' Training Corps, a classic route into the army for a generation brought up in the ethos of volunteering for military service via the Territorial Force.

After graduating with a double first in Classics, Perowne entered the Imperial Civil Service and started a long career in the Federated Malay States. As a member of the Malay Civil Service, he soon joined the Malay States Volunteer Rifles. This was formed in 1911 following a long history of volunteer militias in the Malay and Singapore regions that stretched back to the 1840s. Volunteer militias, the forerunners of the

'I knew my great-uncle when I was at school. I was told he had been lively and outgoing but I remember a solitary man, very withdrawn, damaged by his later years in Changi jail as a prisoner of war.'

ANDREW COE, GREAT-NEPHEW

Territorial Force, were popular in Victorian Britain, and the idea was quickly exported to the Empire to support Britain's small professional army. In 1915 Perowne resigned from the Malay Civil Service, returned to Britain, was awarded a commission as a 2nd Lieutenant and in October that year was in training in the huge camp at Etaples, near Boulogne.

In February 1916 Perowne was wounded in action. Two weeks later he was back in the front line, was wounded again, quickly recovered, and on 30 March 1916 was awarded the Military Cross. In January 1917 he was appointed Brigade Intelligence Officer for the 35th Brigade, which was heavily involved in the Battle of Arras. From this point, apart from a period of absence caused by an attack of German measles, Perowne worked as a Staff Officer, initially as a Temporary Captain with the 3rd Brigade, 12th Division, and then as Brigade Major for various Infantry Brigades in 1918. After the Armistice, he was demobilized in February 1919.

Throughout his war service Perowne took photographs, using the knowledge he had gained through the family business. He also kept many of the photographs that came to him in the course of his duties as a Staff Officer. Today, these remain within the family, as an interesting record of his life, along with albums of photographs that document his life in the Imperial Civil Service.

After a tour which took him to Canada and Singapore, Perowne returned to the Federal Malay Civil Service and in 1929 became Director-General of Post and Telegraph in Kuala Lumpur. In 1941 he was in Singapore when the Japanese invaded, and spent the rest of the war as a prisoner of war in Changi Camp, an experience that deeply affected all those like him, who survived it. Perowne Coe never married, and lived much of his life with his sister. He died in 1974.

Andrew Coe, his great-nephew who now runs the family photography business, knew him when he was a schoolboy but remembers a solitary man, bearing the scars of his Changi experience. Later, looking through his albums and his photographs, Andrew realized that he had to record his great-uncle's extraordinary life before it was forgotten.

Photographs and maps collected by Perowne Coe as a Staff Officer.

THE STORY OF
MY GRANDFATHER'S TRUNK

GOTTFRIED SANDROCK
1882–1918

Throughout the war soldiers on both sides were great correspondents. The letters they sent home, and in some cases received, have often been treasured by their families, offering as they do a tangible, and highly personal link to their lost relatives. For many families, a single letter or postcard, and perhaps

a photograph, is all that remains. Sometimes the legacy is much greater, as a later generation discovers an old box or suitcase filled with documents, photographs and mementoes. However, Gottfried Sandrock's trunk is something quite exceptional containing, as it does, a wealth of letters, documents and objects which tell his story in great detail but also offer an insight into the lives of those who fought in the war, irrespective of nationality.

Gottfried Sandrock was born in September 1882 in Germany. He became a professional soldier in his early twenties and in March 1912 he was a Sergeant in the 49th Infantry Regiment, stationed at Gnesen in East Prussia. In December 1912 he married Else and they had two boys, Gunther and Lothar. The family continued to live in Gnesen until 1918.

'By telling my grandfather's story, I want to show that all those who fought in the war had the same miserable life in the trenches, had the same feelings and had families that were catastrophically destroyed. There was life and tragedy on both sides of No Man's Land. I want to share my family's story, and the objects that tell it, to help us remember that generation in Germany, Britain and in so many other countries that lost so much.'

EGBERT SANDROCK, GRANDSON

After the outbreak of war, Gottfried's regiment left the garrison at Gnesen and travelled westwards. On 25 August 1914 they crossed the French border and were soon in action against the French at Sailly-Saillisel, a village east of the Somme. At this point the German army was advancing rapidly and by early September they were approaching Paris. Stopped by the French at the Battle of the Marne, the Germans were then driven back and forced to abandon all hopes of capturing Paris and bringing the war to an end. By October, the 49th Infantry Regiment was back in Picardy, on the borders of the Somme and the Oise. On 7 October an attack was ordered by General von Linsingen against French forces at Les Loges, Crapeaumesnil, a little village near Tilloloy and to the east of the modern A1 motorway.

Regimental records describe the events of that day:

> The French counter-attacked ... the Germans were mown down by flanking French fire. Death was everywhere ... only very few reached the safety of the trenches south of Crapeaumesnil from where their attack had started. The 49th Infantry Regiment suffered terrible losses this day – a disaster.
>
> All the wounded were close to the French lines, some 700 metres away from us. Recovery operations were not possible due to the deadly flanking fire. Then came the night. We could hear the faint cries for help from the wounded. It broke our hearts but we could not help.

The Germans, decimated by French artillery and machine-gun fire, left 7 officers and 585 men dead or missing, with over 250 wounded. Gottfried fought through the carnage, taking charge of his platoon and being awarded an Iron Cross 2nd Class. In letters to Else, he reported that he 'had saved the honour of the regiment in times of crisis'. When General von Linsingen visited their position on 22 October, he was shaken by the hundreds of dead bodies still lying out in No Man's Land. On 26 October 1914, the regiment was withdrawn to the reserves.

The hundreds of letters sent home by Gottfried are a virtual diary of daily trench life in the German army. A constant theme is the need for cigarettes, cigars and tobacco, 'please send something to smoke more often, there is nothing available here,' 'please send me a parcel with cigarettes,' 'my dear, I am so upset that I cannot give out any cigarettes, cigars or food to my men,' 'please don't send chocolate any more, better something to smoke.'

Gottfried Sandrock's wallet, showing
the damage caused by the shell splinters
that killed him. The photograph shows
his wife and their son Gunther.

By November 1914 the regiment was back in the front line, now facing the British in the Ypres sector. On 14 November, during the fighting at Gheluvelt, Gottfried was seriously wounded by a bullet fired from the opposing trenches, held by the 1st Battalion of the Cheshire Regiment. He was then out of the war until 1917. Gottfried continued to write letters to Else throughout his recovery and convalescence. He often expressed his respect for soldiers on the other side, and referred particularly to 'tough and brave colonial troops', underlining the common theme that many soldiers did not hate their enemy, knowing they had too much in common.

In late 1917 Gottfried, now an Offizierstellvertreter (the equivalent of a Warrant Officer), returned to the trenches near Armentières. On 21 March 1918 the 49th Infantry Regiment was involved in Operation Michael, the German Spring Offensive. Starting near Bourlon, they swept across the old Somme battlefields, passing through Berthincourt, Thilloy, Grevillers and Serre, before being stopped by the Australians near Hebuterne. In April the regiment went north for the Offensive's next phase, the attack on the Lys.

At 14.00 on 1 May 1918 Gottfried was sitting outside his foxhole near Merville, in front of the Bois de Nieppe, making the most of what seemed to be a quiet moment and preparing to write a letter. Without any warning a shell fired at random by a gun crew from D Battery, in the 27th Brigade of the Royal Field Artillery, exploded beside him and Gottfried was killed instantly by shell fragments piercing his chest. His batman, sheltering in the foxhole, was buried alive and seriously wounded. Later, having been dug out and taken to hospital, he gradually recovered, and by 23 July he was able to write to Else from his hospital in Belgium:

> There he was killed on the spot, holding a paper ready to write a letter. I was wounded and buried alive from the same shell ... unfortunately Mr

Sandrock was sitting in front of our hole suspecting nothing. A sudden and fast death hit and he did not need to suffer any pain … Mr Sandrock was always a caring superior and I regret his death vividly.

A second letter, written on 4 August, offered Else a further insight into her husband's death:

Mr Sandrock must have some dark foreboding … Pretty much his last words to me on 1 May were: 'well, Kabitsche, if something will happen to me, take care that all my belongings, watch etc. will be sent home to my wife.'

That sense of foreboding was not uncommon for soldiers at the front. It must have been quite strong for Gottfried as he had written letters to his wife and sons only to be sent in the event of his death. To Else, he wrote:

I cannot tell you much, only that I spent the happiest days with you, days that you have sweetened with your great love. Thank you so very much. Keep me in good memories, and never forget that I always treasured you … and I faithfully loved you in true love. Educate our beloved little ones well, so that they bear our name in honour. God bless you my good wife, it was not meant to be that we spend our lives happily ever after.

To his sons:

You hardly knew me, but your good mother will often tell you how much I loved you. You have been my pride. I wish you so much luck and good fortune for your path in life, be always ambitious but decent … my last wish is that you two learn a good profession and that you will honour our family name. Farewell my dearest sons.

That evening, Gottfried was hastily buried, near where he had died. His was the only death that day in the German lines. His batman drew a map to record the position of his grave, which he sent to Else. Facing the German line was the 1st Battalion of the Duke of Cornwall's Light Infantry (DCLI). The battalion's war diary for 1 May 1918 says, 'Rather dull day,' although two of their men were killed that day, in an equally random manner. Today all three, friend and foe, lie side by side in Merville Communal Cemetery Extension, moved from their temporary battlefield graves after the war.

All Gottfried's papers and possessions, including everything that was on him when he died, were carefully stored in his trunk and sent back to Else, as he had requested. For the rest of her life she guarded this trunk. In December 1918, after Germany's surrender, she and the children were forced to flee their home in Gnesen, narrowly escaping the post-war violence against German families that accompanied the Polish takeover of that region. The family settled in central Germany, and Else raised the boys according to her husband's wishes, despite considerable poverty as her only income came from work as a seamstress.

In the late 1930s Gottfried's elder son Gunther joined the customs service but was swept up in the turmoil of German rearmament instigated by Hitler. He joined the Luftwaffe (the German Air Force) and in 1940 was a 2nd Lieutenant serving as a Reconnaissance Officer in a mobile anti-aircraft unit, the 4th Battery, 43rd Flak Regiment. In May 1940 his unit followed by chance virtually the same route taken by Gottfried in April 1918 during the Battle of the Lys. In 1940 the British held the Lys as they fought a desperate rearguard action to cover the retreat towards Dunkirk, and Gunther was involved in a series of hard-fought battles as the Germans drove the British back. As a result, Gunther was awarded the Iron Cross 2nd Class, the same as his father. Much of the fighting was in the Merville area and one day, making the most of his reconnaissance role, Gunther tried to follow his father's last days. The map drawn by Gottfried's batman brought him to a farm near Merville. There he met the lady owner who told him that, when she was a young girl in 1918, she saw the temporary grave of a German soldier who had been buried near the farm. She also described how he had later been exhumed by the British War Graves Commission and reburied in the Communal Cemetery at Merville. Gunther went there and found his father's grave, marked as an Unknown Soldier. It was the only one which had the correct date of death, and so he was certain. He picked some flowers from the grave to send his mother, and took some photographs.

Later, in 1943, Gunther, by then the Commanding Officer of a motorized anti-aircraft unit, 9th Battery, 23rd Flak Regiment, was fighting with the German army near Kursk in Russia. Just before Christmas his unit was cut off and surrounded by Russian troops. After several days of fierce fighting only Gunther and three others were still alive and they escaped to the German lines. It was Christmas Eve. When the war was finally over, Gunther always spent Christmas Eve in silence, often in tears, reliving the horror of that battle and the memory of his lost men. The Iron Cross 1st Class that he had won was little consolation.

Gunther's son, Egbert, who was born in 1953, followed his father into the German Air Force, rising to the rank of Lieutenant Colonel. He could never persuade his father to talk about his own war or his father's, and so knew little of Gottfried's story until, in due course, he inherited the trunk. Egbert was then absorbed by the trunk and its contents, looking at the hundreds of letters, official and military documents, photographs of his grandparents and his own father as a child, and the many artefacts that Gottfried had preserved: Gunther's baby shoe, watches, pipes, binoculars, a harmonica, a cigar case scarred by shrapnel damage, a wallet containing family photographs all torn by the piece of shrapnel that killed Gottfried. Egbert quickly realized that the trunk and its contents are not just his grandfather's story, but the story of every soldier from every nation killed in the First World War.

In 1979, Gunther took Egbert back to Merville to see Gottfried's grave, 39 years after the chance visit in May 1940. Egbert wrote later:

> As I looked at my father paying his respects at his father's grave, I saw a family tragedy, repeated millions of times. A son, now elderly and visiting the grave of a father he had barely known, killed in action 61 years before in a war that many have forgotten, mourns the dreadful memories of two wars and two generations.

In 2000, thanks to the family records and Egbert's research, Gottfried Sandrock was given a new gravestone. He is no longer Unknown, but is fully identified by name, rank, regiment and date of death, and he rests at peace, a German soldier in a British military cemetery.

Gottfried Sandrock's trunk. Visible are letters and photographs, Gottfried's pipe and harmonica, and a baby's shoe belonging to his son Gunther.

AN OLD BANJO TELLS THE STORY OF CANADA'S WAR

CANADIAN EXPEDITIONARY FORCE

In 2011, Alec Somerville, a retired policeman from Ontario in Canada, found an old five-string banjo for sale in Darwen, Lancashire. The instrument was a wreck but Alec bought it, first because he is a five-string banjo player, and second because the inside of the vellum head was covered with names. A quick look revealed that most of the names were followed by places, and it didn't take Alec long to work out that the places covered every Province of Canada except Prince Edward Island. There was also a place with a date: Paris, Aug 24th, 1917.

This date located the banjo firmly with the Canadian Expeditionary Force in the First World War. This Force, later expanded to form the Canadian Corps, first arrived in France in September 1914. The Canadians first fought at the Battle of Neuve Chapelle in 1915 and then took part in many of the major campaigns on the Western Front. At Vimy Ridge in April 1917, the Canadians first fought as a Corps, and their hard-won success there made a major contribution to their sense of nationhood. The Canadians had a reputation for being hard fighters, and, along with the Australians, they were much feared by the Germans. During the First World War 67,000 Canadians were killed, and 39 per cent of all those who volunteered to serve became casualties.

The purchase of the old banjo was the start of a journey that was to take Alec all over Canada as he tried to trace all the names, unravel their stories and give them back their forgotten place in the story of Canada's contribution to the First World War. Among the most prominent, and

'Twenty-eight Canadians, now long dead – but once very much the flesh and blood of young Canada. I hope that I have not only helped to keep the memory of them alive, but that I have contributed to the effort of keeping all the Great War soldiers' memories alive.'

ALEC SOMERVILLE

The five-string banjo that began Alec Somerville's remarkable journey of discovery about the Canadian Expeditionary Force (see also page 11).

readable, of the names were James Platts, Vineland, and R. Roland, Beamsville, and so they were Alec's starting point.

Vineland is a small place today, and was even smaller in 1917. Two people called Platts are listed today in Vineland, and when Alec called the first one, he found he was talking to the daughter-in-law of the man who had signed the banjo in 1917. Through her, he was able to establish that James had been born in Matlock, Derbyshire and had been sent to Canada in 1906 with a group of 50 orphans to start a new life. On arrival he had been placed on a farm in the Niagara Peninsula, where he grew up. His daughter-in-law also told Alec that James Platts had served as a Gunner, and he then tracked him down via regimental and battery war diaries to E Battery, Royal Canadian Artillery.

Next, Alec traced the attestation papers, the documents signed by everyone who enlisted in the Canadian army in the First World War, for James, as well as for the other 27 names that he could decipher on the banjo that had Canadian connections. This revealed that James Platts had enlisted in Toronto on 9 January 1915. Raymond Roland of Beamsville had enlisted the same day, and so they were probably neighbours or friends, and they were still together in Paris in August 1917, when they signed the banjo. From the attestation papers, Alec established that out of the 28 names, 14 had been born in Canada, 12 in Britain like Platts, one in Belgium and one in Jamaica. One of the Canadian-born names was a First Nation Iroquois.

From this starting point, Alec was able to find out what had happened to some of the names after 1917. Gunner Roland, for example, died in 1933, probably from the long-term effects of being gassed, but Alec has traced his family and his great-niece Linda. Louis Vermeulen, the Canadian born in Belgium, served all through the war, from November 1914, and then died in the Spanish influenza epidemic in January 1919. Also revealed was the fact that James Platts had two brothers, both of whom served in the Canadian army and survived the war.

When Alec visited the Platts, he was shown a photograph of soldiers sitting on the steps of the City Hall at Dour in Belgium, headed The Section, dated November 1918, and presumably taken just after the Armistice. James Platts is seated among them, although the identities of the others are not known. It can be assumed that they are members of E Battery,

Members of E Battery, Royal Canadian Artillery, in Belgium, November 1918. James Platts is in the second row, second from the right.

Royal Canadian Artillery. This was an anti-aircraft battery, operated under the control of Imperial Anti-Aircraft Group Headquarters. It comprised a Headquarters and four field sections, each of which had two 13-pounder guns, mounted on lorries, and 44 officers, Non-Commissioned Officers (NCOs) and other ranks. A fifth field section was added in May 1918. These mobile units were often in the front line, attacking enemy observation and reconnaissance aircraft and fighters operating over the Allied trenches, and took part in most of the major battles, such as Vimy Ridge in April 1917.

It would be gratifying to think that many of the men in the photograph could have signed the banjo, but nothing can be proved until they are identified. Also unknown is how the banjo, a fairly standard instrument of that era, made its way to Lancashire. There are other names on it, unconnected with the war, and some of these have Lancashire, and even Darwen, connections. Perhaps it was taken to England by a soldier recovering from an injury or a gas attack and left there. Perhaps it was left in one of the transit camps after the war during demobilization. Perhaps one of the English-born Canadian names came back to Britain after the war and brought it with them. There is no certain answer but Alec, himself an immigrant from Britain to Canada who had also served in the Artillery, feels that the banjo was waiting for him to find it, so that he could trace its history and bring back to life all those Canadians who had volunteered so willingly to fight in Europe during the First World War.

THE CHAPLAIN WHO WITNESSED THE START AND END OF THE WAR

REVEREND GEORGE KENDALL
1881–1961

For the British nation, the bringing home of the Unknown Warrior in 1920 represented both a powerful moment of shared emotion, and a realization that the war was finally over. Yet, while the Warrior's symbolic power has

never diminished, the actual story is still little known. A man who was present at the moment the Unknown Warrior was chosen was the Reverend George Kendall. Born in West Yorkshire in October 1881, George was one of three children and he was brought up by his grandparents after his father, a police constable, was killed during a colliery riot in 1884. At 14, George got a job in a Sheffield steel works and was later employed in a match factory. In 1905 George went to Manchester to train as a Methodist minister and the following year he married. He and Emily adopted a child after the First World War and, after Emily's death, he married again and had three children.

To practise his ministry George travelled widely and, as a Primitive Methodist, spoke frequently at open-air meetings. While preaching in the street in Windsor, he met Queen Mary, and this was the start of a long

> 'As a Senior Chaplain my grandfather had considerable influence. He was also a very brave man, constantly on the front line. He was hero-worshipped by his children and we grew up knowing him to have been an amazing man, but we didn't really know much about him.'
>
> TIM KENDALL, GRANDSON

association with the royal family. He became Garrison Chaplain at Windsor and formed a lifelong friendship with the Queen, based on their shared passion for antique collecting. George was at Windsor during a state visit by Archduke Franz Ferdinand of Austria, whose assassination shortly afterwards, on 28 June 1914, was the trigger for the series of events that started the First World War.

In 1915 George was appointed as a military chaplain, and was rarely far from the front line, serving in France, Belgium, Salonika, Ireland and Germany. He was present at many of the major battles of the war, including Loos, the Somme and Ypres, becoming one of the army's most senior chaplains. As a Methodist he was aware of the apparent dichotomy between pacifism and his work as a military chaplain, and managed to achieve a balance between the two. Through this period, his influence rose steadily, partly because of his royal connections. He knew General Haig and he had the ear of Herbert Asquith, the Prime Minister until 1916, and later Lloyd George, and was widely respected for his discretion and sensible advice.

In 1916, following the Easter Rising in Dublin, George went to Ireland in his capacity as Chaplain to the 59th Division, sent in to restore order. After being captured one of the leaders of the uprising, James Connolly, was sentenced to death. George was with him on the eve of the execution and helped Connolly, a noted atheist, as he returned to the Catholic faith. During the war, George was attached to many divisions, including the Royal Naval Division. When the war was over, George served with the occupation forces in Cologne and then, in 1920, returned to France and Belgium to oversee, as Senior Chaplain, the exhumations of the war dead and the building of the cemeteries.

On 11 November 1920, the Unknown Warrior passes the newly completed Cenotaph, on the way to Westminster Abbey.

In this capacity, George found himself in charge of the exhumation of the bodies from which the Unknown Warrior was selected. The background to the idea of the Unknown Warrior is well known, as are the details of the Warrior's journey from France to London, and the great procession through London that culminated in the burial in Westminster Abbey. However, until the recent discovery of George's unpublished autobiography, little was known about the way the Unknown Warrior was chosen and, as a result, many myths and inaccuracies have been attached to the story. This is George's account of events:

> Early in November 1920, we received orders from headquarters, for the exhumation of a certain number of bodies of unknown men. No one – and this is very important – was to know from which district a body had been taken. The graves which were opened in all the theatres of war were marked only by a cross which stated that an unknown warrior lay there. If the regiment or division in which the man had served were specified – and there were cases where a man may not have been identified, but his regiment or battalion was known – the grave was untouched. In all some six bodies were finally taken to the headquarters at St Pol, near Arras. Those who awaited the bodies in St Pol did not even know from where they had come. The six coffins were placed in a hut, and each covered with a Union Jack. All night they rested on trestles, with nothing to distinguish one from the other. The door of the hut was locked and sentries posted outside.
>
> In the morning a general entered the hut. He placed his hand on one of the flag-shrouded coffins, and the body therein became 'The Unknown Warrior'. The five other bodies were taken from the hut and reverently reburied. The one selected to receive the tribute of the Empire was conveyed to Boulogne and embarked there on the British destroyer HMS *Verdun*, to be brought to England. On the lid of the coffin, as it was taken on board, was placed a rare and valuable sword taken from the private collection of King George V.

George, like all the others involved in this selection process, did not talk about it, and no record was thought to exist until the discovery of the autobiography. As a result, myths and rumours began to circulate, the most serious of which was that the government knew the identity of the Unknown Warrior. It was in response to these that the government arranged an international press conference in 1930, to which George described the actual sequence of events. Even after this, alternative versions of the story appeared, for example a 1938 article claiming that there were only four bodies. Despite this, the conference was the last time George talked about it, and he turned away all subsequent interview requests.

After the war, George continued to work as a Methodist minister and as an army chaplain. He served among mining communities in South Wales and became involved in public health and education matters. He also worked in London, becoming well known as an orator at Speakers' Corner in Hyde Park. During the Second World War he served again as a military chaplain, becoming the most experienced chaplain in British history. He was awarded the OBE, and continued to enjoy a friendship with the royal family. Later in his life he wrote his autobiography, entitled *Daring All Things*, but made no attempt at finding a publisher. Instead, he put it away in a box, and it remained there unknown and unseen until it was discovered long after his death in 1961.

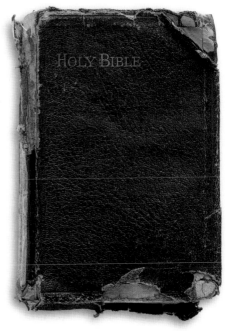

Half of the autobiography describes the First World War. His all-encompassing role in this conflict, and his series of experiences that culminated in the story of the Unknown Warrior, put George Kendall in a unique position. He alone was able to say that, as he looked into the eyes of Archduke Franz Ferdinand in 1914, he saw the start of the war, and as he looked into the eyes of the Unknown Warrior, he saw its end.

The Reverend George Kendall's bible, which he used throughout the war and annotated with the details of his career.

TIMELINE

1914

28 June	Archduke Franz Ferdinand, heir to the throne of the Austro-Hungarian Empire, and his wife Sophie are assassinated in Sarajevo. Serbian revolutionaries are implicated.
20 July	Austro-Hungarian troops are sent to the Serbia frontier.
25 July	Serbian troops mobilize. Russian troops are moved to Austro-Hungarian border in support.
28 July	Austro-Hungary declares war on Serbia.
29 July	Great Britain tells Germany that it cannot remain neutral.
1 August	French troops mobilize. Germany declares war on Russia. Italy and Belgium announce neutrality.
3 August	Germany declares war on France. British troops mobilize.
4 August	Germany declares war on Belgium. Great Britain gives Central Powers, Austro-Hungary and Germany an ultimatum demanding cessation of hostilities. With no satisfactory response received, Britain declares war. United States announces neutrality.
6 August	Cruiser HMS *Amphion* is sunk by a mine, causing the first British casualties of the war.
7 August	British Expeditionary Force (BEF) begins to land in France.
11 August	Lord Kitchener launches campaign to recruit 100,000 new volunteers for his New Army. The call is answered within two weeks.
20 August	Germans occupy Brussels.
26 August	Battle of Le Cateau, first engagement for the BEF. The retreat to Mons.
6 September	First Battle of the Marne checks the German advance.
16 October	British Indian Expeditionary Force sails from Bombay for the Persian Gulf, to defend British interests in Mesopotamia.

19 October	Start of First Battle of Ypres.
29 October	Turkey joins the Central Powers.
22 November	The war of mobility ends as both sides dig in and trench warfare begins.
8 December	The Royal Navy is victorious at the Battle of the Falkland Islands.
16 December	German High Seas fleet bombards Hartlepool, Whitby and Scarborough, bringing civilians into the war.

1915

19 January	First Zeppelin attack on Britain.
18 February	Blockade of Britain started by German submarines, in response to blockade of Germany by Royal Navy.
19 February	Allied naval attack on the Dardanelles.
10 March	Start of British offensive at Neuve Chapelle.
22 April	Start of Second Battle of Ypres. First use of poison gas by Germany.
25 April	Start of the Allied assault on Gallipoli.
7 May	Liner *Lusitania* sunk by German submarine.
23 May	Italy declares war on Austro-Hungary.
25 May	Britain forms coalition government to manage the war.
31 May	First Zeppelin raid on London.
4 June	Battle of Krithia in Gallipoli.
30 June	Germans use flame throwers at Battle of Hooge.
4 August	Germany annexes Warsaw.
6 August	Suvla Bay landings in Gallipoli.
21 August	Final Allied offensive in Gallipoli.
25 September	Start of the British offensive at Loos, and the French offensive in Champagne.

5 October	Austro-Hungary increase attacks on Serbia and Allies land in Salonika to counter German activities in the Balkans.
12 October	Edith Cavell executed.
31 October	Steel helmets are issued to British troops, following the French army's lead.
22 November	Allies defeat Turks at Battle of Ctesiphon, but lack of supplies forces retreat to Kut.
15 December	Sir Douglas Haig takes over as Commander of the British Expeditionary Force.
20 December	Allies complete evacuation from Suvla Bay and ANZAC Cove in Gallipoli.

1916

4 January	First attempt to relieve besieged British garrison in Kut.
8 January	Final evacuation from Helles ends the Dardanelles campaign.
21 February	Germany launches the Verdun offensive against the French.
2 March	Conscription introduced in Britain.
9 March	Germany declares war on Portugal.
29 April	Besieged British garrison at Kut surrenders to the Turks.
31 May	Start of the Battle of Jutland.
4 June	Russia launches Brusilov offensive on the Eastern Front.
1 July	Allies launch the Somme offensive. Britain suffers 60,000 casualties on the first day.
23 July	Battle of Pozières Ridge on the Somme, the first major Australian engagement on the Western Front.
28 August	Italy declares war on Germany.
15 September	Tanks first used during the Battle of Flers–Courcelette.
15 November	End of the Somme campaign.
7 December	Lloyd-George becomes British Prime Minister.
18 December	End of the Battle of Verdun.

1917

31 January	Germany reintroduces unrestricted submarine warfare.
3 February	United States cuts off diplomatic relations with Germany. The Zimmerman telegram, suggesting Mexico might take part on Germany's side, brings the United States closer to war.
21 February	German forces withdraw to the Hindenburg line.
11 March	Baghdad is captured by the Allies.
15 March	Tzar Nicholas of Russia abdicates.
26 March	First Battle of Gaza.
6 April	United States declares war on Germany.
9 April	Start of the Battle of Arras.
16 April	Start of the French Nivelle offensive, leading to mutinies in the French army.
19 April	Second Battle of Gaza.
7 June	Start of Battle of Messines.
13 June	Start of Blitz on London by German bombers.
25 June	First US troops in France.
16 July	T. E. Lawrence and Arab troops capture Aqaba.
31 July	Start of the Third Battle of Ypres.
20 August	French attack in Verdun.
26 October	Start of Battle of Passchendaele.
7 November	Gaza captured.
10 November	Battle of Passchendaele ends.
20 November	Start of the Battle of Cambrai.
11 December	Jerusalem is liberated after six centuries of Turkish rule.

1918

3 March	Treaty of Brest-Litovsk between Soviet Russia and Germany.
21 March	Start of Operation Michael, the German Spring Offensive.
23 March	The Second Battle of the Somme.
28 March	German Offensive on the Scarpe halted, with help of American troops.
5 April	German Spring Offensive halted near Amiens, largely by Australian troops. Operation Michael called off.
9 April	Start of Operation Georgette, the German Offensive on the Lys.
22 April	The Zeebrugge Raid.
29 April	Battle of the Lys ends, Operation Georgette called off.
27 May	Start of Operation Blucher, the German Offensive on the Aisne.
9 June	Start of Operation Gneisnau, the German Offensive on the French near Montdidier. It is called off four days later.
15 June	Start of the Battle of the Piave, the beginning of the end for Austro-Hungary.
15 July	Start of the Second Battle of the Marne, the final phase of the German Spring Offensive.
8 August	Start of the Battle of Amiens, and the beginning of the Allied advance to victory.
22 September	Allied victory in the Balkans.
27 September	Start of Cambrai offensive and Battle of St Quentin. Allied and American troops break through the Hindenburg line.
30 September	Capture of Damascus.
4 October	First German and Austrian request for an armistice.
17 October	Start of the Battle of the Selle. Lille and Belgian Channel coast liberated.
29 October	Mutiny by German sailors.
30 October	Turkish army surrenders in Mesopotamia. Turkey signs Armistice with Allies.

3 November	Austro-Hungary signs Armistice with the Allies.
8 November	Armistice negotiations start at Compiègne.
9 November	Kaiser Wilhelm abdicates and flees to the Netherlands.
11 November	Armistice with Germany signed at 5am, comes into effect at 11am.
14 November	German forces in Africa surrender.
21 November	German High Seas fleet surrenders at Rosyth.
12 December	Allies cross the Rhine and occupy Cologne and other cities.

1919

10 January	Start of Communist revolt in Berlin.
18 January	Start of Paris Peace Conference.
14 February	League of Nations established.
4 April	End of the North Russia Intervention as Allies withdraw.
21 June	German High Seas fleet scuttled at Scapa Flow.
28 June	Treaty of Versailles signed. First World War formally ends.

1920

| 11 November | The Unknown Warrior is buried in Westminster Abbey. |

INDEX

Page numbers in *italic* refer to information contained in captions.

1914 Star (Mons Star) 31, 38, 45, *184*, 258, 363

Aboukir (cruiser) 25–7, *27*
Achiet-le-Grans 220–1
Achiet-le-Petit, battle of 41
Admiralty 76–7, 127, *146*, 147, 177, *276*, 278–9
aerial reconnaissance 84–5, 255
Afghanistan 346, 360–1
Africa 32
air raids 71, 79, 135, 175–7, *236*, 237–9
air supplies 145
Airco DH4 aircraft 314
Airco DH9a aircraft 314–15
Aisne 300
    battle of the 36, 48, 54, 60, 141, 230, 363
Albert 179
Alcock, John 315
Alecto (submarine depot ship) 277–8
Alexandra, Queen *363*, 364
Allenby, General 67, 266
Allied Expeditionary Force 366
Amiens 307
Ancre, battles of 192, 210
Ancre Heights, battle of 40
Anglo-Afghan War, third 360–1
anti-Semitism 312
Anzac Cove 120
Apia, German Samoa 32–3
Arabs 212, 344–5, 346
Archangel 364, 365, 368
Armentières 69, 374
Armistice 117, 267, 275, *288*, 322, 327, 331, 337, 345–6, 366–7, 370
Armstrong Whitworth FK8 aircraft 85
Arras, battle of 44, 61, 212, 223, 225–6, 229, 231–2, 234, 269, 321, 370
Asiago 116, 204
Asquith, Herbert 135, 171, 383
Asquith, Raymond 132, 171

Atterbury, Paul 11
attestation papers 164, 312, 380
Aubers Ridge, battle of 326, 351
Australia 13, 62, 119–20, 125–6
Australian Expeditionary Force 119–20
    Australian Imperial Forces 350, 352
        10th Australian Light Horse
        Regiment 120–1
Australian General Hospital (AGH), No. 3
    96–7
Australian and New Zealand Army Corps
    (ANZAC) 33, 107, 108, 120
        ANZAC Memorial Medallion 118
Austria 125–6
Austro-Hungary 20, 62, 116–17, 212, 275, 367
Authuile Wood 326

badges *111*, 124, 127, *207*, 306, *307*, 321, *359*
Baghdad 280, 334, 344–5
bags
    standard issue kit *294*
    woven hessian 313, *313*
Bailleul 160
Balkans 20
banjos *11*, 378–81, *379*
Bar 40, 41
Barbaros Hayreddin (Turkish battleship) 91
Barrington-Parry, Lieutenant Raymond 157
Bazentin 156–7, 161, 204
BE2 aircraft 285
BE2c aircraft 84–5, 175
Beeskow camp 217, *217*
Beirut 266–7
Belgium 20, 36, 40–1, 62, 116
belts 306, *307*
Bermuda Volunteer Rifle Corps 182–5
bibles 257, *257*, 385
binoculars *267*
Blitz 251, 323
Boer War 44
Bolshevik Revolution 212–13
Bolsheviks 356–7, 364–5, 367–8
Bouchavesnes 303–4
Boy Scouts 22–4, *23*

Brecknockshire (ship) 215–16, 217
Brest-Litovsk, Treaty of 1918 364
Bristol Fighters 254
Britain 13, 20–1, 58, 61, 62, 63, 116, 274, 346
Britannia (battleship) 113
British Army
  Armies
    Fourth Army 307
    New Army 104, 130, 134, 149–50, 156,
      162, 166, 172, 191, 194, 197, 209, 218,
      256, 269, 284, 298, 300, 306
  Corps
    Army Service Corps 323–4, 342–3
    King's Royal Rifle Corps 362–3
    Machine Gun Corps 262–3, 290–1, 364
    Non-Combatant Corps 152, 186, 329–31
    Royal Army Medical Corps 66, 152, 154,
      198, 222, 280, 305, 330, 333–4
    Royal Army Service Corps 128
    Royal Engineers 36–7, 115–16, 203, 340
    Tank Corps 263
  Divisions
    38th Welsh Division 156–7
    47th Division 98, 100
    63rd (Royal Naval) Division 228–9
    Guards Division 54
  Brigades
    2nd Guards Brigade 54
    8th Cavalry Brigade 223
    14th Brigade 350–1
    57th Brigade, Intelligence Section
      209–11
    Rifle Brigade 104
  Regiments and Battalions
    Argyll and Sutherland Highlanders
      206, 225, 227
    Bedfordshire Regiment 60–1, 218–21
    Black Watch 59
    Border Regiment 300
    Coldstream Guards 53–5
    Dorsetshire Regiment 31, 343–5
    Duke of Cornwall's Light Infantry
      172–3, 375
    Essex Regiment 284
    Gloucestershire Regiment 209–10
    Hampshire Regiment 47–9
    Hertfordshire Regiment 38, 40–1
    Highland Light Infantry 231

Isle of Wight Rifles 266
King's (Liverpool) Regiment 320–2
King's Own (Royal Lancaster
  Regiment) 194, 269
Lancashire Fusiliers 298–300
Leicestershire Regiment 233–4
London Irish Rifles 178–9
Manchester Regiment 42–5
Norfolk Regiment 106–9, 145
Northamptonshire Regiment 285
Northumberland Fusiliers 149–51,
  169, 250
Pals battalions 150, 195, 320–1
Prince Albert's (Somerset Light
  Infantry) 256–7, 290
Queen's Own (Royal West Kent
  Regiment) 160–2, 197
Royal Berkshire Regiment 204, 337
Royal Fusiliers (City of London
  Regiment) 19, 162, 303, 312–13, 318
Royal Garrison Artillery, Siege
  Batteries 130–2, 200
Royal Warwickshire Regiment 305–6
Royal Welch Fusiliers 191–3
Seaforth Highlanders 82, 140, 142–3,
  153, 206, 265–6
Tyneside Irish 149–51
Forces, British Expeditionary Force 20,
  30, 36, 38, 40, 48, 54, 58, 60, 166, 179, 225,
  250, 324
cyclist units 358–61, *359*
Gurkhas 345, 361
Jewish Legion 312–13
Remount Service 30–1, 348
Royal Field Artillery 307, 308, 326–7, 348,
  374
brooches
  regimental sweetheart 226, *227*
  Royal Flying Corps sweetheart *315*
  silver anchor 27, *27*
Brooking, General 344
Bruce, Fiona 10, *12*
Brussels 110–12
Buckingham Palace 128
Bulgaria 275
Bullecourt 232
Burns, Robert, poems 55, *55*

Cambrai, battle of 41, 179, 263, 308, 340
cameras 131, *231*, 232, 255
Canada 13, 62, 119–20
Canadian Expeditionary Force 11, 18, 69, 119–20, 378–81
    Royal Canadian Artillery 380–1, *381*
Canal du Nord 340
cap badges *207*, 306, *307*, 321
Capelle 314
Caporetto, battle of 117, 212
Carrick, Alexander 200–3, *201*, *203*
Carton de Wiart, Lieutenant Colonel A 210
Cavell, Edith 13, 110–13, *111*, 204
Central Laboratory, St Omer *78*, 80
Central Powers 21, 275
Certificates of Exemption 328
chalk carvings 180, *180*
Chocolate Hill 261
Christmas presents 195, *195*
Christmas truces, 1914 *46*, 48–9, 141
Churchill, Winston 107, 365, 368
cigarette cases 157, *158*, *299*
City of Cambridge (ship) 243
City of Corinth (ship) *242*, 243
clay tablet, 4000-year-old 344, *344*
coats, leather flying *315*
Collier, Lieutenant Martin Huntly 278
Cologne 337, 383
Colonial Hospital, Gibraltar 113
Combles 19
Commandos 295
Commemorative Scrolls *287*
Commonwealth War Graves Commission 235, 291
    see also Imperial War Graves Commission
Connolly, James 383
Conscientious Objectors 135, 152–5, 186–9, *187*, 325, *328*, 329–31
conscription 135, 186–8, 218, 293, 329–30
Constantinople 62, 91, 107
Cory Hall, battle of 188
Cressy (cruiser) 25–7, 146
cricket 35–6
Cunard 73, 76, 77

daisies, preserved and framed *109*
Dalmatia 117
Damascus 267

Dardanelles 13, 62, 90–3, 106–8, 120, 169, 192, 230, 246, 261–2, 266, 300, 302, 334, 350, 352
David Morris (schooner) 137, 138, 139
death certificates 322, *322*
Death Plaques 28, 31
Delville Wood 156–7, 161, 192, 197–8, 269
demolition 92
Dido (depot ship) 355–6
Discharge Certificates *155*, *368*
disease 59, 66, 96–7, 108, 113, 120, 199, 228–9, 270, 290, 347, 361
Distinguished Conduct Medal 154–5, *155*, 363
ditty boxes *354*, 355, 357
doctors 64–7, *65*
Doughty-Wylie, Lieutenant Colonel Charles 66
Doughty-Wylie, Mrs Lilian 66
Dreadnought (battleship) 348
driving licences 129
Dyer, General Reginald 360

E2 (submarine) 91–2
E11 (submarine) 90–2, *93*
E-Class submarines (British) 90–1
Easter Rising, Dublin 135, 147, 383
Eastern Front 146, 212, 271–2, 346, 364, 368
Edward, VIII 128–9
Edwards, Francis 98–101, 179
    bronze statue of *99*
Edwards, Lionel 30
eggs 123, *123*
Egypt 33, 44–5, 49, 57, 87, 97, 108–9, 120, 153, 169, 262, 266, 340, 350–1
Egypt Expeditionary Force 108
Ellerman Line 240–1, 243
embroideries *359*, 361
Entente Cordiale 20
espionage 63, *86*, 87–9
Euryalus (cruiser) 25–6
explosives 92, 317–18

FE2d aircraft *253*, 254, 255
Festubert, battle of 40, 44, 98, 179, 230, 266
film 131–2
flamethrowers, portable 104
Flers-Courcelette, battle of 61, 126, 132, *133*, 162, 179–81, 183, 198
Foch, Marshal Ferdinand 290

Fokker E.I aircraft 84
Fokker triplane 293
Folkestone 71
Fontaine-les-Croisilles 225–6
football 50, 51, 52, 98, 99, 100–1, 179, 292
footballs 99, 100, 101
Forbes, Stanhope 170, 171–3, 173
Forcaux *see* High Wood
France 20–1, 23, 40, 62, 125–6, 129, 131, 212, 274, 346
Franco-Prussian War 20
Franz Ferdinand, Archduke 383, 385
French, Sir John 40, 179
Fromelles, battle of 350, 351–3

Gallipoli 62, 66, 90, 95–6, 107–8, 118, 120–1, 192, 203, 209, 228, 246, 263, 312, 344
gas attacks 41, 48–9, 61, 63, 69, 79–81, 100, 153, 179, 255, 272, 343, 348
gas masks 80–1, 100
Gaza 266
    first battle of 108
    second battle of 108
    third battle of 108, 266
Gem Line 96
Geneva Convention 51, 247
George V 68, 115, 128, 209, 241, 364, 384
George VI (then Duke of York) 129
German Army, 49th Infantry Regiment 372–4
German Spring Offensive 40–1, 272
Germany 13, 20–1, 23, 24, 32, 62–3, 70, 79, 116–17, 212–13, 274, 275, 346, 360, 367, 368
Gheluvelt 54, 374
Giessen prisoner-of-war camp 69–70
Givenchy 44, 259
Gleichen, Brigadier General Count, *The Doings of the Fifteenth Infantry Brigade* 61, 61
Gommecourt 153–4
Gotha G.IV bombers 71, 237–8
Grave Registration Units 235
Gueudecourt 183–5
Guillemont, battle of 61, 172–3, 198, 269
Gunner, The (Carrick, 1916) 201, 202–3

H10 (submarine) 278–9
Haig, Field Marshal Douglas, 1st Earl Haig 35, 154, 179–81, 290, 383
Haking, Sir Richard 351–2

Halliwell family 12
Hampshire (cruiser) 134, 144, 146–7
Hansa Line 40
Havelberg internment camp 52
Heidenkopf (Quadrilateral) 204, 306
Henry, Prince, Duke of Gloucester 129
High Wood (Forcaux) 61, 156–7, 161–2, 180, 198, 210
Hill 60, battle of 79, 120, 160, 272
Hill 70, battle of 179
Hilton Young, Lieutenant Commander 296–7
Hindenburg Line 212, 263
hip flask, of Haike Janssen 86, 89
Hogue (cruiser) 25–6
Hohenzollern Redoubt 153
Holt tractors 126
Home Guard 243, 335
Hooge, battle of 104, 153
horses 30–1, 222–4, 224, 242, 301, 326–7
Howitzers 131, 132

identity badges 111
Imbros 246
Imperial German Navy, High Seas Fleet 134–5
Imperial War Graves Commission 235, 312, 353
    see also Commonwealth War Graves Commission
Imperial Yeomanry movement 292–3
India 29–30, 35–6, 44–5, 49, 60, 62, 282, 344, 360
Indian Expeditionary Force 84
    7th Meerut (Indian) Division 84
    D 334
injury labels 196, 198
internment camps 24, 50–2, 52, 69–70, 69–71, 193, 217, 217
Iron Cross 271, 273, 337, 337, 373, 376, 377
Isonzo offensives 116
Italy 13, 20, 62, 116–17, 204, 209, 212

Jagger, Charles Sargeant 203
Janssen, Haike 86, 87
Jerusalem 109, 212, 266, 312
Jews 311–13
Joan of Arc, 19th-century biscuit-porcelain figure of 83, 84, 85
Jutland, battle of 134–5, 146, 147, 302

Kemmel, Mount 290
Keyes, Rear Admiral Sir Roger 295
King Edward VII (battleship) 216
Kipling, Rudyard 171
kit bags, standard issue *294*
Kitchener, Field Marshal Herbert, 1st Earl
    Kitchener 63, 104, 128, 130, 134, 146–7, 150,
    172, 192, 209, 218, 269, 312
Kodak Vest Pocket Camera 131
Koikori 365
Kolchak, Admiral 364
Kronprinz Wilhelm (ship) 215, 216
Kronstadt naval base 365
Kurds 282–3
Kut el Amara, siege of 135, 142–3, 231, 334, 344

La Bassée 259
La Boisselle 210
La Couture, battle of 115
Labour Corps 198
Lake, Herbert 223–4, *224*
Lakeside Unit 250–1
Langemarck 79
Laventie, battle of 115
Lawrence, T. E. 212–13, 345
Le Cateau 36, 48, 60, 141, 160, 166
Le Touret Memorial 44
League of Nations 282, 346
Lebanon 282
Lemnos 96–7, 107
Les Loges, Crapeaumesnil 373
Lesboeufs 19
letters *94, 97,* 166–8, *169,* 179–80, *195, 244,*
    246–7, 250, 270, *316,* 372–7, *377*
    telling of soldiers deaths *102,* 104–5, *146,*
    268, 276, 279, 286
Lille *351*
Limburg an der Lahn camp 193
Lloyd George, David 135, 383
lockets *55, 229*
London 71, 135, 237–9, 323
Longueval 61
Loos, battle of 40, 44, 62, *98,* 100–1, 153, 179,
    197, 210, 383
Lozinghem 291
Ludendorff, General 274, 290, 300–1
Luftwaffe (German Air Force) 376–7
Lusitania (liner) 13, 63, 72–7, *75*

Lutyens, Sir Edwin 11, *14,* 17
Lys, battle of the 290, 308, 327, 374, 376

M23 (M-15-class monitor) 367
M-15-class monitors 367
MacDonald, Ramsay 188
Macedonia 209
Mahsud tribe 360–1
Malay Civil Service 369–70
Malta 66–7
Mametz 156–7, 161
Mamora, Sea of 90–3
maps *371*
Marne 300
    battle of the 36, 48, 54, 60, 141, 363, 373
Mary, Queen 383
mascots 205, *205,* 206–7, *207*
Mauretania (liner) 76, 292
Medal for the Epidemics in Silver Gilt 59
medical instruments, army issue *65,* 66
memorial certificates *148*
Memorial to the Missing, Arras 229, 235
Memorial to the Missing of the Somme,
    Thiepval 11, *14,* 17–18, 151, 162, 169, 185
Menin Gate Memorial, Ypres 37, 105, 158
menus, Christmas dinner 160, *163*
Merchant Navy 13, 241
Merchant Services 50–1, 63, 76–7, 95, 113,
    138–9, 213, 214–17, 240–3, 366
Merville 376
Mesopotamia 13, 30, 44, 135, 142, 211, 230–2,
    234, 256, 275, 280–2, 307, 334, 344–5, 365
Messines, battle of 115, 132, 179, 210, 290, 308,
    326–7, 338
Military Cross 129, *253,* 254, 370
Military Medal 40, 41, 48, 49, 59, 71, 210, 322
Military Service Act 186, 329–30
Missy 61
Moewe (commerce raider) 214, 215–17, *217*
Monchy-le-Preux 223
Mons
    battle of 21, 36, 48, 60, 160, 166, 230, 363
    retreat from 54
Montauban 321
Morval, battle of 19, 184
Mosul 282
Mudros, treaty of 282
Mughar Ridge, battle of 266

munitions girls 317–19, *319*

Munnings, Alfred 30

Murmansk 364, 365, 367

Nairana (aircraft carrier) 356–7

Nasmith, Lieutenant Commander Martin 90–2

National Filling Factories 317–18

necklaces 226, 227, *227*

Nek, battle of 120

Neuve Chapelle, battle of 44, 84, 115, 160, 378

Nevill, Captain Wilfred Percy 101

New Zealand 13, 62, 119–20

New Zealand Expeditionary Force 32–3, 119–20

Newbold, Henry 35, 37

Nightingale, Florence 57, 113

Nivelle Offensive 212

No Man's Land 48, 80, 100, 142, 150, 153, 157, 234–5, 246, 249–50, 301, 324, 337, 373

North Russia Intervention 346–7, 356, 364–5, 367

North Sea 26

North West Frontier 13, 346, 358, 360, 367

nurses 57–9, *57*, 64, *65*, 67, 110–13, *111*

oil supplies 334, 360

'Old Contemptibles' 38, 40, 41, 45, 55, 58

Operation Michael 274, 374

Operation Türkenkreuz 237

Ostend 296

Otaki (ship) 217

Ottomans 107, 143, 275, 282, 312

Pacific 32

Padres 249–51

Palestine 13, 108–9, 135, 230, 234, 256, 266, 275, 282, 312, 340, 344

Paris 20–1, 23, 274, 300

Passchendaele (Third Battle of Ypres) 40, 44, 61, 158, 179, 204, 210, 212, 246, 250, 257, 259, 269–70, 290, 321

Passchendaele Ridge 290

patient log books *248*

Pearce-Serocold, Brigadier General 364

Pheasant Wood mass graves 353

Philosophe 198

photography 131–3, *131*, *133*, 254–5, *255*, *371*

Piave 117

plate, silver *288*

pogroms 311

Poland 311, 312

Polygon Wood 36–7, 270

postcards 23–4, *43*, 45, *75*, 89, 120, 139, 146, *160*, 166, 177, 199, 220, 229, *229*, 308–10, 337, *338*, 351, *359*, 372

   embroidered 309, *309–10*

Potaro (ship) 215

Pozières, battle of 204, 210

Preston, Edward Carter 31

Pringel, Herman 322

prisoners-of-war 69–71, 193, 215–17, *244*, 246–7, 257, 301, 313

   escapees 70–1

   royal letters to *68*

   see also internment camps

propaganda 122–3

Quadrilateral (Heidenkopf) 204, 306

Queen Alexandra's Imperial Military Nursing Service 57, 64

Queen's South Africa Medal *43*

Ramadi Ridge 345

rank braids 297, *297*

Rastatt internment camp 52

Ratty the tree rat (mascot) 205, *205*

RE5 aircraft 285

RE8 aircraft 85

Red army 364

Red Cross 66, 112, 177, 235, 247, 250, 310, 353

   parcels 70

Remy 307

Reserved Occupations 127, 290

Rheims cathedral *208*, 211

Ricebourg, battle of 115

rings

   engagement *219*

   German soldier's 324, *324*

   wedding *75*, 76

Roos, Willem 89

Royal Air Force (RAF) 85, 121, 252, 255, 282–3, 314–15, 360–1, 365

Royal Flying Corps 63, 82, 84–5, 121, 145, 166, 176, 181, 198, 205, 221, *221*, 252, 254–5, 285, 293, 314–15

20 Squadron 253, 254
 sweetheart brooches 315
Royal Mail Steam Packet line 215
Royal Marines 146, 295–6, 337, 365
 Royal Marine Artillery 25, 146, 228
 Royal Marine Light Infantry 145–6, 228,
  364–5
Royal Naval Air Service (RNAS) 95, 121, 252,
 314
Royal Naval Division 95, 296, 383
Royal Naval Reserve (RNR) 91, 95–6
Royal Navy 20, 21, 27, 62–3, 91, 92, 95, 126,
 134–5, 139, 275, 277, 302, 348, 355–7, 365, 366
Royal Red Cross 1st Class (medal) 59
Royal Victoria Medal 129
Ruhleben internment camp 50–2
Russell, Bertrand 188
Russia 13, 20, 212–13, 230, 242, 312, 346–7, 356,
 360, 364–8, 376–7
Russian Revolution 364

St John Ambulance Brigade 333, 335
St Omer 78, 80, 160, 196, 198
St Pol 384
St Quentin 179, 321
St Quentin Canal 153
Salonika 303
Savill, Captain Herbert 147
Scarpe, battle of the 223, 232, 340
Schlieffen Plan 20, 40, 45
Schütte-Lanz airships 176–7
Schwieger, Kapitan 77
science 78, 79–81
sculpture 201, 202–3
Second World War 24, 49, 70, 93, 117, 181, 243,
 251, 255, 273, 295, 301, 313, 319, 323, 335, 338,
 346, 348, 365, 370, 376–7, 385
Serre 150, 153–4, 166, 192, 195, 269, 306, 374
shell cases, decorated 51, 52
shell shock 200–2, 306, 318
Shorncliffe 71
signal forms 46
SL-11 airship 174, 176–7
Snaffles 28, 30
Somerville, Alec 11
Somme campaign 11, 14, 17–19, 40–1, 44, 48,
 59, 61, 95, 101, 131, 132, 134–5, 142, 146, 150–1,
 153–4, 156–7, 161–2, 166–7, 172–3, 179–80,

185, 188, 192, 194–5, 197–8, 204, 210, 229, 234,
 246, 250, 252–4, 256, 269, 290, 300, 306, 308,
 318, 321, 326, 337, 351–2, 383
Sopwith Camel fighter 365
South Africa 44, 62, 233, 292–3
Spanish influenza epidemic 59, 113, 199, 270,
 347
spies 63, 86, 87–9
Spring Offensive, 1918 81, 117, 274, 275, 285,
 290, 296, 300–1, 321, 374
spurs 327, 327
stained glass fragments 208, 211
Sterling, Edward 339–40
Sudan 14
Sugarloaf 351–2
suicide 31
suitcases 166–8, 167
Sykes-Picot Agreement 1916 266–7, 282, 346
Syria 108–9, 266–7, 282

tanks 124, 125–7, 132, 133, 179–81
tear gas 79
telegrams 94, 97, 161, 193, 311, 321–2
tennis cups 34
Territorial Force 204, 303, 326, 343, 348, 369–70
 Corps, King's Royal Rifle Corps 303, 304
 Divisions, 46th North Midland Division
  153–4
 Brigades, 137th Staffordshire Brigade 153
 Regiments and Battalions
  Duke of Wellington's (West Riding)
   Regiment 165–6
  London Regiment 18, 19, 153, 159–60
  2nd Bn 252–4
  2/2nd Bn 303
  18th Bn (London Irish Rifles) 98–101
  25th (County of London) Cyclist
   Battalion 358–61, 359
  28th Bn (Artist's Rifles) 159–60, 163,
   339–40
  Queen's Own Surrey Yeomanry 245–6
  Royal Berkshire Regiment 336–7
  Royal Warwickshire Regiment 305
  Seaforth Highlanders 82–4
  Welch Regiment 261–2
Thiepval 40, 166, 326
 see also Memorial to the Missing of the
  Somme, Thiepval

Tower of London, Barrack Wardens 88–9
Townshend, Major-General Charles 142–3, 344
trade wars 62–3, 138–9, 213, 214–17, 241
transatlantic flight 315
Transloy Ridges, battle of the 18, 19
trench warfare, stalemate of 62
Trones 156–7, 161
trophies 34, 51, 52
truncheons, brass 187, 189
trunks 376, 377, 377
Turkey 20, 62, 90–3, 107, 135, 212–13, 275, 312, 334

U-17 (U-boat) 243
U-20 (U-boat) 77
U-28 (U-boat) 96
U-29 (U-boat) 348
U-50 (u-boat) 113
U-75 (U-boat) 147
U-boats 26–7, 63, 77, 91, 213, 214, 241, 295–6
UB-31 (U-boat) 243
United States 13, 63, 77, 213, 241, 250–1, 274–5, 291
Unknown Warrior 347, 382, 383, 384–5

Verdun, battle of 134, 150
Versailles, treaty of 346
Vickers Vimy bomber 315
Victoria, Queen 59
Victoria Cross 91, 175, 210, 225–6, 296, 298, 301
Vimy Ridge, battle of 132, 185, 212, 223, 231–2, 378, 381
Vindictive (cruiser) 295–7
violins 113, 115–17
Vis-en-Artois 307
Vittorio Veneto, battle of 117, 204
von Kluck, General Alexander 40
von Linsingen, General Alexander 373
von Richthofen, Manfred (Red Baron) 273, 275, 292–4, 293
von Spee, Admiral Maximilian 33

walking sticks 363
wallets 39, 40, 41, 374, 377
war artist scheme 275, 280–2, 281, 283
War Office 127, 150, 183, 337
watches 16, 18, 33, 190, 332, 335, 357

Watson, 2nd Lieutenant J. H. 234–5
Watt, Elizabeth Mary 56, 59
Waziristan 346, 360–1
Western Front 13–14, 17, 25, 32, 48, 60, 63, 112–13, 115, 117, 121, 126, 128–9, 133–5, 142, 153, 162, 172, 191, 203, 209, 212, 225, 230, 232, 234, 239, 251, 256, 269, 271–2, 290, 296, 308, 314, 345, 351–2, 360, 363–4, 366, 378
Western Samoa 13
whistles 258–9, 259
White Russians 346, 364, 368
Whitemetal Cup 51, 52
Whitten Brown, Arthur 315
Wiles, B. H. (Official War Artist) 280–2, 281, 283
Wilhelm II 40
William Foster and Company 124, 125, 126, 127
wills 264
Wilson, President Woodrow 364
women 57–9, 57, 63, 64–7, 110–13, 122–3, 127, 221, 221, 225–7, 283, 317–19, 319
Wortley, Major-General Stuart 154

Ypres 79, 84, 132, 153, 185, 200, 259, 272, 274, 285, 290, 308, 310, 327, 351, 374, 383
    first battle of 21, 36–7, 38, 40, 54, 141, 363
    second battle of 18, 61, 62, 69, 84, 142
    third battle of (Passchendaele) 40, 44, 61, 158, 179, 204, 210, 212, 246, 250, 257, 259, 269–70, 290, 321

Zeebrugge Raid 275, 295–7
Zeppelins 135, 174, 175–7, 237, 238–9
Zonnebeke Wood 270

1 3 5 7 9 10 8 6 4 2

Published in 2014 by BBC Books,
an imprint of Ebury Publishing.
A Random House Group Company.

Text by Paul Atterbury
Copyright © Woodlands Books Ltd.

The Random House Group Limited
Reg. No. 954009

Addresses for companies within the
Random House Group can be found at
www.randomhouse.co.uk

A CIP catalogue record for this book is available
from the British Library.

ISBN: 9781849907262

The Random House Group Limited supports
the Forest Stewardship Council® (FSC®), the
leading international forest-certification
organisation. Our books carrying the FSC label
are printed on FSC®-certified paper. FSC is the
only forest-certification scheme supported by the
leading environmental organisations, including
Greenpeace. Our paper procurement policy can be
found at www.randomhouse.co.uk/environment

Designed by Andrew Barron, Thextension
Colour origination by AltaImage, London
Printed and bound in Germany by
Mohn Media GmbH

All pictures by Karl Adamson or supplied by
the contributors with the exception of:
15 Getty images/Cultura Travel/Chris Whitehead;
187 Welsh Pictorial, courtesy of Cardiff Libraries;
239 William Whiffin, Tower Hamlets Council;
293 Australian War Memorial;
379 Canadian War Museum;
381 Platts Family Collection, Vineland, Ontario.

To buy books by your favourite authors and
register for offers visit www.randomhouse.co.uk

ACKNOWLEDGEMENTS

As someone long fascinated by the First World
War, and with a particular passion for the Somme,
I was delighted to be given the task of writing
this book. The original idea came from Simon
Shaw, the executive producer of the *Antiques
Roadshow*, and I am eternally grateful to him
for my involvement. I am also indebted to Jan
Waldron and Sally Dyas, along with many other
Roadshow friends and colleagues, for their
support and enthusiasm but particular thanks
are due to Graham Lay and Martin Pegler, friends
and militaria specialists on the programme, who
took on the onerous task of checking all my facts.
Any errors or inaccuracies that remain are entirely
my own.

Working with Lorna Russell and Kate Fox at
BBC Books has always been a pleasure, and their
support at all stages of the production has been
invaluable. Sarah Chatwin, an excellent editor,
also helped to make a difficult and demanding
task enjoyable.

However, the most important thanks must
go to the 100 families whose stories feature in
this book. They have without exception been
enthusiastic, helpful and always willing to be
bothered about that final detail. Some I have
met, others have been voices on the telephone, or
email partners, but all have given generously of
their time and knowledge. Many have expressed
delight that their family story is finally being
shared, and I feel it a privilege to have been part
of that process.

This book is published to accompany the
Antiques Roadshow World War I Specials,
first broadcast on BBC One in 2014.

Simon Shaw, Series Editor
Julia Foot, Producer/Director
Simon Brant, Director
Michèle Burgess, Producer
Sally Dyas, Assistant Producer
Jan Waldron, Assistant Producer
Pam McIntyre, Researcher